KLOPPITE

KLOPPITE

ONE MAN'S QUEST TO TURN DOUBTERS INTO BELIEVERS

DAVID SEGAR

First published by Pitch Publishing, 2017

Pitch Publishing
A2 Yeoman Gate
Yeoman Way
Worthing
Sussex
BN13 3QZ
www.pitchpublishing.co.uk
info@pitchpublishing.co.uk

ISBN 978-1-78531-306-6

Typesetting and origination by Pitch Publishing

Printed in Denmark by Nørhaven, Viborg

Contents

This book is dedicated to Raymond Clifford Segar (1950–2011), without whom it would never have been possible. You started and nurtured a love of football and writing.

Thanks for everything, Dad.

Acknowledgements

THE first thanks have to go to Paul and Jane Camillin at Pitch Publishing for showing enough faith in a previously unpublished writer to cover a topic as exhaustive as this. Also for showing patience when I asked what were, in hindsight, probably pretty daft questions.

Also to Duncan Olner for an excellent cover design. I gave him a vague description of what I was after and he somehow managed to produce exactly what was in my mind's eye.

An absolutely enormous thank you to Gareth Roberts, Neil Atkinson and everyone at *The Anfield Wrap*, not just for contributing to this book, but for allowing me to be a small part of *TAW* and to get my writing out there in the first place. I first spoke to Gareth about writing for his former labour of love, *Well Red Magazine*, and he's allowed me to continue writing for *TAW* ever since. It's very much appreciated, mate.

A big thank you to Sandra Goldschmidt for also contributing and for lovely chats about Liverpool and BVB. I owe you a beer or two next time you're in London.

Also to Rory Smith, who is far too big and important to talk to the likes of me. Thanks for your involvement and for what was a really interesting chat about Klopp, football in general and the delights of walking through Bradford.

I'm also tremendously grateful to Joe, Matt, John and Pep at LFC for their time and efforts in helping with this book.

I'd be in big trouble if I didn't thank my mum, who has put up with so much football nonsense over the last few years that I'd forgive her if she couldn't bring herself to actually read this book. Also thanks to my brother, Paul, who's been my match-going mate for life.

A shout as well to my writing partner in crime, Faz. We've had so many chats down the years about football and writing that they undoubtedly shaped the idea of doing a book in the first place.

I have to give special thanks to Rich, Lawrence and James as well, though I can't for the life of me remember what for.

And of course the final thank you has to go to Jürgen Norbert Klopp, without whom this book would have been fairly empty.

Introduction

'I am the normal one, if you want this.'

AND there it was. Jürgen Klopp had thrown the media a bone and they were more than willing to take it. It was his first press conference since being announced as manager of Liverpool Football Club and the charismatic German coach had already made very clear that he wasn't in England for the sake of the press. He wasn't dismissive, he knew he had a duty to do the media side of things, but he wanted to set the tone from the off. 'Everyone has told me about the British press, so it's up to you to show me they are all liars!'

The room echoed with laughter, but as with most jokes, there was a truth behind it. Klopp wasn't here for the media, he was here to work with footballers.

On 16 June 1967, not quite one year after England had beaten West Germany in the World Cup Final, a baby boy by the name of Jürgen Norbert Klopp was born in the city of Stuttgart to parents Norbert and Elisabeth. Soon after, they moved to the countryside where little Jürgen would grow up in the Black Forest village of Glatten near Freudenstadt with his two older sisters.

Norbert was a travelling salesman of wall fittings by trade, but had shown promise in his early years of making a career in professional football as a goalkeeper. He had even had a trial at Kaiserslautern, but it was ultimately not to be and once Jürgen arrived, Norbert felt it was his duty to give his son the best chance at succeeding where he hadn't.

Where most dads would play sport with their child and let them win to build self-esteem, Norbert believed this wouldn't bear the necessary results and character, and so decided to thrash poor Jürgen at everything. Skiing, running, and in particular tennis, where he regularly beat his young son 6-0, 6-0.

In 2009, Klopp was interviewed by German national weekly paper *Die Zeit* where he said of his father, 'He was ruthless. When we went skiing, I only ever saw his red anorak from behind. He never waited for me. It didn't matter that I was just a beginner. He wanted me to become the perfect skier.'

While it was not much fun for the youngster at the time, it was this harsh method of learning and motivating that would shape the expectation that Klopp has had of every player he has worked with. Give me everything you have to win. 'For me, attitude was always more important than talent.'

In October 2015, Klopp was sitting in the press room at Melwood fielding questions from more journalists than could reasonably fit. More than an hour before the press conference began there was already no space to move in the media room. People were used to having to navigate past a handful of cameras, but there were now almost 20 of them.

This was big news. Jürgen Klopp had been named as manager of Liverpool Football Club, and the world wanted to see his unveiling, whether it was to hear how he believed he could turn the fortunes of a once great club around, again, or just to see if he would come out with any characteristic 'Klopp-isms'.

His quotes had become legendary, from describing new signing at Borussia Dortmund, Henrikh Mkhitaryan, as fitting his side 'like an arse in a bucket' to claiming that he once told a fourth official, 'How many mistakes are allowed here? If it's 15, you have one more!'

The journalists asking the questions were begging for a golden nugget from Klopp on his first outing in front of them, and set him up with a predictable question based around José Mourinho's infamous assertion that he was 'A Special One'.

Klopp batted it away by saying that he was a normal person from the Black Forest, a quiet part of Germany. That his mother was maybe watching the press conference but would have not understood any of it, but is proud nonetheless, and reiterated that he was just a normal guy. Then he threw it out there. 'I am the normal one, if you want this.'

Of course the parading of the new manager wasn't just for the benefit of the press. The Liverpool fans wanted to see their new man and hear what he had planned for their team. One of his closest friends at Mainz was Thomas Ziemer, who told the *Daily Telegraph* that he and Klopp had once put together a boy band to recreate All-4-One's 1994 hit 'I Swear'. 'He was a friend of everybody at the club, from the president to the bus driver,' says Ziemer. 'That's the personality of Jürgen Klopp. He only has friends.'

By the end of that first press conference, Klopp had tens of millions more.

He also let out a soundbite that would stick, that would bring everyone on board, suggesting that all involved at LFC would have a responsibility if success was going to follow. It was something people needed to hear. He shone a mirror up to Liverpool players and fans alike and said, 'We have to change from doubters to believers. Now.

'At this moment all the LFC family is a little bit too nervous, a little bit too pessimistic, a little bit too much in doubt. They all celebrate the game and there is a fantastic atmosphere in the stadium, But they don't believe at the moment. They only see five years ago, ten years ago, twenty years ago.

History is great. But only to remember. Now we have the possibility to write a new story if we want, but we have to clear a few things and maybe we can do this and be as successful as we can be.'

The gauntlet had been laid down. The work was to begin.

1

'I always said in that moment where I believe I am not the perfect coach any more for this extraordinary club, I will say so.'

KLOPP is the first to admit that he had an unremarkable playing career. As a youngster he played for several lower league clubs, and in 1987 moved from 1. FC Pforzheim to Eintracht Frankfurt, where he multitasked expertly by playing for the amateur side, studying sport science and coaching the club's under-13 team.

Over the next couple of years he would also play for Viktoria Sindlingen and Rot-Weiss Frankfurt, before eventually ending up at FSV Mainz 05 in 1990, where he would remain for the rest of his career.

As a young VfB Stuttgart fan, Klopp's favourite player was centre-back Karlheinz Förster. He was an unspectacular, no-nonsense kind of defender, and Klopp was drawn to that. He was dedicated, intelligent, and above all else, played at full throttle. He was also only 5ft 10in, not ideal for a centre-back, but he made up for this with his attitude and it earned him 81 caps for West Germany. He was Stuttgart through and through, making over 300 appearances for Die Roten, and even managed over 100 appearances at his only other senior club, Olympique de Marseille.

Klopp began playing life as a striker, and has often described himself as an average player, but he eventually became a defender who embodied everything that he had loved about Förster. He wasn't as successful and never made an appearance for the national side, but he played with heart, desire, passion and commitment, and also managed to score 52 goals in 346 appearances.

Ziemer says of his former teammate, 'He was not a good technical player, but he always played with aggression. He was a big team man, a very good friend of all the players.

'He had many, many ideas, but he also got many ideas from Wolfgang Frank. He would speak many times with him about tactics. At this time, we already knew he was born to make a trainer.'

Wolfgang Frank had two spells in the 1990s as manager at Mainz, and he was one of the first coaches in Germany to stop utilising the sweeper position. Frank preferred to use a four-man backline with a diamond midfield, and strongly believed in a high press, immaculate organisation of the defence and overloading the flanks.

Klopp has said that Frank was the coach he learned most from during his playing days, and had an on-air catch-up with his old boss on the German football review show *Sky90* in March 2013. Frank sadly passed away just six months later.

Early on in his playing days Klopp decided he would eventually go into coaching, and twice a week would make the 250-mile round trip to Cologne to take classes at the fabled coaching school of Erich Rutemöller.

Rutemöller trained his students through the Deutscher Fußball-Bund (DFB) Football Teacher course, the German FA's equivalent to UEFA's top coaching qualification, with other graduates including Thomas Tuchel, Mirko Slomka, Christian Streich and Paul Lambert.

Klopp had been a striker at Rot-Weiss Frankfurt, noted for his pace and ability in the air, which is why Mainz manager Robert Jung brought him to Die Nullfünfer (the 05s). In 11 years at the Rhine club he made 325 appearances, and over that time gradually moved from striker to right midfield, and finally to right-back.

It was Frank who moved Klopp to defence, and it was he who had more influence on how Klopp would develop both as a player and as a future coach than anyone.

As a player, Frank himself had been a striker, playing for the likes of Stuttgart and Borussia Dortmund. He went on to manage in Switzerland and at German second division side Rot-Weiss Essen, who he guided to the 1994 DFB-Pokal (German Cup) Final. Once he became Mainz boss, Frank's effect was immediate. His influence on the players he managed became apparent in later years as a large number of them would go on to become coaches themselves.

Frank was a big fan of Klopp, as Klopp was of Frank, who believed that Klopp's passion and desire came from his own frustrations at his limited technical ability. What Klopp lacked in skill, he more than made up for in intelligence and effort.

In the early 1990s football was obsessed with the '*libero*' system – the use of a sweeper – and no country encompassed the system as much as Germany. From the legendary Franz Beckenbauer to Lothar Matthäus and Matthias Sammer, the idea of using any other system was practically unthinkable. Some coaches had tried back fours, but were quickly shouted back down and eventually relented. That was apart from Frank. He was convinced the *libero* system was dated and on its way out, and had enjoyed success with a back four in Switzerland where there was less resistance to change.

Mainz had been struggling so badly before Frank's arrival that they were willing to try anything. Frank himself was influenced by the great Milan coach Arrigo Sacchi and showed his players drills that the Italian used in making a back-four system as solid and effective as the sweeper one. The players embraced the ideas and practised hard in training. In their first game utilising it against FC Saarbrücken, they found themselves 4-0 up after half an hour. They ended up winning 5-0.

Frank's tactics didn't just involve a back four, but zonal marking, high pressing, and a dedication to winning the ball as high up the pitch as possible. It was clear years later where Klopp had first found what would be the inspiration to his own football philosophy.

A bad run of results saw Frank leave the club after a couple of years, but following a series of other managerial failures, he returned in the late '90s. The fans were so happy to have him back they chanted 'Messiah! Messiah!' at his first home game, and enjoyed another near three years using his preferred pressing tactics. However, after flirting with a move to MSV Duisburg, he was out the door again.

More managers came and went, including Eckhard Krautzun, who had got the job after a conversation with Klopp gave him enough inside information on the state of the team to impress in his interview. However, Krautzun was less successful once in charge, and it wasn't long before Mainz sporting director Christian Heidel decided he might need to make a change.

He couldn't find a manager that inspired him, and could not figure out who would be best to take the reins after Krautzun. It was pointed out to him that the dressing room was full of leaders, including Klopp. Heidel decided to offer Klopp the role of player-manager, which Klopp said yes to immediately, though he made one demand, that the role of player was removed. Klopp was now a manager.

The initial public reaction was not as effusive as Heidel had been. At his first press conference the assembled journalists jokingly asked if Klopp was lost when they saw him sat next to Heidel. He had sceptics to convince, and convince them he did.

On the training pitch Klopp was mirroring his mentor, Frank, making sure the players were well drilled in a back-four system and that the main philosophy of the team was of high pressing and counter-pressing (known as '*gegenpressing*' in Germany), and results turned around immediately. He won six of his first seven games.

While Klopp followed Frank's principles, he also added his own. The young coach allowed his players more freedom to express their individual abilities, but with the caveat that the team always came first.

He steered Mainz clear of relegation from the second division and in his first two seasons nearly led them to unlikely promotions. They were both heartbreaking scenarios as failure to win on the last day of the 2001/02 season stopped them going up, and the following year it was an injury-time goal from Klopp's former club, Eintracht Frankfurt, that denied them on goal difference.

Some suggested it was a curse, but the manager and his team would not be kept down. In 2003/04 they enjoyed the fortune of results elsewhere themselves and a 3-0 win over Eintracht Trier saw them earn the club's first ever promotion to the Bundesliga.

Against all the odds, they managed to spend three seasons in the top division, finishing 11th in their first two.

Coming top of the fair play league in their first season meant a place in the UEFA Cup in 2005/06. Klopp led them to a historic 4-0 win over FC Mika of Armenia in the club's first ever European game, before overcoming Icelandic outfit Keflavík in the final qualifying round. They were eventually eliminated by Sevilla in the first round, but had represented themselves well.

However, by the third season the players who had been overachieving were being poached by bigger clubs. Mainz only gathered 11 points in the first half of the 2006/07 season, and despite a slight recovery, including winning five of their first six games after the winter break, they were relegated at the season's end.

The following year, their fate again came down to the final day of the season. They needed to win and hope that Hoffenheim didn't if they were to gain immediate promotion back to the Bundesliga. Klopp's men battered Hamburg 5-1, but unfortunately Hoffenheim went one better and won 5-0 against Greuther Fürth. Klopp was in tears, and not just because he hadn't managed to get his team back to the top flight. He had promised Heidel that he would resign if he didn't gain promotion. After his final game at Bruchwegstadion, Klopp and his players sat on the pitch as the Mainz fans sang 'You'll Never Walk Alone'. It was an omen of things to come later in his career.

Somewhere close to 20,000 people gathered in Guternbergplatz in Mainz town centre to say goodbye to their iconic boss. They chanted his name as an emotional Klopp gave an impassioned speech to the club that had raised him in football. The loudspeakers belted out the Trude Herr song 'Niemals geht man so ganz' ('Nobody ever completely leaves').

It was inevitable that Klopp wouldn't be out of work for long. He'd made a name for himself. Not just in the way he had overachieved at Mainz with his revolutionary style of football, but with his cult of personality. He had taken to press conferences straight away. His infectious enthusiasm charmed all who observed, and it wasn't just in his work at Mainz.

The 2006 World Cup in Germany took the country by storm, not just in the way the national side came so close to glory before dramatic elimination by Italy in the semi-finals, but the overall spirit of the competition. At the centre of the national coverage was Klopp, who had agreed to be a pundit for the summer. The way he talked about the game, broke it down in common sense terms compared to other pundits, and did it all with an obvious love for the sport meant that he had become close to a national darling by the tournament's end. Interest in him was high, and once he became available, Bundesliga clubs starting circling.

Hamburg, Bayer Leverkusen and Bayern Munich had all shown an interest due to his results and popularity. Bayern felt he was more of a motivator than a tactician, and decided to go with Jürgen Klinsmann instead. However, another club made their interest known and straight away Klopp knew it had the potential to be the perfect match.

As new Borussia Dortmund manager, he had a big job on his hands. He replaced the outgoing Thomas Doll, who had struggled with an ageing squad. BVB were one of the biggest clubs in Germany – they had won the Champions League just 11 years earlier – but were coming fresh off a 13th-place finish in the league. Klopp was tasked with overhauling the squad, filling it with new young talent and getting them to play the kind of football he had brought in at Mainz, but to a higher level.

The biggest early move of this new era was when Klopp got rid of elder statesmen centre-backs Christian Worns and Robert Kovać and replaced them with two teenagers, Mats Hummels and Neven Subotić, the latter of which had followed him from Mainz.

It was a curious change as Dortmund had shipped 62 goals the previous season, but the necessary improvement would not just be down to Hummels and Subotić. Klopp made sure to drill into everyone that every single player on the pitch had a responsibility to defend.

His first competitive game saw him come up against Bayern Munich in the T-Home Supercup – the German equivalent to the Community Shield. Dortmund won 2-1.

From there optimism flowed. Dortmund did indeed play like a higher-level version of Mainz. It was far from a faultless season but an eventual sixth-place finish was a lot better than what had gone before.

Klopp was building, slowly but surely, and assured fans that success would follow. The next season saw a slight improvement as they finished fifth and earned European qualification, but it was from there that everything clicked for Klopp and BVB.

Dortmund started the 2010/11 season with a 2-0 loss to Bayer Leverkusen, but went on to win 14 of their next 15 games, and the young exhilarating team that Klopp had put together over three years went on to win the league with two weeks to spare after a 2-0 win over Nürnberg.

The likes of Hummels, Subotić, Roman Weidenfeller, Sven Bender, Łukasz Piszczek, Marcel Schmelzer, Kevin Großkreutz, Shinji Kagawa, Nuri Şahin, Mario Götze and Lucas Barrios had either been brought through the youth system or been signed for comparative peanuts compared to what Bayern had spent on their squad, but Dortmund had overcome them with ease.

The following season needed to be one of continuity, though two big changes were necessary. Şahin left for Real Madrid and was replaced by İlkay Gündoğan, while Barrios made room for an unknown young Polish striker by the name of Robert Lewandowski.

As often happens in football when a team achieves unexpected success, what follows quickly is scepticism as to whether it was a fluke. Dortmund did nothing to quell the questions at the start of the 2011/12 season as they experienced early defeats to Hoffenheim, Hertha Berlin and Hannover. They suffered more defeats in the first six games than they had in the entire previous campaign.

The surprise factor had gone, and teams were playing Dortmund with the same determination to stop them as they did with Bayern.

They needed to evolve, and Klopp made sure they did. They started to move the ball around more, were less reliant on trying to counter-attack as they weren't being given the space to do so, and they needed to use more weapons.

After an inauspicious start, Lewandowski went on to cement the place of centre-forward. Barrios was out injured after a muscle tear during the summer, but failed to ever get back into the team due to the form of the Pole, who scored 22 times in his first proper season.

Once the goals started flowing, the points followed. Dortmund soared back towards the top of the league and found themselves in a three-way title race with Bayern and Borussia Mönchengladbach. A Dortmund home win over Bayern on matchday 30 saw them go six points clear, which was followed by a derby victory at Schalke 04 and then another three points against Gladbach that clinched a second consecutive Bundesliga title. A week after their last league game of the season – a 4-0 win over Freiburg – they took on Bayern again, this time in the DFB-Pokal Final. They hammered Jupp Heynckes's men 5-2 in Berlin to secure the double.

This was no fluke, this was a genuinely top-class team that Klopp had built and coached to the top of German football.

All over the world people were fascinated by the resurgence of BVB. Klopp had revived them and turned them into a German powerhouse again, and without lavishly spending money, but by finding hungry and talented players and coaching them, instilling his tactics and fearing no one.

It would turn out to be Klopp's last league title win with Dortmund, but it didn't stop his team impressing further. After domestic success, the next stop was Europe, and the 2012/13 season saw them very nearly get all the way to the summit.

Dortmund embarked on a daunting Champions League campaign as they drew Ajax, Manchester City and Real Madrid in the group stages. They ended up topping the group.

After beating Shakhtar Donetsk in the last 16, they took on the newly-rich Spanish side Málaga. After a 0-0 in Spain, the second leg provided enough drama to last a lifetime. Klopp's men went 2-1 down with eight minutes to play. They needed two goals to go through, and got them in the 91st and 93rd minutes.

In the semi-final they made the world sit up and take notice as they hammered the mighty Real Madrid 4-1 in the first leg, with all four goals scored by Lewandowski, before eventually securing a 4-3 aggregate win.

Inevitably, they were to play Bayern in the final at Wembley Stadium. Every non-Bayern fan seemed to want Dortmund to triumph. They had become the football hipster's favourite team, and the second team of many who just enjoyed watching them overachieve against the odds with exciting fast-paced football.

Klopp had beaten Heynckes in the DFB-Pokal Final the year before, but Bayern and their team of megastars went in as favourites having beaten Klopp's men to the Bundesliga title by 25 points and scored nearly 100 goals in their 34 league games.

This was a special Bayern team, and despite a spirited fightback to 1-1 having gone a goal down, Dortmund succumbed to a late Arjen Robben strike and were denied Champions League glory. It was another kick in the teeth for Klopp after he had learned just a few weeks earlier that one of his star players, Götze, had decided to leave Dortmund to join Bayern.

This was an issue that Klopp needed to deal with. As great as the spirit was that he had built at the club, it was inevitable that with success would come admirers, and he was fighting a losing battle to keep hold of his star players. Since the first title win he had lost Şahin to Real Madrid, Kagawa to Manchester United, Götze to Bayern and a year later, Lewandowski followed.

The likes of Marco Reus, Henrikh Mkhitaryan and Pierre-Emerick Aubameyang came in as replacements and were largely success stories, but they weren't quite able to replicate the heights of their predecessors in terms of trophies.

The 2013/14 season saw a slightly improved league campaign, but it was ultimately another runners-up spot as Pep Guardiola steamrolled Bayern to the title. There was also another final defeat in the DFB-Pokal to their old enemy.

Dortmund were still playing entertaining football and winning plenty of games, but Bayern's relentless suffocation of the league meant the motivation of thinking the title was possible was rarely there. However, no one anticipated what would happen the following season.

The 2014/15 campaign began with a trophy, beating Bayern 2-0 in the German Supercup, but the league campaign started as it meant to go on, with a dour 2-0 loss at home to Bayer Leverkusen. The opening goal of the game came just nine seconds into the season.

Nothing seemed to work for Dortmund. Teams had started realising that sitting deep and forcing Klopp's side to break their parked bus was stifling them. There were also numerous injuries to deal with, and despite the returns of Şahin and Kagawa, they could not rediscover the form that had brought them so much success years earlier.

At the halfway stage of the season, Dortmund were second from bottom of the league. However, one of the reasons Klopp had cited for the difficulties was the lack of time he'd had with his players in pre-season following the 2014 World Cup. He now had six weeks to work with them in training and to try and get them prepared for the second half of the campaign.

Dortmund did recover and managed to climb their way from 17th to 7th in the final Bundesliga table.

A few weeks before the end of the season, the club called a press conference. No one was certain why, but the media assembled. There were rumours, there was speculation, and soon enough it was confirmed by CEO Hans-Joachim Watzke. At the end of the season, Jürgen Klopp would be leaving Borussia Dortmund.

Klopp explained, 'This decision feels absolutely right … I believe that BVB needs a change. There will be other influences on the team, which will be positive.

'It's not that I'm tired, I've not had contact with another club but don't plan to take a sabbatical.

'I always said in that moment where I believe I am not the perfect coach any more for this extraordinary club, I will say so. I really think the decision is the right one. This club deserves to be coached from the 100 per cent right manager.'

Fittingly in his last game at Signal Iduna Park, his team won 3-2 against Werder Bremen. It allowed there to be nothing but bittersweet smiles in his final goodbye to the fans in the stadium where he had resided for seven years. Klopp was in tears, as were the fans, who unfurled a large banner across the legendary Yellow Wall part of the stadium that simply read 'Danke Jürgen'.

There was though one more game to go. It would have been the perfect way to say goodbye to win one last trophy, but unfortunately despite going 1-0 up, Klopp's team were beaten 3-1 by Wolfsburg in the DFB-Pokal Final. The Dortmund chapter of Klopp's career was at an end.

In spite of making it clear in his goodbye press conference that he did not want to take a sabbatical from football, he decided that before he came back to the game he wanted to have a long holiday to spend time with his family.

Stories of an immediate return would not cease of course. In fact both Klopp and Fenerbahçe felt forced to release separate statements that he would not be joining the Turkish club straight after he packed his bags in Dortmund, such was the level of media reporting that Istanbul would be his next destination.

There had been extensive media coverage in Germany around the future of Klopp, and many felt it almost inevitable that he was merely biding his time until he could come back and manage Bayern once Dortmund had moved on and Pep Guardiola had vacated his seat. Even BVB sporting director Michael Zorc felt it was possible, telling *Sport Bild* ahead of *Der Klassiker* that Klopp to Bayern was 'factually conceivable'.

Instead of the Allianz Arena hotseat though, Klopp was offered the chance of taking charge of the Mexican national side, but Mexico Football Federation general secretary Guillermo Cantú revealed that he turned them down. 'We sought him out through his agent, but he told us it would not be possible because he wants to continue to take a break for right now,' Cantú said on TV Azteca.

Just over a week later, Klopp was officially announced as Liverpool manager.

2

'As a human being we always think about
faults, we don't think about the good things.
That is what we have to learn again.'

I T took many by surprise. Just hours after Liverpool had earned
a hard-fought 1-1 draw with Everton in the Merseyside derby
at Goodison Park, Brendan Rodgers was sacked as first-team
manager. Arsenal had just beaten Manchester United 3-0 at the
Emirates Stadium, and as the *Sky Sports* pundits were making their
analyses, the news broke that Rodgers had gone. Among the pundit
team were Graeme Souness, Jamie Carragher and Thierry Henry,
whose instinctive reaction to grab Carragher's leg in shock became
viral across social media within minutes.

After the initial surprise had subsided, Liverpool legends Souness
and Carragher reluctantly agreed that the dismissal was just, and
Carragher in particular made an impassioned plea to the club's owners
to make the right decision when it came to hiring the next coach.

'They've made a lot of decisions that haven't worked ... At this
moment, the owners' track record of making decisions for Liverpool
Football Club over the last two or three years has not been good
enough. It's miles off.'

Carragher was alluding to decisions such as bringing in Damian
Comolli as a director of football, the handling of the appointment
and then dismissal of Kenny Dalglish, forming a transfer committee
with no clear direction and the decision to keep Rodgers the previous
summer after a season where they fell four places in the table and
ended with defeats to the likes of Hull City, Crystal Palace and Stoke
City, who thrashed them 6-1 on the last day of the campaign.

Carragher went on to say, 'Liverpool are becoming Tottenham. Think they're a big club, but the real big clubs are not too worried about them, and that included when I was there towards the end. I'm not just picking on Rodgers and these players.

'What are these owners going to do to get Liverpool back to where they need to be, which is consistently in the Champions League and challenging for trophies? At this moment we've become a team who think we're big, but we're not.'

The former Reds defender was heartfelt in his view on the club, and in particular the way the owners were running it. Many decisions had been taken since they seized power in 2011, and several of them had failed to result in success on the pitch. Carragher's call was echoed by many Kopites who were eager to see whether Fenway Sports Group were going to show the ambition necessary to take Liverpool to the next level.

Within the hour, Jürgen Klopp was the clear favourite with the bookies. Former Chelsea and Real Madrid manager Carlo Ancelotti was also heavily backed, and the fans became immediately hopeful that a world-class manager was on the way, whether it be Klopp or Ancelotti.

Many had fretted that the owners would go down the same route as before and go for a bright young manager with potential, as they had done with Rodgers, when the club was crying out for experience and a figure of authority to guide what was a very young squad.

It appeared to be a two-horse race. The fan polls just gave Klopp the edge over the Italian, but near enough every person you asked conceded that choosing between Klopp and Ancelotti was akin to choosing between a Mercedes Benz and a Ferrari. A no-lose scenario.

It became apparent by the middle of the week that the Merseyside club favoured the German, and soon enough you couldn't move for Klopp-talk. The fans were excited, the media anticipated the arrival of a man who would practically do their jobs for them, and the dark cloud that had been hanging over L4 since the end of the previous season had finally started to lift.

On Thursday, 8 October 2015, Jürgen Klopp was officially announced as manager of Liverpool Football Club.

There had already been an incredible number of articles written about the man by the time he was named as boss. Several editors would have been left pretty red-faced if the deal had not materialised. The world, not just Liverpool fans, was encapsulated by idea of Klopp arriving in English football.

By the time of his first press conference on the Friday morning, social media had exploded. Klopp to LFC had more than two million mentions on Twitter, at the time it was the most ever about a managerial appointment (the next highest being 1.7m for José Mourinho returning to Chelsea).

The reason there was such a clamour for 'Klopp to the Kop' and why his name had been incessantly linked with the role even when he was happily contracted to Dortmund and Rodgers was thriving on Merseyside, was that it seemed from a distance to be an ideal marriage.

The history of the club has been littered with great managers. Bill Shankly, Bob Paisley, Joe Fagan, Kenny Dalglish, Gerard Houllier and Rafa Benitez all won multiple trophies, and they were all such different characters. And yet, they were in many ways all the same.

It was far from the only quality that these great coaches had needed to succeed, but all of them in their own way had a cult of personality about them. They were figures the fans could relate to, could worship and could support in both good times and bad. In moments of doubt, fans could look over to the man standing in the dugout and believe that everything was going to be okay.

It was arguable whether there were any managers in world football at the time who embodied that cult of personality quite as much as Klopp.

He had been loved at Dortmund like a father figure, and Liverpool fans wanted that. They had admired Rodgers, but there had never really been that same closeness between the Northern Irishman and the Kop, more a mutual appreciation. Anfield wanted to love again.

Klopp was a man who often stated that his passion for football came purely from a romantic sense, a desire to experience the game through emotion rather than finance.

Both he and his agent, Mark Kosicke, had mentioned more than once that his next job after Dortmund could well be in England as he wanted to manage in a country where he spoke the language and could communicate easily with his players. That left only German and English speaking countries as possibilities.

It was also made clear that Klopp would happily go to a club who were not necessarily at the very top of the game.

Speaking to *SPOX.com* four months before Klopp's appointment, Kosicke said, 'The Premier League is very exciting, and we do not only think about the top four because there are some other great clubs below them.

'It is always all about the challenge. When Jürgen signed for Dortmund there were other clubs who had better prestige and were in better financial mood at this time. Nevertheless he decided for Dortmund.

'He has the great ability to develop things. If he goes into a stadium, feels the energy and thinks that he can make a difference here, this could be more attractive to him than going with the big deals and aiming for the treble.'

To many it seemed as if Kosicke was directly describing Liverpool, and had stopped just short of adding 'and they must play in all red, be based in the north-west and have a famous stand that rhymes with Klopp'.

Christian Heidel, Klopp's general manager at Mainz 05 and now performing the same role at Schalke 04, was convinced that the appointment suited both parties.

'If you've worked in Mainz before, then in Dortmund, then maybe Liverpool is the only club left to coach,' Heidel told *LFCTV*.

'There are many, many great emotions, that's what Kloppo needs and I think that's part of the reason he chose to go there.

'I'm just very happy for him, that a boy who played football in Mainz, who became a head coach in Mainz, who then went and became a Bundesliga champion at Dortmund and played a Champions League Final, now moves over to one of the most famous stadiums in Europe at Anfield. Actually I'm pretty sure the people in Liverpool will love him because he's just the right type of guy for Liverpool.

'I think he can do it, he's just got this aura that can excite people – not just the players but everyone around him – and I'm pretty sure that in a couple of days or maybe a few weeks, Jürgen Klopp will be a household name in the UK.'

It didn't even take that long.

The packed-out press room at Anfield played host to Klopp's unveiling, and within those 25 minutes he had metaphorically 'broken the Internet' with his soundbites, wooed the photographers with his tooth-filled smile (before chastising them for taking so many that he couldn't hear one journalist's question), and impressed the world's media with how he handled himself and the occasion.

He was paraded like a new signing, which in a sense he was. He went to the pitch for photo opportunities with chairman Tom Werner and chief executive Ian Ayre. Such was his relaxed approach to everything he even got both men, who were essentially his bosses, in a friendly double headlock, and they both just smiled.

However, Klopp was clearly not enamoured with the excessive attention he was getting from the media.

'All the photographs. This is not what I want. I only want to work with the team. But this is part of the deal. So, okay, we do this today. Let's start tomorrow to work with the team.'

Klopp was making all the right noises, and continued that in his interviews with the press away from the cameras afterwards.

'I am not the guy who is going to go out and shout "we are going to conquer the world" or something like this,' he later told journalists.

'But we will conquer the ball, yeah? Each fucking time!

'We will chase the ball. We will run more, fight more. We will work more together, better together. We will have better organisation in defence than the other teams.

'We have to find our own way to play. Our performances have to be enjoyable for ourselves.'

He described how he had watched the team's previous three games against Aston Villa, FC Sion and Everton.

'You can see it in their eyes, they are not free. Football is about creating chances, not to make 20 goals a game. It is not possible.

'If you feel "yes I can miss, the next chance we will get" then you are free and you can stay confident.

'That is very important. In the game against Sion, you saw many of the problems because there was so much pressure on the players. We have to work so that they feel good. I couldn't see any fun in this game in no faces and that is not so good.'

That night he was caught on camera again as he visited a bar on Hardman Street near the centre of Liverpool with his wife. A group of women on a night out recognised the German and took the chance to have their photo taken with him. Within seconds it was on Twitter, and retweeted across the world. Klopp was on the town, and people loved it. He wasn't hiding away in his hotel room as he had been forced to do the night before his unveiling. He was among the people.

However, Klopp would state at his press conference ahead of the Tottenham game that due to every photo of him being shared all over social media and getting into newspapers, he would have to stop agreeing to take them as they were making it appear as if he spent all his spare time in bars.

The media circus was over for now, and finally he could get on the training field at Melwood and start working with his new set of players. As it happened to be an international week he only had the skeleton of a squad in attendance, with most of his players away with their national sides. They would not come back until two days before the game.

There was another immediate issue as Klopp's assistant Željko Buvač, whom he had worked with in Mainz and Dortmund, had to wait until the Wednesday before he was granted his work permit to enter the country. The Bosnian was on the training ground that afternoon to work with the squad.

The initial effect on the players was apparent, with Lucas Leiva commenting on his first impressions of the new boss in an interview with the official club website, saying that he expected them to work hard, but that he was already enjoying it.

From afar, Adam Lallana and Jordon Ibe, who had both enjoyed close relationships with Rodgers, expressed their excitement at returning from international duty to work under Klopp. Spurs striker Harry Kane stated in an interview that the Liverpool players in the England squad were 'buzzing' about the appointment and couldn't wait to get back to their club.

However, two players would not be looking forward to training with Klopp for long. Youngster Joe Gomez tore his anterior cruciate ligament while playing for England U21s, and was ruled out for the season. The next day, Danny Ings suffered exactly the same injury in his first session with Klopp, and was also out for the campaign.

It was not an ideal start for the new coach, who was already missing Christian Benteke, and would not be able to use Daniel Sturridge after he picked up a knee injury in training.

It was with a bit of a sad expression that Klopp kicked off his first pre-match press conference as he spent a large amount of time talking about injuries to players he had not yet worked with and had barely said 'hallo' to.

The media room was packed yet again, and Klopp understandably sounded tired of the attention he had been getting all week. Once he started talking about the football he was generally positive about his players and believed he had seen enough to ascertain that they were willing to put the work in he demanded.

He stated that he wanted to make the players braver, and made a more general comment that people are too afraid of faults.

'As a human being we always think about faults, we don't think about the good things. That is what we have to learn again.'

The talk was over. It was time to see how brave his new players could be.

3

*'They work so hard, they are full of
concentration, full of readiness, full of passion,
everything is there... You can come back always
and that's what we have to understand.'*

THE time had come. It had been eight days since Klopp's
unveiling but after the international break, he had barely three
days with his squad. The eyes of the world were now on him and
his charges though, expecting to see the first signs of what a Klopp-led
Liverpool side would look like.

The trip to White Hart Lane to play Tottenham was inevitably
the first kick-off of the weekend in the Premier League. As the
teams warmed up, Klopp stood in the centre circle watching his
men go through their paces. Then he turned around and watched
the opposition. Then it was back into the dressing room for one last
motivational team talk before heading out to be greeted by an obscene
number of cameras pointed at the dugout before the game. There were
more cameras pointed at Klopp than at the pitch when the whistle blew.

The first Klopp line-up was in a 4-3-2-1 formation, with Mignolet,
Clyne, Škrtel, Sakho, Moreno, Lucas, Can, Milner, Lallana, Coutinho
and Origi. It was a first league start for Divock Origi, a £10m signing
from Lille the previous summer. The Belgian striker had impressed
at the 2014 World Cup as a 19-year-old, and several clubs had been
chasing him, including Klopp's Dortmund. He signed for Liverpool
before heading back to France for a further year on loan with Lille.
Since arriving properly at Anfield in the summer of 2015 he had
struggled to get game time, only being trusted for cameos from the
bench late in games, and two starts in the Europa League.

He started here though, largely due to necessity. The fourth-choice striker had become the first choice, with fifth choice Jerome Sinclair on the bench.

Klopp took his seat and the game kicked off. The Klopp era was under way, and for the first time since his arrival, all eyes were on the players rather than the German.

The sceptics who had questioned what impact Klopp and his coaches could have in such limited time were soon silenced as, for the first 15 minutes, the influence of those few days of training were clear. Just 90 seconds in and after Clyne had given the ball away to the Spurs midfield, five Liverpool players were sprinting toward the ball carrier. He panicked and laid it back to a centre-back, who also panicked and laid it to his fellow centre-back, who also panicked and hit the ball long and out for a throw-in. Liverpool were *gegenpressing* already.

For the opening period the away side were harrying their hosts, winning possession, winning corners from nothing, one of which nearly bore fruit as a flick from Emre Can found Origi, whose header smacked the underside of the crossbar. Hugo Lloris in the Spurs goal managed to pat the ball away from Martin Škrtel on the rebound, and Origi was unable to react before it was cleared.

Under Mauricio Pochettino, Spurs had become statistically the hardest working side in the league, covering more ground than anyone. They had routinely been winning games late on due to their superior fitness levels and tiring the opposition out. This was the perfect test for Klopp's men so early on. If they could stay on the same level of effort, then they would have a great chance of winning.

As it turned out, they exceeded Tottenham in this regard, covering 116km during the game. It was the first time in the season that Spurs had been outrun during a game. This could have been put down to the inevitable 'bounce' that a team experiences with a new manager, trying to impress early on. However, the Reds also outsprinted their hosts, 614 times to 564. This wasn't just bounce, this was a deliberate change of style, and it had occurred after three days of work.

It wasn't enough for the win though. Mignolet made a save from Kane in the second half, while Can flashed a shot wide near the end, but it was a game short of quality in the final third and the points were shared.

Klopp had thrown Joe Allen on for Lallana, who had run himself ragged, and then brought Ibe on for Philippe Coutinho with just five minutes remaining. Ibe was the first public recipient of Klopp's temper as he shouted at the teenager for not being ready to come on quickly enough. It may have been the reason why Ibe put in his best performance of the season, albeit in a short cameo. He took players on with confidence, opened up the play and threatened to break the deadlock himself. Klopp had also readied young Sinclair to be his final change in stoppage time, but the whistle blew before it could be made.

The general opinion was that Liverpool still lacked something, especially in an attacking sense, but that overall it was a positive outing, especially considering how clearly the players had bought into Klopp's methods so early and adapted so quickly. He was smiling in his first post-match press conference.

'I am satisfied with the start, which is not the worst sign,' he said.

'I did not have the biggest expectations for the game because I knew we only had three days to prepare, and that Tottenham are a very strong, tuned team. I knew it could be difficult, but I am really satisfied.

'The start was brilliant. I think we surprised them a little bit.

'We were there for the second balls – Divock, Adam and Phil were perfect in their timing, and got into good positions.

'But then, the problem was that when we had the ball, we were not cool enough. We didn't use our skills, we were a little bit too hectic and we didn't see the right option.

'We had our moments, hit the bar, and had some other situations where we could have done better, but it's okay. After three or four days, it's brilliant. Now we have our own experience together, and now we can go on working.'

The first game was out the way, but the next was just round the corner as Liverpool's involvement in the Europa League meant that playing midweek would be a regular occurrence.

The Reds had made a stuttering start in their Europa League group campaign, with back-to-back 1-1 draws away at Bordeaux and then at home to FC Sion. The listless display against the Swiss side at home was one of the final nails in the coffin of Rodgers's reign, a team they had been expected to beat with ease. Much the same was expected against Rubin Kazan, who had been struggling in their domestic league.

The home fans were good to their word and made Anfield loud for the new manager, who took his place in the dugout for the first time and surveyed all that he now led.

Against the script, Liverpool fell behind early on. However, the game turned on Kazan captain Oleg Kuzmin living up to his reputation as a brash force with two wild tackles leading to a first-half red card. The second had been a cynical body-check on Emre Can, and from the resulting free kick, the German midfielder slammed home the equaliser from close range after Origi's header flicked off a defender.

The first goal of the Klopp reign had fittingly been scored by the only German in the squad.

Liverpool dominated the second half with the extra man, but the same issues of a lack of calmness and generally poor decision making was costing them again. They registered 35 shots on the visitors' goal, but managed just six on target. They failed to break through again and were forced to settle for another draw.

One positive was the return from injury of summer signings Christian Benteke and Roberto Firmino, who came on as second-half substitutes.

After the game, Klopp was open-minded about the performance.

'When you come for the first time in a new house, normally you have a present,' the German said. 'I am not quite satisfied with my present tonight but it was only the first time and I will come again.'

Just three days later and he was back at Anfield for his first Premier League game on home turf, with Ronald Koeman's impressive Southampton providing the opposition.

As they had done in their previous two games, Liverpool started well. Ultimately though, the end product was still lacking.

Chances were few and far between, and Benteke was brought on for Origi at half-time. The big Belgian gave his side more of a target to aim for, and with 13 minutes to go, he showed just what a target he could be. James Milner retrieved a ball that had been deflected back downfield, before turning and whipping a pinpoint cross from deep into the penalty area, where Benteke rose in trademark fashion and bulleted a header into the top corner of the net.

Anfield erupted, as did Klopp, who ran down the touchline, leapt up and punched the air in his trademark fashion. For the first time in his tenure, his team had taken the lead.

They very nearly gave it away moments later as Sadio Mané was allowed in but his shot went high and wide.

Liverpool looked nervous as Southampton pressed, and sure enough it led to an equaliser shortly after. Milner had sloppily given away a free kick out on the left. The ball in wasn't dealt with and eventually found its way to an unmarked Mané, who headed in from close range. Silence once more, and several fans made for the exits.

It was another 1-1 draw. The seventh out of their last nine games. Out of those seven, six had been occasions where the Reds had taken the lead only to concede an equaliser shortly after. Klopp recognised the problem straight away. He could see that the mentality in key moments wasn't right, namely in moments where they went ahead and then their inability to respond to a setback.

'They work so hard, they are full of concentration, full of readiness, full of passion, everything is there. They [Southampton] get one goal, and it felt like the end of the world, and it was not the end of the world. You can come back always and that's what we have to understand.'

After the game there were murmurs of discontent from some, saying that nothing had changed from the Rodgers era. This ignored the fact that Klopp had barely had three weeks to work with a team that was low on confidence and high on injuries, but it was also a sign that the German was going to be heavily scrutinised right from the off. Almost a victim of the fanfare that had welcomed his appointment.

Many expected the 'new manager bounce'. While Klopp quite often bounced in a literal sense, his new team were not yet replicating that positivity on the pitch.

The fans, the players and none more than Klopp were aching for that first win to get the ball rolling.

Klopp wanted to turn doubters into believers, but it was clear that this was going to be much easier said than done.

4

'I don't think that it's better that we win the first game and don't know why. I think that it's important that we find a way that we win games in the future and we know why.'

JUST a few days later, Liverpool welcomed another south-coast club to Anfield in the form of Bournemouth for a League Cup fourth-round tie.

The Reds had already hosted Eddie Howe's newly promoted side earlier in the season, earning a hard-fought 1-0 win thanks to a solitary Christian Benteke goal.

The Cherries had revenge in their sights and may have fancied their chances when the starting line-ups were announced. Klopp had stated in his pre-match press conference that this competition was the most important one as it was 'the next game', but he had still taken the chance to rest key players and blood some youngsters.

Connor Randall, João Teixeira and Cameron Brannagan were all handed their first starts for the first team, as was back-up goalkeeper Ádám Bogdán, who had been signed on a free transfer from Bolton Wanderers in the summer.

Randall sat in at right-back, which meant Nathaniel Clyne moving over to play at left-back for the first time at his new club.

Benteke was unable to play as he had picked up another knock against Southampton so Divock Origi was back in, with Roberto Firmino in behind him.

The Brazilian was outstanding, and for the first time since his big-money move from Hoffenheim in the summer, he was playing with confidence and leadership. He wanted the ball all the time, was comfortable with it and created chances for himself and others. He had dragged a shot wide in the opening minute, and seen another drive from range fly just over the bar.

Then came the breakthrough as Firmino played a delightful ball to Teixeira, who showed confidence as his touch took him wide to improvise and back-heel the ball into the ground and over the onrushing goalkeeper. The ball was about to go in, but the young Portuguese midfielder was denied by a goal-line clearance. However, Clyne was coming in from the left and calmly side-footed the loose ball into the empty net to give his side the lead.

The Reds held on for the win and earned their passage through to the quarter-finals.

Klopp went on to the pitch at the final whistle and shook every Bournemouth player's hand, before hugging each member of his own team. He made sure he went to the youngsters to praise them on their efforts, ruffling the hair of Randall as a dad would his five-year-old son.

It was Klopp's first win in English football. It was far from a classic but it was significant. With an understrength side, the Reds had shown a steely resilience matched with a willingness for flair that had been missing for some time.

It was very much on to the next one for Klopp, who just three days later took his side to Stamford Bridge to take on Premier League champions Chelsea.

José Mourinho's side had been uncharacteristically poor in the opening two months of the season, finding themselves in the bottom half of the table having lost five of their first ten league games, and had also been knocked out of the League Cup by Stoke the previous Tuesday.

However, it was still Chelsea and it was still Mourinho. Liverpool's record in west London had not been great in recent years, and it was soon apparent that this game wasn't going to be a typical game against a struggling team as Ramires headed the Blues in front within the opening three minutes. Straight away Klopp was telling his players to keep their chins up. There was still a long way to go.

Benteke was still not fit enough to start, and there had been much debate pre-match after the side had been named, with no Origi either. Liverpool appeared to be playing without a recognised striker with the assumption that Firmino would play a false-nine role.

That turned out to be the case and it was being heavily criticised as an approach by BT Sport commentators Ian Darke and Trevor

Francis as Chelsea dominated the first ten minutes, suggesting that without a focal point, Liverpool wouldn't be able to break down the home defence to find the equaliser.

However, what it did allow the Reds to do was control the ball. They enjoyed a lot of possession, and were also able to nullify any counter-attacks that Mourinho's side attempted. As the first half went on, Liverpool came more and more into the game, and by the time two minutes of stoppage time was announced they had seen 64 per cent of the ball and taken six shots to Chelsea's one.

Then as the clock ticked over the extra two minutes, Klopp's men broke down the right. The ball came to Firmino, who laid it back to fellow countryman Coutinho. The little magician, as he was known to the Kop, turned on to his left foot, completely flummoxing Ramires, and curled a sumptuous effort past the reach of Asmir Begović and into the far corner for the equaliser.

It was an ideal time to score, and the home fans were not happy, claiming that the whistle should have gone for half-time before Coutinho was allowed to score.

In the second half it was much of the same. Possession dominance from Liverpool and blunt counter-attacking from Chelsea. Once Klopp introduced Benteke from the bench, the game was there to be won, and it was.

A long ball from Mamadou Sakho was brought down by the big Belgian. The ball found its way to Coutinho on the edge of the penalty area, and this time he turned on to his right foot, before side-footing past Begović, courtesy of a John Terry deflection, to give Liverpool the lead.

The game was then sealed when a Jordon Ibe cross ended up at the feet of Benteke, who with all the time and space in the world, set himself and put the ball into the far corner to make it 3-1.

It felt like a big win, in spite of Chelsea's problems. They had beaten the champions on their own patch. José Mourinho's champions, and they'd beaten them well. It wasn't a smash and grab, it was a dominant and deserved victory.

It was Klopp's first win in the Premier League and it had come at Stamford Bridge, where the Reds hadn't scored more than twice in a game since 1989.

It was soon time for Liverpool to resume Europa League duty. It has often been seen as a chore in England, especially for games such as this where they were going to have to travel all the way to Russia.

However, Klopp did not understand this dismissal of a premier European competition. In spite of the added stipulation that the winner of the tournament would get a place in the Champions League, teams such as West Ham and Southampton had been eliminated in the qualifying rounds and seemed to be more relieved than disappointed, fearing that prolonged commitments on Thursday nights would affect their league form.

It was the first game in Rubin's new stadium, the Kazan Arena, and a big turnout came to see the world-famous Liverpool FC as the first opponents.

Klopp's men controlled the game throughout, though it took an excellent run and finish from Ibe to make the difference in the second half.

It was the teenager's first goal for the club, and pleased his manager so much that on the final whistle he came over to his players and simply shouted 'Ibeeee!' as he ran up and embraced him in a bear hug.

Barring a couple of scares near the end, it was a comfortable win for Liverpool, their first of this Europa League campaign. This made it three wins in a row, and all of a sudden the Klopp machine appeared to be up and running. Six games, three draws followed by three wins, with only three goals conceded in that time.

Klopp's next challenge three days later was against a particular thorn in Liverpool's side, Crystal Palace.

The London club had been a regular source of pain for the Reds in previous years, having extinguished their 2013/14 title challenge with a comeback 3-3 draw, and then beaten them home and away in the league the following season, although Liverpool had put them out of the FA Cup.

Palace defeated Liverpool 3-1 in Steven Gerrard's final game at Anfield, and they were determined to ruin the Klopp party as well.

As fate would have it, Gerrard was back at Anfield on the day. The Liverpool legend had come to the end of his first season in the MLS with LA Galaxy, and was back in England to see his former team-mates play.

Inevitably, the media was full of stories about how Gerrard was ready to return to the club, either as a player or a coach. Klopp was quick to pour water on the claims, saying that while he would happily have the former Reds captain train with them to keep his fitness up before returning to the US, he would not be coming back in a playing capacity.

Gerrard was in the stands, and will have had the same sinking feeling as he had six months prior as Yannick Bolasie took advantage of an error from Emre Can to fire Palace into an early lead.

In spite of the support around him, Benteke was unable to get into the game, as Palace defended deep. It was that deepness though that allowed Liverpool to get back level as a ball in from the right from Ibe was touched on by Lallana, and an onrushing Coutinho buried the chance with the inside of his right foot.

The expectation was that they would do as they did at Stamford Bridge in the second half as well and go on to win.

However, having looked like a new team in recent games, all the old frustrations and concerns came flooding back as the visitors won a corner, which was headed home at the second attempt by Scott Dann.

It was a sloppy goal to concede just eight minutes from time, and all of a sudden fans were out of their seats and leaving the stadium.

The minutes ticked down and Liverpool were unable to find another equaliser. It was Klopp's first defeat as Reds manager, and it had come at home.

Seeing the fans leaving when there was still over ten minutes to play, Klopp said after the game, 'Eighty-two minutes – game over.

'I turned around and I felt pretty alone at this moment. We have to decide when it is over ... I am not disappointed about this, the fans leaving, they have reasons, but we are responsible that nobody can leave the stadium a minute before the last whistle because everything can happen.

'Between 82 minutes and 94 you can make eight goals, if you want, but you have to work for it ... That is what we have to show and we didn't.'

Klopp felt alone, at Anfield of all places.

5

'They are football maniacs.'

L IVERPOOL'S dominance from the early days of the great Bill Shankly up to the start of the 1990s owed much to the fabled 'boot room', where legendary figures such as Shankly, Bob Paisley, Joe Fagan, Ronnie Moran and Roy Evans masterminded decades of success.

As time went on the manager changed, but the boot room remained. It was a term that referred to an actual boot room where the manager and his staff would have meetings and conjure up the ideas and strategies that would win the Reds domestic and European titles by the bucketful, but it was also a concept that coaches could be far more important than just motivators who put the cones out.

Having a close bond with his coaching staff has always been something that Klopp credits his achievements in the game to. In 2011 after being named manager of the year in Germany, he told *11 Freunde* magazine, 'The three of us together make one really good Bundesliga manager.'

He was referring to his closest football allies, Željko Buvač and Peter Krawietz. They worked together in Mainz and Dortmund, and on their appointments at Liverpool, Klopp told the club website, 'They are football maniacs. They work pretty hard and they are my perfect partners in this job, because as a manager you always have to make decisions and always have to think about so many different things.

'In my opinion, it's very important that you have somebody you can talk to. We can talk about everything. I make the decisions, of course, but I need very good people around me.'

Klopp had brought his own boot room to Merseyside, the *'schuhraum'* if you will.

Buvač was born in what is now known as Bosnia and Herzegovina, and enjoyed a 13-year playing career in his homeland and then in Germany with Rot-Weiss Erfurt, Mainz 05 and SC Neukirchen, where he took over as manager in 1998. He remained in Neukirchen for three seasons, before Klopp came along with a proposition.

The duo formed a close friendship during their years playing together at Mainz, and had come to an arrangement. When they went into professional management, one would follow and be the other's assistant. Klopp made the call and Buvač was soon on his way back to Mainz.

Buvač is also a keen believer in the art of *gegenpressing*, and Klopp credits him with being the man who refined it to allow his teams to reach the levels they did.

Dortmund midfielder Nuri Şahin once said of Buvač that he was 'basically Klopp's twin' when he took charge of a Champions League tie in 2013 due to Klopp serving a suspension.

Colin Bell was the reserve team manager at Mainz during Klopp's tenure, and he told *The Times* about the effect of Buvač on Klopp's teams, 'When Mainz started to play 4-3-3 it was different to the Dutch way where you have a central striker and two out-and-out wingers.

'Andriy Voronin [who went on to play for Liverpool] scored 20 goals for Mainz [in 2002/03] and he was all over the pitch, working really hard from central striker or right wing and left wing and it was so difficult for opponents to stop him and others.

'I can see those sorts of aspects in the Liverpool style now, especially with the quality of player they have.

'Closing down, surrounding opponents, going hunting for the ball – that all started in Mainz. That was one of Željko's big things and he did specific training forms for that.'

While Klopp is always front and centre for the media, who lap up his every word, Buvač is notoriously low-key when it comes to the limelight. He leaves that side of things to his good friend and can only ever really be heard on the training field. However, in January 2016 he did give a very rare interview to *The Express*, where he spoke about his relationship with 'Kloppo'.

'As players there was a direct connection straight away,' he said. 'Kloppo as a player was the same as he is as a manager. His character was the same, he wants to win. You cannot help but like him.

'Both of us were looking to become managers and we promised each other, "If I am the first manager, I will take you and if you are the first manager you will take me." He came first. It is a friendship.

'Before every training session and after every training session we talk together. Before every match and after every match we talk.

'In training I am observing and watching and if I have the feeling something needs to be changed I will speak to Kloppo. We discuss it, "Why should this be? Why that?" But it is a decision we come to together. That is the way in training and that is the way in the match.

'If it is necessary, I get up from the bench and that is okay. I don't need to ask. Together with Peter we have six eyes. You see more than if only one man is looking.'

Buvač was visiting his parents when he received a call from a familiar voice with a new opportunity.

'I was enjoying the sunshine, but I always knew that I could get a call from Kloppo if he had been contacted by an interesting club,' he said.

'Liverpool is more than an interesting club that is clear. I knew that after Dortmund this was a good step as the next club. I don't think he needed a long time to think about Liverpool. You must say "yes".

'Liverpool has big tradition and the feeling was that with hard work you can create maybe a new era, new successes. That was part of the attraction.'

Due to work permit complications, Buvač didn't arrive in England until almost a week after Klopp did, but once everything was sorted he was flown in on a chartered private jet at the insistence of the manager, and the work could truly begin.

Fellow Liverpool first-team coach Pepijn Lijnders has described Buvač as 'the human computer', but it was Klopp who gave him his famous nickname, 'The Brain'.

Klopp sees the triumvirate of himself, Buvač and Krawietz as one perfect manager, with a brain (Buvač), mouth (Klopp) and eyes (Krawietz).

Unlike Buvač, Krawietz did not enjoy a career as a player, but had joined Mainz straight out of the local university after securing a degree in sport.

While Klopp was a player at the club, Krawietz was the team's video analyst, and his abilities in the role were not lost on a younger Klopp, who promoted him from within the scouting team once he became manager, eventually making him his chief scout. Once at Dortmund, Klopp made Krawietz his opposition analyst.

The Telegraph's Chris Bascombe was able to obtain an interview with Krawietz in January 2016 where the German explained his role in more detail.

'It is very collaborative how we work. We've been this way since we started together,' Krawietz revealed.

'We are all part of the team here but it is different in Germany to England. Here, as a manager, there are so many more tasks around the club so me and Željko try to help as much as we can.

'In Mainz and Dortmund video analysis was my main task. Here it is different because we already have a department doing all this stuff and I try to prepare – filter all the information we need and prepare meetings for the team.

'Now we have the computer in the dressing room on a match day, a projector and then the screen.

'I don't know if we were the first to do it when we started at Mainz but we like to immediately show the players what we mean. A manager can explain a situation, ask the player about it and then we can show him. You've got it there to see it. It makes it easy for players to understand.

'Hopefully it should mean you correct the faults every time. I'm making the list during the game seeing what is important for us, working out if the problem is one scene or a trend – maybe a defensive problem or spaces we are not using, or the opponent has changed their setup.

'We use this, especially at the moment, to improve the development. It is very important to be able to react at half-time and show what we can do better. We also have the cameras outside on the training pitch to use if necessary.

'I began as a student in the University of Mainz and [Wolfgang Frank] worked with my professor. I became part of the scouting team. That's how I met Jürgen.

'When I started my work there was a situation where I presented my analysis, telling him what he should have done.

'It was my task to tell him what he'd done wrong. Then we had a "discussion" – if I can put it like that – as he asked me why I suggested this. It was the first time we spoke about football I can remember. It was the start.

'I always saw the possibility of him becoming a manager. He was an important player for his team but not the best player, but he had the attitude, leadership skills and understanding of his game to know what he could and could not do. He was always thinking for the team.

'He was very interested in the tactics and it was clear he was an outstanding person.

'He called me and said there was the possibility of Liverpool and what did I think? He said he thought we should go and I was invited.

'I was enjoying the sabbatical so it was a surprising moment but I felt his conviction that Liverpool is the right place to go. I thought for two hours and then said "okay".'

While having Buvač and Krawietz was absolutely crucial in Klopp taking the job, he would need more.

In the aftermath of Brendan Rodgers's departure, some of his coaching staff had left as well. Assistant Sean O'Driscoll followed Rodgers out the door, and former Liverpool player Gary McAllister was also relieved of his coaching duties but was offered an ambassadorial role instead, which he took.

That left goalkeeper coach John Achterberg and newly appointed first-team coach Pepijn Lijnders. Despite the fact that both are Dutch and the notorious football rivalry between Germany and the Netherlands, Klopp was happy to take them on as part of his coaching team.

Achterberg joined Liverpool's backroom staff in June 2009 under Rafa Benitez having previously been a goalkeeper and coach at nearby Tranmere Rovers. After initially working with the youngsters, he was promoted to first-team goalkeeper coach in 2011, and has remained in the role ever since.

In December 2015, Klopp told the club website, 'I really trust John Achterberg because he does a brilliant job here. He is one of the hardest working people I have ever met. He is a goalkeeper coach 25 hours a day.'

I was given the opportunity to ask Achterberg about life working with the German coach. 'When a new manager first comes through the door, it's always a case of wait and see. You need to work with him on his philosophy and ultimately see what his ways of doing things are as one manager's ways of working are different to another's. But, I distinctly remember during my first meeting with him, I felt like I had already known him 20 years. It has been great working with him and for him; he is always asking for my opinion both on the goalkeepers inside and outside of the club, as well as how they are progressing. I always give my opinion and he always says what he thinks – he is very straight to the point, which is cool as that's how it should be. It's a healthy way of working.

'He is so relaxed and has a great personality that instils such a warm feeling throughout the club. He has created a one-club mentality, everyone in every role at Liverpool is respected; we are part of a family. He also sets very high expectations. You have to function in the job as he expects; everyone has to be at their best day in, day out, just like him, in order for the team to succeed.'

Achterberg also reflected on how he felt when Klopp was first appointed. 'He had a big reputation and had such an illustrious career at Dortmund, and during our first meeting he was so relaxed and calm – straight away there was a good feeling when we were talking. We were just talking about football, goalkeepers and players that were here, all to try and help provide him with information on the English game, as well as life values in the United Kingdom.

'He has instilled more belief in the players. They have a clear game plan of what they have to do and what he wants from them and is always trying to improve their knowledge of the game; including making them think quicker to find solutions, make faster movements and increase the pace of ball circulation. The intensity has gone up both in games and team training to bring the individuals and team up to a higher level.'

I asked Achterberg about how the coaching staff works as a team, and how Klopp compares to the other managers he has worked under at Liverpool. 'We openly discuss things during each part of the day before and after training, or when we are together for a more casual, relaxed meet up. We communicate consistently on all aspects. That's really important and, as I said, Jürgen is a manager who values your opinion on matters.

'Every manager is different and they all have their own way of working. With Jürgen, he is so focused and consistent on not letting any player relax or not give 100 per cent each day for the team, he pushes every player to give absolutely everything they have got. He tells them all straight and they know exactly what's expected of them. He knows you need to build a rapport and friendship with each player, but at the same time, knows there is a line, as he needs to pick a team that can win the next game. He is a winner and this is what he wants to transmit into each player – that belief and that passion that they can use in each game and make them feel unbeatable.'

Liverpool acquired the services of upcoming young coach Pep Lijnders from FC Porto in August 2014, where he spent seven seasons. Prior to that, he coached at PSV Eindhoven for five years.

Lijnders came in initially to work with the club's under-16 side, but it wasn't long before his exceptional coaching promise saw him promoted to the first team under Brendan Rodgers. It was a newly created role of first-team development coach, though he was still in charge of certain aspects of youth development, being the go-between for the club's most talented youngsters and the first team.

Lijnders spoke to me about what it was like when Klopp first arrived at the club. 'There is a saying that there are only two types of coaches in this world: the ones with guts and the ones without. We are lucky Jürgen is with us. To innovate you need guts, and to adapt you need an open mind. He only thinks about preparing the team, step by step, towards playing more and better football – in his first meeting he made this very clear. He also told the team counter-pressing isn't a proposal, it's a law under him. With this first meeting he defined our identity as a team: terrible, enthusiastic, ambitious, mentally strong machines.

'Also, he defined the character he searches for with an unbelievably smart trick. All the staff at Melwood were told to walk through one door and out the other during the first meeting with the squad. He then addressed the team saying "all these people work so hard, day in, day out, so you can develop to your maximum, respect this by giving everything". You only have one chance to make a first impression and that was a perfect first impression for the team.

'He is a coach who wants to be dominant, who wants control in all game moments. The way he, Željko and Peter set up training and set up meetings is only possible because they know exactly what they are trying to achieve. That's something they are searching for constantly: improvement. But only in order to win the next game – as he says: "hauptsache drei Punkte" (the main thing is three points). I believe this, in the short, short, short-term, automatically creates the perfect long-term, because you can only influence now. The three are like a jigsaw; they only fit together – and therefore work – with each other, and that is something that can only grow with time.

'There is a saying, you're a product of your own environment, and this is so true. But some people, just a few have the gift to create an environment just by themselves, giving colour to a whole organisation.'

I also asked Lijnders about how he has enjoyed working with Klopp and the rest of the coaching team. 'I'm proud to be part of this project and of this group of special people at Melwood. It's up to us to create momentum because the ones who win are the ones who think they can. Anfield deserves his mentality; it's such a special place that deserves special coaches. If as a manager after so many years you still believe in training and in development, that says everything because that means you go for the hardest but most valuable way. You feel every day at Melwood that we are not in this job to participate; we are in the job to win. He is the captain and gives directions – I just try and help him as much as I can.

'The manager's job is a job that has evolved so quickly in the last few years. With a club like Liverpool, you need to delegate and create trust with the people around you. That's why better people make a better team. He is very good at cutting out and ignoring what is beyond his control. The power and passion supported by our pressing and counter-pressing structure is what makes our team different to all other teams in world football, in my opinion. They say that the force of character is cumulative and I believe that the character of the team is defined by the character of the coach.

'In life you meet many people, most of them walk by, some of them give you direction and help you in difficult moments, but just one or two make an impact you couldn't imagine.'

Despite Klopp being happy with his coaching staff, there was still one that got away, at least according to reports.

David Wagner managed the reserve team at Dortmund, and was best man at Klopp's wedding. Upon Klopp's appointment at Liverpool, it was reported that Klopp wanted his long-time friend to join him at Anfield to manage the club's under-23 team.

However, Wagner had another offer from England to manage Huddersfield Town, which he took.

While Klopp may have been left disappointed by his friend not being a part of his setup at Liverpool, there was little doubt that Wagner made the right choice when he guided the Terriers to an unlikely promotion to the Premier League at the end of the 2016/17 season after a dramatic penalty shoot-out win against Jaap Stam's Reading at Wembley Stadium.

6

'I don't know if proud is the right word, but of course I'm really satisfied with the performance. It was far away from perfect, but it was in many moments really, really good.'

K LOPP felt alone, but Chris Morgan, the club's head of physiotherapy, certainly didn't. His room was getting fuller by the game. Joe Gomez, Danny Ings, Jon Flanagan, Jordan Rossiter and Jordan Henderson had now been joined by Mamadou Sakho on the sidelines.

However, one perennially injured player was on the brink of a return. Daniel Sturridge, who had barely managed a handful of games since being injured on England duty over a year earlier, was fit enough to be named on the bench for the trip to his former club Manchester City.

Klopp had already expressed his surprise at how often he was asked about Sturridge, but now he finally had him ready to be a part of his squad. He'd be able to see what all the fuss was about.

In spite of being able to add another striker to the bench, Klopp started the game at the Etihad Stadium with no recognised striker, as he had done at Chelsea. Firmino played as a false nine again with Coutinho and Lallana working around him.

Manuel Pellegrini's men had experienced some setbacks early on in the season, but had been looking imperious since then, winning 12 of their previous 13 home games. They had also taken Raheem Sterling from the Anfield club in the transfer saga of the summer. This would be the 20-year-old's first game against his former club since the move, but was not one he'd remember fondly.

The Reds started all guns blazing, chasing and harrying straight from the first whistle. City were flustered, and that manifested itself in the opening goal when Coutinho linked with Firmino in the penalty area. Firmino pulled the ball back, and a panicky Eliaquim Mangala diverted the ball into his own net. Liverpool were ahead, and on fire.

Firmino linked with his Brazilian teammate again as he chased a ball down and dribbled toward the penalty area. He then played an outrageous ball into the perfect area for Coutinho to run on to it and side-foot the second through the legs of Joe Hart. Klopp's men were rampant, and City had no idea how to combat it.

The same link-up led to number three as a wonderfully imaginative back-heel from Emre Can released Coutinho in the area. He committed Hart, before selflessly passing to Firmino for a simple tap in and his first goal in a Liverpool shirt.

This was incredible. Manchester City, with Yaya Touré, Sterling, Kevin De Bruyne and Sergio Agüero in their side, were being absolutely destroyed by a Liverpool team that had recently been beaten at home by Crystal Palace. The visitors were all over them, and Firmino could have scored two more before half-time.

However, City were given hope before the break as Agüero in trademark fashion curled a right-footed effort into the corner from 25 yards to make it 3-1.

That changed the mood of the second half as Klopp's men retreated from their 100mph start. They found their shape and largely kept City at bay, restricting them to fleeting moments of threat.

Klopp's starting XI meant he had the luxury of being able to call on his strikers from the bench later on if he needed, and in spite of leading, he decided to introduce Christian Benteke for the closing stages. His ability at defending from set pieces as well as attacking them may have been a factor, and it was the Belgian's work that led to the game being wrapped up.

After being played through on goal, he dallied and only just managed to get a shot away. It was pushed behind by Hart, but from the resulting corner, Benteke brought the ball down and Martin Škrtel smashed it in to make it 4-1.

The away fans cheered as the players ran over in their direction. Škrtel wanted to jump in with them but was thwarted by the photographers' area that separated fans and pitch.

The game was over and Liverpool had thoroughly outplayed Manchester City on their own ground. It was a masterclass from Klopp, and Pellegrini conceded as much in his post-match interview, suggesting that his team could have conceded a lot more than the four they did.

For the German, while he was obviously pleased with the result and aspects of the performance, he was not entirely content. Talking to NBC after the game, he said, 'I don't know if proud is the right word, but of course I'm really satisfied with the performance. It was far away from perfect, but it was in many moments really, really good.

'What we had to do was disturb their build-up play, because if you let them play how they want, you have no chance. That's what we tried to do. This was the first step in this game. It's really not easy because we didn't defend perfectly, we had some problems at the wing, in the centre we didn't move enough on the ball side. But when we got the ball, our counter-attack was not too bad tonight, it was really good.'

When asked about the development of his side, he added, 'We are not at the end of this way, it's a long way we have to go. It's not easy because there is no time to train. When we have time, all the players are around the world with the national teams.

'The character of the team is really good, they want to work. I knew about the character, when you watch Liverpool you see they're ready for work. But of course we have to work at the mentality, and it's a different thing. I said to my players at half-time, "It looks a little like you're surprised we're in the lead". We have to learn to win, to be in the lead. It's far away from perfect, but it was a big step. The points, and style of play, we can do better and that's very important.'

An added bonus for Klopp was that he didn't have to use Sturridge, allowing him extra time to train before being thrown into a game situation.

'To have Sturridge on the bench, and you don't have to bring him in, because four days in training is nothing. It was more "come on, Studge [Sturridge's nickname], feel it, you are with us" and now he can make the next step, four more days training against Bordeaux, then another two. To bring him in the shape so he's robust enough for the long season.'

The next few days were filled with papers and pundits sitting up and taking notice of Liverpool's performance. While there was an acceptance that City had been poor, there was no ignoring the performance of Klopp's men, particularly in the first half.

However, it was yet another example of how well Klopp had his team playing on the road in games where they would be able to press and counter-attack. It was at home where the problems remained, and their next two games would be tests of how good this team was at taking the initiative rather than picking teams off.

The first was the visit of Bordeaux in the Europa League. Despite falling behind to a farcical goal from an indirect free kick when Mignolet held on to the ball for too long, goals from Benteke and Milner (penalty) saw the Reds win the game 2-1. They had secured passage through to the knockout stages, even leapfrogging Sion into first place after the Swiss side lost to Rubin Kazan.

It was not a vintage performance but the win was important, and the same was to be said three days later when Swansea City came to town. It was a ferociously windy day on Merseyside, with local road closures and some fixtures around the ground needing to be cordoned off and tied down.

To the surprise of many, the name of Daniel Sturridge appeared once again on the subs bench. There had been no news of the results of his scan, or that he had even had one, but the day after the Bordeaux game, Klopp made some interesting comments about a player who had previously been accused by fans and even ex-team-mates of being 'too cautious' whenever he felt a bit of pain.

However, Klopp stated in his pre-match press conference, 'If it wasn't for Daniel's quality no one would think about him being back on the pitch after such a short time. What you need in times like this is training. Your body has to learn new intensity of training and you have to learn what is serious pain or what is only pain.'

He didn't want to rush Sturridge back, especially as his body was only just getting used to a new type of training regime. With Benteke hitting form, it wasn't as drastic as it had seemed earlier in the season to rush Sturridge back, and it was the Belgian named up top on his own again against the Swans.

The Reds dominated the ball as Garry Monk's side sat back and tried to soak up the pressure. This was exactly the sort of thing Liverpool had been struggling with, and they once again found it difficult to create meaningful openings. Swansea were showing no interest in getting forward, and it was frustrating Klopp. You cannot press a team that doesn't want the ball, and this style was completely against what you would have normally expected from Swansea, who prided themselves on a philosophy of possession-based football. However, Monk was under pressure after a poor run of recent results and was doing what he thought necessary to get something from the game.

That may have been what led him to being so angry about the decision to award Liverpool a penalty after a cross from Ibe struck the arm of Neil Taylor. As he had done three days earlier, Milner stepped up and coolly put it in the net.

It was a crucial three points for Liverpool, with several of the teams above them dropping points earlier that weekend. The win moved them up to sixth in the table, only four points from the Champions League places, and only six from the top.

Klopp expressed his delight after the game, admitting that it was a good win considering the windy conditions. In both home games across the four days his side had laboured somewhat, but had won both of them and until they were able to find the performances to match their away showings, the points would have to be a suitable consolation.

It will perhaps have been a relief that their next game came away, a League Cup trip to Southampton. It was a long trip down to the south coast for a midweek game, but the journey would prove worthwhile for those who made it.

Klopp had made clear ahead of the previous round of the competition that he was taking it seriously, realising that as the first winnable trophy of his Liverpool tenure, it was a great chance to get his reign off to an ideal start.

It wasn't an ideal start to the game though as after just 40 seconds, sloppy play on the right allowed a cross to come in and Sadio Mané gave the Saints a very early lead.

The first ten minutes were dominated by Southampton, threatening to double their lead on a couple of occasions. Then all of a sudden the game changed dramatically.

Allen played a terrific ball over to Sturridge, whose control forced him out wide. He set himself and fired past Maarten Stekelenburg from a tight angle to equalise. From then on, it was Liverpool's night.

Sturridge bagged his second after getting on the end of a wonderful ball from Emre Can, and Alberto Moreno thought he'd scored the third after firing in from the edge of the area following a corner. However, the goal would be awarded to Origi, who had deflected it slightly.

After soaking up a few moments of pressure in the second half, the Reds put their foot down again and a thunderbolt from Origi, a well-taken strike by Ibe and a final header from Origi to complete his hat-trick sealed an incredible 6-1 victory for Klopp.

Southampton had not been at peak form, but they were still a fine side, as shown in their well-earned 1-1 draw at Anfield just a few weeks prior. Liverpool had absolutely decimated them, as they had done to Manchester City, only this was in spite of missing the likes of Coutinho, Firmino, Sakho, Benteke, Mignolet and Clyne. It was another top-class away display that made people sit up and take notice.

The questions post-game for Klopp though were predictably about Sturridge, who looked like he had not missed a beat, taking both goals in such a nonchalant manner. Klopp said, 'I said to Sturridge after the game, "Now I know what everybody is talking about so thank you."'

Ahead of the tie, Klopp had said something that not only gave the collective journalists a chuckle, but also gave a clear insight into the mind of the man. He constantly played down the importance of setbacks to the media, saying things like 'this is football', and the basic message being that you should never get too carried away by wins or become too despondent in defeat.

However, when asked about his start to life at Anfield, with just one defeat in his first ten games, he replied, 'I would really like to change my personality but I can't forget this fucking loss against Crystal Palace.'

For all his insistence that people not overreact and keep their heads, he appeared to have been as affected as anyone by that particular loss. It was the sign of a perfectionist, and a personality trait that had partly led to his successes in Germany.

It was something that would be tested again as Liverpool travelled to Newcastle, who were in a woeful run of form having registered just two wins in the league before December, and were fresh off a 5-1 hammering by – coincidentally – Crystal Palace.

All the signs pointed to a comfortable away win, but then 'this is football'.

Klopp's side were awful from first whistle to last. Misplacing passes throughout the game, they failed to create anything by way of meaningful chances. An own goal from Martin Škrtel and a late strike by Giorginio Wijnaldum were enough to see Liverpool off.

They looked a world away from the electric form of the side that had ripped apart Southampton just four days earlier, and was comfortably the worst performance of the Klopp era so far.

Klopp could not forget the 'fucking loss against Crystal Palace'. It was anyone's guess what word he was going to use to describe this defeat.

In a matter of days, the mood had gone from that of jubilant optimism, to a crashing back down to earth. There was an appreciation that this was still very much a work in progress and that hiccups such as this were inevitable, but nonetheless the Liverpool fans were deflated by the defeat and performance.

Theirs and Klopp's moods weren't helped at all by the news that came out just two days later.

Daniel Sturridge was injured again.

7

'I think if anyone is capable of finally winning the Premier League with Liverpool it's Jürgen Klopp.' Sandra Goldschmidt – Borussia Dortmund fan

L IVERPOOL Football Club is one of the biggest in the world. With nearly 30 million followers on Facebook, 7.5million followers on Twitter and a season ticket waiting list that stretches over decades, you are never too far away from a Liverpool supporter.

With that amount of interest, it inevitably leads to high levels of demand to watch, talk and listen to anything and everything LFC, and one independent club podcast and website has become a must for Reds fans far and wide in recent years.

The Anfield Wrap is a free twice-weekly podcast, with a separate subscription service (TAW Player) for those who want even more of their multi-award-winning shows.

Neil Atkinson (presenter) and Gareth Roberts (editor) are match-going Reds who believe in Jürgen Klopp and are thoroughly enjoying the journey the club is on under the German coach, and both were sure that he was the right appointment at the right time.

NA: 'It's important not to overstate the similarities between Liverpool and Dortmund in the context of what they were like as clubs when Klopp arrived at both places. Dortmund are a medium-level European power whereas Liverpool's European profile is second only to that of Real Madrid. That neither were punching their weight when Klopp arrived is the main thing they have in common, that and a wider perception that there is a fervent fan-base.

'But what Klopp would be able to bring, I thought, was a collective clarity of purpose. Liverpool needed a manager it could unite behind. From halfway through the Benitez era onwards Liverpool had lacked that barring two half-seasons for Dalglish and Rodgers and even the latter was failing to unite internally while playing the best football we had seen in years. Klopp would be able to demand more of everyone.'

GR: 'I was delighted because I thought Jürgen Klopp was the perfect fit for Liverpool; in terms of the style of football, in terms of his passion, in terms of a history of going toe-to-toe with big clubs and beating them. I think the Liverpool job is such a difficult one for a manager – we have huge expectations of style and results and of how the manager should act and behave.

'Klopp had the track record, the attitude and the passion – I was convinced Liverpool fans would take to him quite quickly. It was a statement, too. He had been linked to a string of top jobs; he was one of the most coveted managers in the world. As fans we'll always say Liverpool are one of the biggest and best in the world but the club's owners need to act that way too and back it up with their actions. By landing Klopp they made a much-needed signal of ambition.'

Neil and Gareth's first impressions of life under Klopp only served to back up that confidence in him.

NA: 'He had jokes and he couldn't believe how mad it was. He was someone who just wanted to do the job in front of him and could quickly grow annoyed if blocked from that. I was slightly worried at first. This didn't look a laugh for him at all.'

GR: 'I was sold! I was fortunate enough to be present at his opening press conference and he handled it brilliantly. How managers deal with the media is a big part of the job in the modern age and it was clear that Klopp could take it all in his stride. He was charismatic, he was charming but he also had a clear vision and he wasn't shy in telling someone if he thought they were wrong or crossing a line with a question. It was a public demonstration of his leadership.

'I like also that he recognised what Liverpool the club, Liverpool the city and Liverpool the fans can be when they come together. He's tried to foster that spirit of togetherness, of support, ever since. Liverpool is at its best when it's acting as one and shaking a fist in the direction of the opposition. That's what Klopp wants and that's what we want.'

I also asked Neil and Gareth whether Klopp had surprised them at all in the way he set the team up during his early games in charge.

NA: 'There was a ton of defensive shape early and at times almost too much rigidity especially at home against poorer sides. We could be excellent one minute and poor the next.'

GR: 'I think even for someone like me who doesn't watch hours on end of football away from Liverpool and the Premier League it was hard to have missed what Klopp did at Dortmund and the way he had them playing football. It was fairly clear he would come in, rev up the side, get them working harder than ever before and lift them from the doldrums we had ended up in at the end of Brendan Rodgers.

'From his first game in charge, away at Tottenham, it was clear his methods were sinking in with Adam Lallana in particular almost falling into the manager's arms when he left the pitch such was the effort he had put in. It was obvious fairly quickly that the players bought into what Klopp was about.'

It has not just been England where people have been fascinated by Klopp and how he has adapted to the Premier League. Sandra Goldschmidt has been going to Borussia Dortmund games since her dad first took her in 1994. Now she is the CCO of *Buzz09*, an app for Borussia Dortmund fans that covers news, rumours and live updates for every BVB game in both German and English.

Sandra was kind enough to give me her opinions on Klopp, what he achieved at Dortmund and what he might achieve at Liverpool.

What was the general opinion of Borussia Dortmund fans when Klopp was appointed in 2008?

'All BVB fans were very excited. We just had a tricky time behind us with three different managers in the space of six months. I still remember the moment we first heard about it. We made it into the DFB-Pokal Final in Berlin in 2008 and me and my friends were just in McDonald's when they showed it on TV inside the restaurant that Klopp was rumoured to take over and there were cheers everywhere. I don't know a single fan who wasn't happy with his appointment.'

Was much patience shown by fans in his first two seasons when the club finished sixth and fifth?

'Yes. Our squad really wasn't great back then and we were simply glad to see things looking up again. Even though it was a shame when we just missed out on qualifying for the Europa League in his first season the fans still stayed patient. Everyone could see that he was just forming his own squad and that of course needed some time.'

Was there ever much unrest with the style he had his team playing or were fans mostly happy with it?

'At first not at all. Everyone loved the "full speed" football and it was great to watch. I can only remember unrest in his last season when we had a very tough first half of the season and fans began to question whether he had a "plan B", but I think overall everyone enjoyed the style of football we were playing. People might argue now that [Thomas] Tuchel's tactics were even more successful, but I personally think we were much more fun to watch under Klopp.'

How much of an influence do you think Željko Buvač and Peter Krawietz had on Dortmund's success?

'A lot. After we won the German championship and then the double a year later Klopp always said, "It wasn't just me who won it, it was us three." I think they are a really good team.'

Just how much was Klopp loved by fans during the peak of his success at the club?

'I'd say it's fair to say more than any other BVB manager before him. Klopp and Dortmund were just perfect for each other. The club started their *"Echte Liebe"* (real love) slogan during this time and right there and then it was really fitting, because it was truly love between the fans, the club and Klopp. To watch how he gave all those young players a chance and how he formed them into a title-winning team was a great experience. I don't think any league win will ever be as emotional as the one in 2011, because it was so unexpected.'

What was the consensus of his final season? What did people put the dramatic drop in form down to?

'That's something everyone probably still wonders about now. The World Cup and injuries played their part, but it should have still not caused such a drop in form. Everyone kept saying, "Surely they'll win their next game, they have too much quality," and maybe the players told themselves that too. But the more games went by without winning, the more doubts everyone had. Luckily we had a really good second half of the season, but the awful form in the first half of the season will always be one big question mark.'

Did fans agree that the time was right for Klopp and BVB to part ways?

'There were mixed feelings. Some thought that it was time for a change, because like I mentioned earlier they believed Klopp only had one tactic plan and that all the pressing football took its toll on the players. However, even when we were at the bottom of the table none of the fans openly demanded him to be sacked. He was loved even during the worst moments of the last season and his farewell was very emotional. I'd say most BVB fans still hope that he'll be back one day.'

How did Dortmund fans feel about him going to Liverpool?

'I think everyone was really excited for him. If there was another club as perfect for Klopp as Dortmund it had to be Liverpool. He was previously linked to Bayern in the German press, so of course it was also a relief that never happened, everyone would have hated him to go there. Liverpool are very popular with the Dortmund fans, so we all still keeping our fingers crossed for him.'

Do you think he is capable of winning that elusive Premier League title?

'Absolutely yes! I think if anyone is capable of finally winning the Premier League with Liverpool it is Jürgen Klopp. I hope that the fans will continue to be patient with him and at Dortmund he won us the league in his third season in charge, so who knows, it could possibly happen next year already.'

8

'Like all things in life, you can wait for the moment or you can create the moment.'

D ANIEL Sturridge had been ruled out yet again after suffering a hamstring injury in the loss at Newcastle. The prognosis was not as bad as first feared and it was estimated that the striker would be back in time for the turn of the year, but it was yet more frustration for a player who had missed so much football in the previous 15 months, and a team who were still quite reliant on his natural goalscoring ability.

The fixtures were still coming thick and fast for Klopp and his team, with the final game of their Europa League group campaign to navigate.

A dull 0-0 away to Sion was good enough for Liverpool. They had won the group. After the match, Klopp said, 'It was difficult. The ground was very difficult to play and for both teams the first thing to do was show you were prepared for a game like this and that is what my team did.

'We wanted to be first after this game and that is what we did. A few weeks ago it was far away from us that we could reach this place but we did it and it is really good. Everyone will have to change their mind about this tournament now as everyone will see it is something like a small Champions League.'

Liverpool were deemed fortunate to have been given several home games immediately after Europa League fixtures, though Klopp may not have felt so lucky given that it was at home where they were struggling to pick up wins. Their next game was against West Brom, managed by Tony Pulis, whose teams were notoriously hard-working and favoured a more direct approach.

Klopp was asked about this in his pre-match press conference and admitted that it would be up to his side to break through that system, though this was something they had struggled to do for most of the season.

He also chose that moment to again address the issue of the atmosphere at Anfield.

'It is close to Christmas and people are maybe concentrating on other things. But when we come together on Sunday, we should all be prepared for a very special moment. Maybe we can create the best atmosphere in the last ten years.

'Like all things in life, you can wait for the moment or you can create the moment. And hopefully we can create the moment on Sunday.

'I'm always close to a good atmosphere in myself. If other people can join us in this, then that would be cool.'

Reds fans took Klopp's pre-match comments on board. The atmosphere was as good as it had been since the German was appointed, and was in full voice as Jordan Henderson swept home the opening goal following a lovely move. For once it felt like Liverpool were taking a home game by the scruff of the neck.

However, after being warned about the dangers that West Brom posed from set pieces, they succumbed to two, firstly as Mignolet came out to claim a cross, completely missed it, and Craig Dawson bundled home the loose ball to equalise for the visitors. Then midway through the second half an unmarked Jonas Olsson header from a corner made it 2-1.

It was yet another set-piece goal conceded, and this time the entire defence was to blame, with defenders strewn all over the place and none stopping the big Swede from scoring.

The Reds had been on top for most of the contest, and the fans maintained their noise levels, roaring their team on in hope of a comeback.

Eight minutes of stoppage time were given, and just as hope appeared lost, Divock Origi picked the ball up on the left and evaded a challenge, before hitting a speculative effort from range that took a heavy deflection and sent the ball into the far corner of the net.

Liverpool were level, the Kop went crazy and the manager exploded with joy, with his trademark punching of the air and racing around the technical area.

The game ended level, which was not the ideal outcome for Liverpool, but the nature of the draw had made it feel like a win.

That was not the end of the story though as Klopp ignored the post-match handshake with Pulis, only reluctantly giving one to a West Brom coach who had followed him and practically forced him to do so. Klopp explained to him why he wasn't willing to shake Pulis's hand, and went on to the field to be with his players.

He gathered them round, before taking them to the Kop, making them join hands and salute the crowd. It was reminiscent of the traditional post-match celebrations seen in the Bundesliga, and the home fans were appreciative of the gesture.

It was widely scrutinised after the game by rival fans and pundits alike, with the misconception being that Klopp was celebrating a draw with West Brom as if he'd won a trophy. This was far from the case, as he explained in his post-match press conference, 'It was the best atmosphere since I've been here, it was great. People were disappointed or frustrated but they didn't let us feel it. They saw the lads tried everything.'

In spite of being seen as a draw scraped out of a potential loss, Liverpool could consider themselves unlucky not to have won all three points. They had 70 per cent possession and 28 shots on goal compared to West Brom's four. It was yet another tale of errant finishing and erratic defending. The signs were there though that Klopp was starting to get his team playing with more belief and in the style he wanted. However, he made it abundantly clear that he did not have any interest in replicating the style of his opposite number.

'I have no problem with losing in football, you have to accept it. But this was not a game to lose, because they only played long balls and if you get points like this, do it. It's not bad. But not here. So we have to stop this. If you want to defend against us no problem, but when your only plan is to play long balls you're not allowed to win against us.

'I didn't see him [Pulis] after the game. I can say nothing. We had some words in the game; sometimes it takes more than a few seconds to cool down.

'If you want to make a big story, then please. Sometimes it is like this. Usually I shake hands; I did not today because it was not a friendly game.'

Klopp seemed satisfied with his team's work, and now for the first time since taking over would get an early Christmas present with a whole week to work with his squad before the next game.

With international breaks, Europa League commitments and League Cup ties to negotiate, the German was yet to have a full seven days with his entire squad at Melwood.

Away from the pitch, the club's official charity organisation, The Liverpool FC Foundation, had held its inaugural LFC Foundation Day on the day of the West Brom game, and Klopp made his feelings clear on the duty that he and his players had to be a part of it.

He told the club website, 'What responsibility does a football club have? Every football club needs to win matches, that's no secret. But there has to be more to it than that.

'We all know football is not the most important thing in life. The only thing you really have to do is care for each other, it's your responsibility. You can give back some of the things you got from all of the people around you. As a football club it's important you don't forget this.

'Young people are our future and they need help. Of course, we needed help when we were young and we all know that nobody is born and has the same chances, and we need to try that little bit more so that everybody has the same.

'Everything we could do, everything we have the power for, we should try.

'Our players here know where they come from and they are really good lads, and everybody should know that not only are they professional football players but they are human beings behind the shirt.

'If we can help by only being there and only showing our respect then it's easy to do and so football is very important.

'All these things we are doing without a bigger reason behind, we don't want to get something back, so we are the people who give back so everybody who is with us can get our help.'

Klopp even provided something for the related charity auction; an opportunity for the Reds manager to come to your house for dinner.

There were some inventive experiences put up for grabs by the players as well. People could bid to play a round of golf with James Milner, go for a curry with Danny Ings, have Kolo Touré cook them a meal, watch *Home Alone* with Nathaniel Clyne, Joe Gomez and Jordon Ibe, have a Brazilian meal with Lucas, Coutinho and Firmino, and even play table tennis with Alberto Moreno and João Teixeira.

One of the more popular annual Christmas activities at the club is visiting Alder Hey Children's Hospital. The manager and first team squad traditionally take presents every year to the young patients to give them a special pre-Christmas treat. Klopp and his players spoke to the children, handed out presents and posed for photographs.

Liverpool continued to be charitable when they went to Vicarage Road to play Watford. The Hornets had been quietly going about their business while Leicester City were capturing the country's imagination at the top of the league. Quique Sánchez Flores had guided his side into the top half of the table and they sat ahead of Liverpool before the game.

The front pairing of Troy Deeney and Odion Ighalo were terrorising defences up and down the land, and so the Reds would likely need to be at their best to navigate this fixture safely.

Klopp had lost three players to injury leading up to the game, with Lovren, Milner and Mignolet all missing out. Ádám Bogdán started in goal, with some fans suggesting that the Hungarian should have been selected regardless given Mignolet's recent dip in form.

However, that was no longer the general consensus just three minutes into the game as Bogdán dropped a corner and Chelsea loanee Nathan Aké prodded Watford ahead. There was an argument that Aké had kicked the ball out of Bogdan's hands, but it was a disastrous moment for the reserve keeper, and the team, who never fully recovered.

Watford dominated the game from first to last, bullying Liverpool into countless mistakes. The Reds were comfortably dispatched 3-0.

Understandably, the manager was not happy, pointing out that while the first goal shouldn't have stood, it was the players to blame for the performance,

'You have to have both hands on the ball and he had both hands on the ball, so it's a foul. But I have to say that we made bigger faults than the ref today. Mistakes, fouls, refs, whatever, can happen. That's football. Our reaction has to be better. We lost our mind after the first goal. We lost our compact formation after the first goal, and we didn't play easy, as we should have done.

'I would say, hopefully, this is the most disappointing moment in my whole Liverpool FC life, from now. We don't feel good today, of course, because we came here to do something really different to what you saw. There was a big space between what we wanted to do and what you see, and that's what we have to fill before the next game against Leicester.'

9

'For me as a young coach learning from the best it's the same as [the young players]. It's like a masterclass every day.' Pep Lijnders

W HEN people talk about working with Jürgen Klopp there is an inevitable gushing that comes with it. His former players have never been shy in speaking about how highly they rate the German coach.

One player whom Klopp had brought to Dortmund back in 2007 was Polish winger Jakub Błaszczykowski, or 'Kuba', and after Klopp's appointment at Liverpool, he had some extremely high praise for his former manager.

'He was, he is, and he always will be a special guy,' Kuba told *FourFourTwo* magazine. 'He's changed me, not only as a footballer but as a human being.

'No one had more influence than Klopp on who I became as a player. I owe him a lot. He always taught me that in all this craziness and competition, there is also a human side inside all of us that we need to cherish. Liverpool couldn't have hired a better manager. They have already won by appointing him.

'He's not only a great coach; he's a great psychologist and a great man. He made decisions based on what he sees, not what other people are telling him. That's extremely important, because he is honest with people and we could sense that. He knows how to deal with different characters and different egos.

'I'm pretty sure he will [succeed], but only if the players buy into his philosophy. That's what we did at Borussia and it paid off. They just need to trust him. He knows what he's doing, on and off the field.

We had to work and make a lot of sacrifices, but we accomplished a lot with Dortmund.'

Pep Lijnders was appointed as first-team coach in the summer of 2015 by Brendan Rodgers as a 32-year-old, less than a year after being brought to the club to work with the under-16 team.

He was very highly regarded by the powers that be at Anfield, and Klopp was more than happy to keep him on as part of his backroom team. It wasn't long before Lijnders was expressing his happiness at getting to work with Klopp.

'For me as a young coach learning from the best it's the same as [the young players]. It's like a masterclass every day,' he told the club website.

'You go to a congress and you see that one speaker and you like him and you think "wow".

'If you can work with that speaker every day that would be [fantastic] and that's the situation I'm in at the moment.'

Lijnders's role includes being in charge of the Talent Group, a selection of the best players from the youth setup brought to Melwood to train with the first team. He speaks highly of the concept, suggesting that having these young players work with Klopp early in their development is key to their transition to possible options for the first team.

'First of all, the character of the team is mainly developed by the character of the coach,' he said.

'You can train loads of things and develop but how you are as a person influences so much the players, how they are, how they approach the game, how they are in the game.

'If you look to the sessions, the games, the character of Jürgen and how he approaches every single thing, is very clear.

'The bravery and the passion of "this is how we are going to do it" makes an impact. That's one, that impact of the character, and then the impact of "this is what I want when we have the ball", "this is what I want when we lose the ball" so it gives the players a clear game idea.

'There are certain ways to create development, the most important one is knowing exactly how we approach the game as a collective, and creating an identity in terms of, if we wore different shirts, you would recognise us.'

The last comment is almost a word for word reflection of something Klopp said himself about his Borussia Dortmund side, that the team would be recognised by their way of playing rather than their iconic yellow and black kit.

The key to this would be to have the players buy into his methods early on, and it was clear from interviews with some of his first team players that he was succeeding in doing this.

Defensive midfielder Lucas Leiva had experienced something of a mixed career at Anfield. The Brazilian arrived as a youngster under Rafa Benitez in 2007, and following the exit of Steven Gerrard in 2015 he became the longest-serving player at the club.

After struggling in his first few years, he eventually became a key part of the teams of Kenny Dalglish and Brendan Rodgers, evolving from a promising attacking midfielder during his time at his boyhood club Grêmio into a destructive and efficient defensive midfielder on Merseyside.

In spite of his experience, Lucas periodically fell out of favour under Rodgers, and there was more than one occasion, including the summer of 2015, where it appeared as if the club were willing to sell him.

However, he managed to outlast the Northern Irishman at Anfield and had already established himself as a favourite under his new boss.

Klopp had utilised similar players at Dortmund in Sven Bender and Sebastian Kehl, and seemed eager to make Lucas an integral part of his team, certainly in the early games.

Speaking to Brazilian news outlet *Globo Esporte*, Lucas gushed about the effect Klopp's presence was having on him.

'I believe that the arrival of Klopp has given me a new energy, a new gas, he said. 'He shows he has enough confidence in me. I have learned a lot from him.

'He's very demanding, but has clear ideas about football. I've gotten along well with him in the first month.

'He is a direct guy, as I imagined, knowing the German culture, but he is open too. I feel close [to him], knowing he is the boss.'

It was not just the older players who were enthused about working under Klopp. Young Belgian striker Divock Origi, in his first season at the club, was already playing under his second manager having been brought in by Rodgers.

However, he appeared to be flourishing under the German, scoring his first goals in the remarkable win at Southampton.

'Every trainer has his own way of managing and his own methods. The thing I like is that he's very direct and can show his plan and convince everybody with his ideas very quickly,' said Origi.

'That is the one thing that struck me from the start of his training sessions: he is very clear in his way of explaining and his vision.'

One opinion that always has more sway than most at Liverpool is that of club legend Steven Gerrard. The iconic midfielder left Anfield the previous summer for the sunnier climes of Los Angeles, where he turned out for LA Galaxy in Major League Soccer.

However, at the end of his first campaign in America, he returned to England where he was allowed to train with his former Reds teammates to maintain his fitness levels. This also gave the former England international the opportunity to meet with Klopp for the first time, and he was blown away.

'I had coffee with him and when I came out of the room I just felt happy,' Gerrard told the *London Evening Standard*. 'I felt taller, and I'm not one of the players so I can only imagine what he has done to those players in the dressing room.

'The atmosphere at the club is brilliant. The players are buzzing around the training ground and there are smiles all over the place. I think he has lifted the whole place. He wants to be around players who are enjoying it. He does not want players to be tense, worried or concerned. He wants to take all that pressure on his shoulders.

'My impressions from the outside were that I loved him. I loved how charismatic he was on camera, I loved his tactics and I always appreciated Borussia Dortmund, who I watched quite closely in the Champions League. So I was a huge fan anyway. But now that I have met him and worked with him, it has gone up a notch.

'Of course. If I was a player at Liverpool – either a young player or one at my peak – and Jürgen Klopp walked through the door I would be licking my lips.

'The players should be excited. I think to myself, imagine being 25 or 26 and how happy and excited I would be to be working with him.

'So the players should be sitting themselves down and realising what an opportunity they have to achieve success in the next two, three, four or however many years he is here.

'If the players are not feeling it then there is something wrong.'

One team that had certainly been feeling it was Leicester City. The Foxes had struggled in their first campaign back in the top flight, but under the guidance of Nigel Pearson they had just about clawed their way to safety with an impressive second half to the season. However, Pearson had left the club in the summer and to the surprise of many, Claudio Ranieri had been brought in.

The experienced Italian had managed some of the top clubs in European football in his time, but his reputation had taken somewhat of a battering after a disastrous spell in charge of the Greek national team, with the lowest point being a shock defeat at home to the Faroe Islands during World Cup qualifying.

He was written off by many before he had taken charge of a game at the King Power Stadium, but it wasn't long before he was silencing those critics and severely disrupting the status quo in English football.

Ranieri turned his Leicester side into an efficient and effective counter-attacking outfit, the sort that Klopp would have been proud of, and thanks in particular to the explosive attacking talents of Riyad Mahrez and Jamie Vardy, who had broken an all-time Premier League record by scoring in 11 consecutive games that had helped take Leicester to the top of the league at Christmas.

On paper, it seemed to be the last game Klopp would have wanted on Boxing Day, with his side struggling in recent games and appearing to be low on confidence. Klopp was soon cursing his luck after a promising start as Origi went down with a hamstring injury. Liverpool's main threat would have to come off and was replaced by the talented, but less mobile, Christian Benteke.

Questions had been raised by many as to whether Benteke would suit the way Liverpool generally played. His finishing ability was almost without doubt, banging in on average a goal every other game at previous club Aston Villa, but there had been a clear issue with his presence in this Liverpool team. He had scored some goals, but the side never seemed to play with the same pace and cohesion when he was up front compared to when Origi, Firmino or Sturridge were at the tip of the attack.

Liverpool continued to dominate but without getting much in the way of service to Benteke, and the potential threat of Mahrez and Vardy was keeping the home fans anxious.

Then, almost from nowhere, Firmino collected the ball on the left side of the penalty area, and poked it towards the middle. Benteke had pulled away from his marker and side-footed the ball into the corner of the net. Liverpool had the lead and Benteke was the man to give it to them. They closed out a 1-0 win and became the first team to keep a clean sheet against the league leaders since the start of the season.

Klopp was happy, and said after the game, 'Everybody knows about the quality of Leicester and we had to always be very concentrated.

'It was a very intense game. The set pieces were very dangerous, especially the throw-ins. But we got the win and it was perfect.

'There are more pluses from this game. It was deserved. We made the game we should make against this opponent. We knew if we stayed concentrated we would get our chances.'

In spite of Benteke getting the winner, Klopp made it known that he was still not entirely satisfied with the striker's contribution. The Belgian had not helped his cause by fluffing a chance to seal the game at the end when Kasper Schmeichel had been left stranded upfield, but Benteke could only place his shot straight at the backtracking Morgan.

'There is no doubt he brings goals,' the Liverpool manager said after the game. 'We need his goals but I don't only think about him and goals. We are not a team that can play with a striker who scores a goal but is not involved in the game for the other 89 minutes. We need the striker for the other options too, to work for the other minutes. I know Christian can do this, that's what I said. We had a really good talk in the week. He knows what he has to do. He came in and had a really good game, and decided the game. So well done!'

A few days later Benteke would also make reference to what he described as a 'man conversation' with his manager, and admitted that he needed to add more to his game if he was to succeed at Anfield.

'I have to run more and I have to be there for my team-mates,' said the striker.

'I spoke with the manager a few days ago about where I can improve and what he is expecting from me.

'Sometimes when you are a little bit on the side you try to understand what the manager needs and what he wants, and we had a very good chat.

'You could see [against Leicester] that I showed I understand his message and now I have to keep going like that.

'Of course I am still a young player and I want to learn. He is the right manager for me to help me in my development.

'I am not saying every player can play like Barcelona but I have been in England a long time so I can adapt.'

At the other end of the field, Klopp also had injury issues, with Martin Škrtel picking up a problem in the Watford defeat that would keep him out over the busy Christmas and New Year period. This meant that Klopp would have to pair Dejan Lovren and Mamadou Sakho together and the manager had praise for them after they managed to shut out Leicester, though wasn't as pleased with both players' tendency to play short balls out from the back every time.

'It was not easy for the two of them coming straight back in after injuries but they did really good. The one thing I did say to them was, "Don't play these passes. If you want to kill me, use a knife, don't play these passes!" They both played them, it's an invitation for a counter-attack. But they played good otherwise and a clean sheet is really good.'

The duo would line up again four days later as Klopp took his team to Sunderland, who were languishing at the bottom of the table, though after replacing Dick Advocaat with Sam Allardyce, had inevitably become a more organised and solid outfit.

However, another solitary Benteke goal, another 1-0 win and another clean sheet took Liverpool level with Manchester United at the halfway stage of the season.

One sore point of the game for Klopp was a late challenge by Sunderland winger Jeremain Lens on Sakho, which had left the French defender in agony. Klopp was outraged by the foul, and in particular, that Lens only received a booking for it.

Allardyce, who had also had a frosty relationship with former Liverpool boss Rafa Benitez, labelled Klopp a 'soft German' after the game if he believed such a challenge was worthy of dismissal.

Klopp laughed off the comment a day later during his next press conference, asserting that he had been called far worse in his time, but it was yet another example of Klopp's concern at the physicality of some of England's lower teams.

During the same press conference, looking ahead to the first game of 2016 away to West Ham, Klopp, whether intentional or not, called Allardyce's style into question. The Englishman had been in charge of West Ham the previous season, and was replaced by Croatian Slaven Bilić in the summer of 2015.

Klopp claimed that he had seen plenty of the Hammers under both Allardyce and Bilić, and said that they had evolved their style since Bilić had arrived so that they were now capable of playing two ways, which would make the match more difficult for his team.

On the back of two wins and two clean sheets, Klopp was hoping to start the New Year with another solid performance. He didn't get one.

A dreadful Liverpool showing saw them succumb to a 2-0 defeat, their third loss in four away games.

Klopp's reaction to the game, as ever, was interesting, 'It's not a day for being disappointed, it's a day for being angry. You cannot win a football match with 90 per cent, you have to do everything. I don't like it.'

He clarified in his post-match press conference, 'It was not enough from my team today. The decisive moments we were there, but we were not there 100 per cent. We could have done much better. We had our moments, we tried, but if you fight at 95 per cent then it's not enough.

'It's my responsibility. I'm angry about myself today.'

Some news outlets later reported that Klopp had given his players their first proper rollicking after the game. There had apparently been games where he had unleashed Buvač on them instead, but this time it was him dishing out the tellings off.

He wanted a reaction from his players, and he needed one if Liverpool were going to salvage their season.

10

'I know Jürgen from UEFA meetings and he has always liked Liverpool. He had a passion for the club.' Gerard Houllier

MOST of Liverpool's past managers remain highly revered by the fans long after they have left. While there may have been disagreements and voices of discontent at the time, many appreciate after the event that everyone just wanted what was best for the football club, and remember the good times.

Gerard Houllier cemented his place in Red hearts when he guided his team to a historic treble in the 2000/01 season, winning the League Cup, FA Cup and UEFA Cup.

Fans who had been starved of success, winning just one League Cup in the previous eight seasons, were all of a sudden watching their team win finals one after the other.

The Frenchman was ultimately unable to give them what they really wanted, a league title, but his time at the club is still remembered fondly by most, especially after the dignified way he recovered from suffering heart problems in the 2001/02 season.

His opinion on matters at the club are always welcomed, and he had his say on the new man in charge.

'Jürgen has personality,' Houllier told *Express Sport*.

'I know Jürgen from UEFA meetings and he has always liked Liverpool. He had a passion for the club. He was always talking about Liverpool; what we did, how we lived. I can tell you he was a true fan of Liverpool and he was following the results before going there. In a way, he will bring something different. And the way he plays is a very modern way; high pressing, offensive football and quick transition.

'They are in the semi-final of the [League] Cup, which could give a lot of confidence for the rest of the season.

'We saw that when we won and you saw that with Chelsea. When Mourinho won that trophy [in 2005], he won the title on the back of it.

'Sometimes with a competition like that you get a sense of relief first because you win something and then it gives you confidence.'

While in charge at Anfield, Houllier took his Liverpool side to face Stoke at the Britannia Stadium in a League Cup tie. He won 8-0.

In fairness, Stoke were in the third tier at the time, and it would be another 15 years before they could boast having a handful of Champions League winners in their side.

Klopp knew that he would have to guide his team through an incredible eight fixtures in the month of January, at least, and the last thing he needed was his players starting to pick up injuries.

Joe Gomez and Danny Ings were already on the long-term absentee list, while Daniel Sturridge was spending much more time in the physio room than on the pitch. Jordan Henderson had spent some time out with a heel problem, Jon Flanagan was only just coming back from an injury that had kept him out for well over a year, Martin Škrtel had picked up a hamstring strain at Watford, Divock Origi had the same problem in the win over Leicester and Mamadou Sakho picked up a minor knee injury before the game at Stoke.

Klopp was still able to put out a strong side, putting his 'LFC' front three of Lallana, Firmino and Coutinho at the top end of the pitch and leaving Benteke on the bench.

The German had demanded a response from his players following the meek showing at West Ham, and he got one. Liverpool were outstanding in the first half, pressing Stoke from the first whistle.

However, it was not all positive for the visitors in the first half as Coutinho pulled his hamstring trying to put a cross into the box, and had to be replaced by Jordon Ibe.

Then just moments later, Dejan Lovren went down clutching his hamstring after overstretching in a tackle. The Croat was replaced by James Milner, who himself was just coming back from injury, with Lucas going back into defence.

It was starting to become farcical for Klopp, forced to play people out of position, having to rush the likes of Milner back to cover for new injuries, and just as his side were facing a heavy workload of games in front of them.

In spite of these setbacks, Liverpool's bench was soon cheering as Adam Lallana broke down the right. His cutback was sliced by Joe

Allen into the path of Ibe, who fired in what turned out to be the only goal of the game.

Even with a makeshift centre-back pairing of Lucas and Kolo Touré – who were both outstanding on the night – the Reds held on to take a one-goal lead back with them in the return leg at Anfield.

It was a good win for Klopp and a much-improved performance from his team, but by the end of the game the headlines were being written about the war-wounded rather than the victory. The injury list at the club was getting ridiculous, and it was notable that a number of those had been struck down by hamstring issues.

Immediately the accusations were levelled at Klopp that his training methods were too severe, and that he was running his players into the ground.

Lallana leapt to his manager's defence, stating that given the number of games in recent weeks they'd barely had time to do any intensive training. The schedule had forced them to pretty much only do recovery sessions, which were much lighter. Lallana blamed the number of games they were being forced to play for the injury crisis.

However, it was not the first time that a Klopp side had faced such problems. In his final season at Dortmund, one of the reasons attributed to the team's stuttering first half of the campaign was the number of injuries to key players.

Klopp was forever having to juggle his players, move them around, play them out of position, and never really had all of his main stars available to him at any one time. However, their fitness and availability improved in the second half of the season, and sure enough, so did Dortmund's form.

Since Klopp had taken over, Liverpool had on average covered around 6km more per game than they had under Brendan Rodgers, and made around 70 more sprints. However, of the five players who had been covering the most ground in that time, only one of them (Coutinho) had picked up a hamstring injury.

Whatever the reason, Klopp had some thinking to do. Not only was he going to have big players missing big games in the coming weeks, but in the immediate situation he had no fit centre-backs available to him.

Škrtel was already out, Sakho picked up a knock before the Stoke game, Lovren was injured during that game, and Touré was also feeling his hamstring by the end of it.

Klopp cursed his luck, and put it down to his players having suffered injuries before the season had begun, disrupting their pre-season preparations. However, he also admitted that he needed to share some of the blame.

He said, 'Two weeks ago we had three centre-backs, at the start of the season we had five, now we have none. The problem is if all the players in this moment had no injuries in pre-season, they are still in the race and can cope with this intensity. But they had little things and had no chance to recover.

'Maybe we would have to change our training methods. I am responsible, certainly.'

Klopp had downplayed suggestions that he was going to spend big in the January transfer window, but conceded after the Stoke game that given the problems with injuries, especially to centre-backs, he would be left with no choice but to do something in the winter transfer market.

One other avenue available to him was to try and get some players back from loan spells, and that's exactly what he did.

Within two days the club had recalled Ryan Kent from Coventry, Sheyi Ojo from Wolves, and Tiago Ilori from Aston Villa.

Klopp admitted before the game against Exeter that he would be forced to make a lot of changes to his team, especially with big matches against Arsenal and Manchester United on the horizon, and said that many of his younger players would be given a chance.

Touré would not be fit, Lovren was ruled out until after the United game, and Coutinho was likely to be out for the rest of the month of January.

Liverpool's list of absent first-teamers now stood at 12, and Klopp joked, 'We have to take the situation like it is and we'll go to Exeter. I will be there for sure! I will take a few players with me!'

Klopp spoke about the situation and fixture pile-up, but also revealed just how happy he was with his team's efforts at Stoke, 'In this moment there is a little bit of work to be honest, and not too much joy! Now it is Exeter. Then we have five or six days until we play again. It's nearly a break. I can think about flying on holiday!

'Then we play against Arsenal and Manchester United. Of course, they are big games. I have played a few times before against Arsenal, but it'll be my first against Manchester United. There will be no big space to enjoy all that stuff in the moment.

'But we should not forget what we saw at Stoke – it was a brilliant performance from my team, especially the first half.

'It was great and I think everybody who watches football thought, "That's the kind of football I could love." That's very important and

I didn't forget that in all the things that happened afterwards such as thinking about who'd be available for the next game.

'We will always have a team on the pitch. We will always have good players, sometimes with a little bit less experience of course, but we will have a good team. It's an intensive moment, but I am really looking forward to the next week.'

A very inexperienced side wobbled at times against a determined Exeter, but goals in each half from Jerome Sinclair and Brad Smith saw them salvage a 2-2 draw having gone behind twice. Of course a replay meant that Klopp would have yet another match to fit into the schedule, during the week where he had joked he could go on holiday. It took Liverpool's scheduled fixtures in January to nine.

'I have had a similar situation before with injuries, but with the winter break, they come back,' he told *The Telegraph*. 'The number of games is the biggest difference. When I came here, I didn't know there were two rounds in the semi-final of the [League] Cup. I had people in Germany, saying, "Yeah, you're in the final again!"

'In Germany, when you tell people about the FA Cup that if you draw you play again, they say, "What?" Here you have penalties and extra time, but only after the second game. That's the thing, it's the number of games, football, football, football. With a perfect pre-season you are prepared for a long, long journey. What I can say about here is very positive, great country, great people, the food is much better than everybody said. Okay, the weather is not great – like everyone said!'

The Reds's punishing schedule meant that an average of just 2.9 days separated their fixtures between 2 December 2015 and 26 January 2016.

Klopp needed the injury gods to start smiling on him, and some positive news came ahead of the match with Arsenal. Kolo Touré was fit to play, and Mamadou Sakho was insisting that he was.

However, Klopp still felt the need to dip into the transfer market and over the space of a few hours, the loan signing of QPR centre-back Steven Caulker was wrapped up.

Caulker had joined Southampton on loan at the start of the campaign, but the subsequent signing of Virgil van Dijk from Celtic meant that his minutes were limited at St Mary's. His last appearance for the Saints actually came in the 6-1 loss to Liverpool.

The 24-year-old was even signed in time to be included in the squad for the Arsenal game, which would be an intriguing encounter between Arsène Wenger's 'symphony' and Klopp's 'heavy metal'.

The German expressed his admiration for his French counterpart in his pre-match press conference.

'My respect [for Wenger] goes up day by day because it's really intensive to work in the Premier League, especially in a team with international matches [for their players] too.

'He always had my biggest respect but now it's a little bit bigger since I'm here. That's really a brilliant job he's done – 19 and a half years.

'He's a high-quality manager, one of the best in the world for sure. This long period, it's really rare that you can do this but he did. He's a football maniac, in the best [sense of the word].'

There was a buzz around Anfield ahead of Arsenal's visit. The Reds had been stuttering against the lower sides, but thriving in the big games against their traditional rivals. The question on everyone's lips was, which Liverpool would turn up?

Klopp unsurprisingly made 11 changes from the team that drew at Exeter, with Touré, Sakho and Henderson among those named, while Firmino was back in attack.

The Brazilian had struggled to make the impact in England that he had in Germany, where he was the talismanic superstar at Hoffenheim. In 2013/14 he had scored 22 goals and managed 15 assists in 37 games, mostly from an attacking midfield position. Big things were expected when he signed for Liverpool for a reported £29m, but apart from outstanding showings at Manchester City and in the League Cup tie against Bournemouth, his impact had been minimal, scoring just once in 17 appearances.

However, something clicked on this night, and all of a sudden Firmino was on fire. He gave Liverpool the lead when he followed up a parried Emre Can effort, turning the ball past a stricken Petr Čech.

Arsenal levelled shortly after through Aaron Ramsey but then following good work from Henderson to win the ball back, Firmino wowed the crowd as he curled an effort accurately round Čech and into the top corner to restore Liverpool's lead. There was a real sense that the fans were finally seeing the Firmino they had been told was so good in the Bundesliga.

Once again though Klopp's men caused their own downfall as a Gunners corner was whipped in at the near post, and a flick from Olivier Giroud was enough to take it past Mignolet and make it 2-2.

The visitors improved in the second half and went in front for the first time in the game after a kind deflection in the box took the ball to Giroud, who turned Touré well and slammed the ball into the far corner.

Klopp decided to turn to his bench. Benteke, Allen and Caulker were brought on, with Caulker being introduced in the last few minutes and remarkably being sent straight up front on debut. However, it was the influence of the two other changes that made the difference as a long ball in the 90th minute from Henderson found Benteke, who headed the ball across the box for Allen to run on to, and the Welshman got enough on the shot to take it past Čech and make it 3-3.

Klopp raced down the touchline and punched the air, beating his chest and roaring to the crowd, who roared back. It was only a draw, but as with the West Brom game, it had been snatched from the jaws of defeat in the dying embers of the game.

After the match, Klopp said, 'It was a great football game, how it should be.

'The beginning was really good. Not perfect, of course, but not too far away from it because we knew how they play and at the start we were better in the game and played really good football.

'We lost control and it wasn't too easy, we lost the ball easily. They are strong on counter-attacks, everybody knows this and so we had to defend.

'In the second half we were again in the game; it was a little bit more open than the beginning of the first half but we came back into the game. At the end, it was brilliant from Giroud but in the beginning we have to defend it better – it was not too difficult. We have to be more concentrated in situations like this.

'Then you need a little bit of luck and we had it. We changed players and it was a perfect ball for Christian, a perfect header and a perfect finish. I think it was a well-deserved draw in an all-time spectacular game.'

Klopp also reserved particular praise for Firmino's performance, 'I could talk about this for half an hour, but to be honest I think it should be normal because I know how good he is. If you are good, you have to show it and tonight he did.

'It was very important for us because for 95 minutes, he was always thinking about playing in different positions and in all of them was really good.

'He made perfect goals – the first was really good, the second spectacular, brilliant … whatever you want to say! It was a really good game, but he wasn't the only one.

'If we talk tonight about special performances, Kolo Touré... I have to show more than my respect because it is not easy and he did great, as did a lot of other players. You saw it.

'It was a good football game. A draw can be really good to watch, and that was one of these games. Now it's recovery and again like this, or better, against Manchester United.'

11

'I love derbies, to be honest. It's the salt in the soup. They are the best matches to perform in.'

THE midweek game against Arsenal under the Anfield floodlights had felt like an occasion. The fans were loud, the goals were flowing – at both ends – and a late equaliser sent the crowd home relatively happy with what they had seen.

However, next up was Manchester United. The big one. The biggest one for some.

In spite of the fall from grace that both clubs had suffered in recent years, this was still the biggest grudge match in English football.

Klopp showed straight away that he appreciated the thrill of the conflict, and compared it to the *Revierderby,* the clashes he had faced numerous times between fierce rivals Borussia Dortmund and Schalke 04.

'A game against Manchester United is a little bit like Dortmund-Schalke. You can play the whole season the way you want, but in these games you have to be prepared and you have to be there and show your best. Obviously it is important for the table, we are close together and both teams need the points to stay close with the top teams in the table. For this, it's important.

'But it is Manchester United. If we were 20 points in the lead of the whole table, it would [still] be important. That's how I understand derbies. I love derbies, to be honest. It's the salt in the soup. They are the best matches to perform in.'

It may have been an unfamiliar rivalry, but it was a familiar foe to Klopp as he came head-to-head with Louis van Gaal. It would be the first time they had faced one another since Klopp's Dortmund bested van Gaal's Bayern Munich side 3-1 in February 2011 in the Allianz

Arena, a result that would lead to the Dutchman's sacking a short time after and a Bundesliga title for Dortmund.

There were similarities in van Gaal's situation at Manchester United. Although results had not been too bad, the style of play had been largely criticised not just by the media, but by significant portions of the Red Devils's fan-base, and some newspapers were speculating that defeat to Klopp could lead to van Gaal's dismissal yet again.

United started the stronger of the two, keeping the ball and managing to threaten the Liverpool goal with a couple of speculative efforts.

However, it didn't last long as the Reds soon found their rhythm, and Firmino was once again making a nuisance of himself at the head of the attack. His movement opened a space for Adam Lallana to run into, and Lucas played a perfect through ball to the England international. David de Gea raced from his goal and Lallana attempted to head the ball over him, but couldn't get enough on it and the Spaniard saved comfortably.

This would be a theme of the first half. Liverpool played well and United could not keep up with them. It appeared as if Klopp's game plan was working perfectly, it just needed the ball to go in the goal. However, this was looking harder than it had been against Arsenal.

Firmino, Henderson and Can all had attempts but wayward finishing was costing them, and not for the first time.

Liverpool continued to create, and Emre Can was unlucky not to break the deadlock as a beautiful step-over got him into the box, only to see his left-foot effort hit the back of de Gea's heel and skew wide. The German midfielder tried the same with his right foot minutes later from distance, which de Gea was at full stretch to palm away.

It felt like one of those days for Liverpool, and in the 78th minute that feeling was cemented.

The hosts had dealt with set pieces well in the game. However, this time a short corner had been taken. Ibe, who had just been subbed on, had not closed down Juan Mata quickly enough and the Spaniard whipped a dangerous ball into the box. Marouane Fellaini, who Lucas had kept quiet the entire game, was able to leap and reach the header, which struck the crossbar. The ball fell to an unmarked Wayne Rooney, who made no mistake in smashing it home to send the travelling fans into delirium. United had scored with their first shot on target.

Klopp tried to remain upbeat in his press conference, but it was clear that this defeat really bothered him, especially as it was in a derby game.

'I think if Manchester United were to talk about their performance, they'd say it was not that good but they won so they are really happy,' he said.

'We played better but feel really frustrated because of the result. Our performance and a lot of things we did today were really good. Creating chances was good, but the finishing was not good otherwise we would have scored a goal.

'The set play was unlucky because we changed two positions for defending set plays a few moments before. We didn't avoid the cross, lose Fellaini, bar, lose Rooney – goal.

'Three mistakes around the goal, which is obviously too much against a team with the quality of Manchester United. Today there was not enough time to come back in the game.

'At this moment it is frustrating, how it should be, but we have to carry on and that's what we'll do.'

It was yet another setback for Klopp's Liverpool, but unlike in games at Watford, Newcastle and West Ham, his team had at least come away in defeat feeling they were very unlucky to do so.

Over the days that followed numerous articles were written on the quality that Klopp had been given in his squad by predecessor Brendan Rodgers, who had returned to the spotlight by appearing on Sky Sports over that weekend.

Among the numerous things the Irishman raised about his time in the Anfield hotseat was his relationship with the transfer committee at the club, and how he had sometimes been vetoed on players he had wanted, while he was almost forced to accept players who he didn't really want, such as Mario Balotelli.

The press and fan sites generally did not blame Klopp for not being able to produce steady results with the players he had. Injuries and a perceived lack of quality were credited with Liverpool's inconsistency, and the question was raised at the next press conference ahead of the Exeter replay as to whether the club's background setup when it came to transfers would hinder Klopp in his redevelopment of the squad in his image, and whether he would get the final say in any future dealings.

Klopp said, 'Does anybody have the final say? For example, say I wanted to take Zlatan Ibrahimović and we have to pay £100m plus a big contract at 35 ... I think I would have to ask first!'

The January transfer window was still open, and inevitable questions about bringing in a new striker were raised in relation to Liverpool failing to take their chances and injuries to Sturridge, Ings and Origi, while Benteke had been struggling.

'We have to see the situation: from five strikers, two are left, and I think in the beginning of the season Roberto Firmino maybe was not planned as a striker. But in our situation we thought because of his skills, it's a really good formation for creating chances in these games.

'For scoring it's more than only one player, we didn't score enough from different positions. We don't have enough goals from the offensive midfield but the players know about it. It's sometimes being a little more greedy in the right situations. We shoot in situations we don't have to shoot, you can see we are greedy on goals but not cool enough to [find] the better player in the better position.

'We had these situations against Manchester United, even when we had big chances we could have had – with an easy pass – a nearly 100 per cent goal. That's football. We talk about this, we show the players and we work on this. We can change in how we can help.'

A third game at Anfield in a row beckoned, this time against slightly less high-profile opposition in Exeter. The unwelcome replay fell in the midweek that Klopp had earmarked as a rare one where he could rest, but the 2-2 draw a couple of weeks earlier meant that yet another fixture was added to the growing list.

Understandably, Klopp once again named a young side, but with three crucial changes from the first game. First-teamers Mignolet, Allen and Ibe came in for Bogdán, Kent and Sinclair. That extra experience would tell.

Liverpool were comfortable throughout the return match at Anfield, with goals from Allen, Ojo and Teixeira sealing a 3-0 success.

It was a positive run-out for the young Reds, and in particular Ojo, who had announced himself with a wonderful strike to seal the game for Klopp's team in the second half.

That set up a fourth-round tie with West Ham, but that would have to wait as the following Saturday saw a trip down to Norwich.

The two sides had been a part of some fairly high-scoring battles over the years, usually involving Luis Suárez putting the Canaries to the sword – once scoring four against them – but this was like no other match the two had ever encountered.

Klopp had his work cut out at half-time with his side trailing 2-1. Then followed a crazy second half.

Crazy was the word as Moreno was caught the wrong side of Naismith and inexplicably tried a lunging tackle. Remarkably, the referee didn't give a penalty, so Moreno gave the Scot another kick, and the spot was pointed to. Wes Hoolahan made it 3-1 and it appeared to be game over.

However, Kolo Touré took the ball out of the net and raced it back to the halfway line. The Reds weren't going to take this lying down.

Moments later, it was 3-2 as Jordan Henderson swept home a cross from the right. From there on, the game was very much on.

Liverpool were all over the hosts, and the introduction of Adam Lallana, who had been prevented from starting with a muscle problem, was instrumental. The former Southampton midfielder laid a precise ball on to Firmino, who calmly lofted the ball over the onrushing keeper to level it up at 3-3.

There wasn't much build-up play in the next twist as Russell Martin played a blind backpass, which James Milner took in his stride and ran through to round the goalkeeper and give Liverpool a 4-3 lead.

That appeared to be that until an incomprehensible five minutes were added on at the end. Two minutes into it, Norwich were level again.

A long free kick was punted upfield and fell kindly to centre-back Sebastian Bassong, who fired in from 25 yards to make it 4-4.

A Norwich side trying to avoid relegation seemed to have rescued a point in the dying minutes of the game, but that wasn't everything.

Liverpool went right up the other end and a ball into the box fell to substitute Caulker, whose shot was blocked. It ricocheted back across the goal to Lallana, who hit an effort into the ground. The ball looped over the goalkeeper and into the corner of the net for 5-4.

The resulting celebration was epic, with Lallana ripping his shirt off, Touré screaming 'fucking hell!' in disbelief over and over again in the mass-player hug, and Klopp racing down the pitch to put himself in the middle of the melee, even having his glasses accidentally broken by an overly excited Benteke.

The whole bench had gone crazy, with Buvač, Krawietz and Lijnders all exuding joy from every pore. An away win at lowly Norwich shouldn't have been such a big deal, but the drama of it all, the never-say-die attitude and the togetherness in celebration had meant more than even the resulting three points.

When asked about the celebrations, Klopp said 'I don't know, I saw nothing. Usually I have a second pair [of glasses], but I couldn't find them. It's really difficult looking for glasses without glasses.

'We won [at Dortmund] for the first time against Bayern Munich and Nuri Şahin broke my glasses. Today it was Adam,' he added, not realising at the time that it had been Benteke.

The defending Klopp had seen before the late winner though was less amusing to the German.

'We've made different mistakes. If you win 5-4 it's a funny story, but it's not that funny. We have to solve it.

'Today we conceded four goals after set plays, but we defended them better. We got all the goals after second-ball set plays. Things like this can happen. That's how life is: solve one problem and you have another one.

'They do what we have to do, defend the first ball, but because of our history they all stay in the box.

'The first [Norwich] goal, with the heel, you have to be offside if you stay there. It's unbelievable. It's not possible. I am not happy with this situation, for sure.'

Klopp would go on to be more damning about his side's defending in the days that followed. It was perhaps a good time to finally put his cards on the table, after a morale-boosting win, and say what needed to be said about the state of his team's defending.

They were conceding an inordinate amount of goals from set pieces, and after the Norwich game, had incredibly conceded from every one of the last seven shots on target they had faced. They would need to improve and fast as next up was the second leg of the League Cup semi-final against Stoke.

There wasn't much evidence of improvement though as a 1-0 defeat after extra time thanks to a Marko Arnautović strike meant the tie would have to be settled on penalties.

Stoke had won the toss and the kicks were to be taken in front of their boisterous travelling fans. Jonathan Walters, a boyhood Everton fan, stepped up to score the first. Lallana went for Liverpool and also scored. Former Red, Peter Crouch, took the next one for the visitors, and had it saved. Mignolet guessed correctly and it was advantage Liverpool. Emre Can stepped up next, but hit the post.

From there it was a series of good penalties, with Glenn Whelan, Ibrahim Afellay, Xherdan Shaqiri and Marco van Ginkel scoring for Stoke, and Benteke, Firmino, Milner and Lucas all successful for Liverpool.

Centre-back Marc Muniesa then came up for Stoke, and it was saved magnificently by Mignolet, diving full-stretch to his left and tipping it round the post.

That meant that if Joe Allen, who had come on as a substitute and was coming off the back of two rare goals in the last few weeks, was able to keep his cool Liverpool would be in the final.

The Welshman nestled his penalty into the top corner of the net. Liverpool and Klopp were heading to Wembley.

After the post-game celebrations died down, Klopp admitted that he had been unable to watch the penalties.

'I didn't see one shot. I was behind the wall of my players so I had to watch it from there. I will watch it on television at home but it was good watching the crowd instead.

'Their goal was double offside but, in the end, we had luck in the penalty shoot-out. Over the whole 120 minutes, the players, crowd and Liverpool deserved it.

'Wembley is a cool place to play football … but we go there to win. It's not much fun to lose.'

His predecessor had not made a final in his three years at the club. Klopp had managed to do so in just over three months.

12

*'That's the thing with Liverpool – you can't
become someone in this club without being
a great person. For everyone in this club,
football is important but they want the
whole person. Either you are that person or
they make you that person, always caring
about the club, always humble.'*

THE fourth round of the FA Cup was the next port of call, and
Klopp made it clear before the game that he would be forced
to play a similar team to the young and inexperienced one that
was used in the Exeter games.

However, they were not playing League Two opposition again.
It would be West Ham, who were actually above Liverpool in the
Premier League.

True to his word, Klopp made significant changes and once again
youngsters were given an opportunity. One piece of good news was
that Dejan Lovren was fit to return, while Steven Caulker made his
first start for the club.

By comparison, Slaven Bilić named a relatively strong Hammers
team, with star players Dimitri Payet and Enner Valencia providing
the attacking threat.

Liverpool had been comfortably beaten in both league games with
the east London side, so it was anticipated that they would struggle in
this one too, especially with a weakened team out. However, the young
Reds largely dominated proceedings. It was the same old story though
as their possession didn't count for anything on the scoreboard.

Brad Smith and Caulker both avoided penalty shouts for handball, but otherwise Klopp's men were rarely troubled and the game played out to a 0-0 draw.

The replay meant yet another fixture to add to the growing list. Klopp semi-joked after the game that it would need to be played on the morning of a day when they have another game in the evening, such was the extent of his side's fixture congestion.

Just two days later was the final day of the January transfer window. The club had not been as active as many expected in Klopp's first window, with Caulker the only new name, other than young Serbian midfielder Marko Grujić, who went straight back on loan to Red Star Belgrade.

However, rumours had been rampant for the previous week and a half that Liverpool were looking to sign Shakhtar Donetsk attacker Alex Teixeira. The Brazilian had been widely expected to join Chelsea, but all of a sudden it appeared that the Reds were at the front of the queue and a bid of £25m was reportedly made, and swiftly rejected.

Various reports and comments from the Shakhtar CEO priced Teixeira at between £38m and £53m, and it became apparent as the window drew to a close that Liverpool were unwilling to pay that much. Teixeira ended up moving to China for £38m.

Some fans vented their fury at the perceived failure to bring a high-quality attacking talent to a squad that desperately needed it. The player had even given fairly candid interviews where he was practically begging the Ukrainian side to accept Liverpool's bid, citing his long-standing friendship with Philippe Coutinho and Lucas Leiva as one of the reasons, as well as his desire to play in England.

However, Klopp explained that it was a decision taken by him as well as the others involved in transfer dealings at the club.

He said, 'We made offers – I won't say too much about that but they were realistic, absolutely, with the pluses of it being January, the Premier League, all the pluses you have when you make negotiations with other clubs. But it was a case of, "If you don't want it, okay, we can't change the situation, do what you want." You have to work respectfully and responsibly.'

Klopp also revealed that due to the high player turnover in the Premier League, he decided to view new signings as being on a one-year contract, 'I know they have them for longer, but for me I say, "Okay, yes, you are in my team and if you don't play the biggest rubbish in your life, I will trust you, you have to trust me." And after a year, we'll look. Maybe he wants somewhere else, maybe I want him to go somewhere else. That's football.'

One piece of news that the club hoped would appease fans that had been hungry for a signing was the imminent return to full training of quartet Coutinho, Škrtel, Origi and Sturridge. It would be the first time Sturridge had been allowed to take part in full training since the Newcastle game in mid-December.

There was another round of midweek Premier League matches scheduled after a cup weekend, and the Reds were due to travel to the King Power Stadium to face the surprise league leaders Leicester City.

Klopp and Claudio Ranieri shared a laugh and a handshake before the game, but only one was smiling by the final whistle.

The German was able to make multiple changes and bring back some of his key players after a seven-day break. However, the rest didn't seem to do them much good.

The game was level at the break, but shortly after the restart the home fans were bouncing.

After a Liverpool attack had broken down in the Leicester half, Riyad Mahrez played a long ball for Jamie Vardy to run on to. Vardy raced to the ball out on the right ahead of Lovren, and without thinking, hammered it towards goal from all of 30 yards. The strike looped over Mignolet and Leicester were in front. It was a remarkable goal from Vardy, but had come from another Liverpool attack that had sloppily broken down.

It wasn't long before the hosts' lead was doubled and the game was over. Another long ball was only headed partially away by Sakho. Okazaki picked the ball up and fired towards goal. It deflected off Moreno and fell perfectly for Vardy, who made no mistake.

Klopp's men offered little by way of reply and the night ended with a routine 2-0 win for Leicester.

The Reds had actually been in the game for large periods, and still enjoyed the vast majority of possession, but Leicester had become an efficient counter-attacking unit, much like the Liverpool side that had nearly won the league two years earlier. Their superstars Mahrez and Vardy made all the difference, and Klopp acknowledged this after the game.

'He [Vardy] made the difference tonight. I think our plan was good, it was obviously good,' he said.

'We forced ourselves to play, we knew about their kind of defending; sometimes they had higher pressing and things like this. Then you can, and have to, play over the wings.

'We had time, we had the ball, we had opportunities in the box, but everybody could see we didn't make the right decision often enough.

'The longer the game was, we didn't get cooler and the decisions didn't get better.

'That's the problem. We had the ball in their box, we didn't shoot and one second later, Vardy shot from 35 yards and the ball was in. That says most about the game.

'I don't feel too good in this moment, because I know we lost and we have to accept it, absolutely no problem. But, I think, with a few things we would have done differently today, we could have won this game.

'If you can win a game, you should do it. We didn't. So I need a few minutes to cool down.'

He also mentioned that the two-games-a-week fixture pile-up was taking its toll, in spite of the rotation utilised in the FA Cup ties.

'Maybe the reason is we had six games more in January,' Klopp continued.

'The intensity we played with, we had a lot of good situations. Our problem today was not to run more or to run more intensively, our problem was when we had the ball in the right position we made the wrong decision. That's all.

'They [Leicester] had ten days off and we had three games, so if we could have played at the same intensity, absolutely even, like them then I think they would have done something wrong.'

The defeat didn't help the mood among the fans, who had been left disappointed that the club hadn't made any significant moves in the transfer window. The team were showing promise in some games, and then were completely without inspiration in others. They had scored three against Arsenal and then failed to score against United, then scored five at Norwich, only to not score in any of their next three outings. The attack was looking blunt.

Liverpool would have a chance to make up for the Leicester defeat shortly after as their next game was a fairly straightforward looking home clash against relegation-threatened Sunderland. However, 'straightforward' is not really the word to be used to describe what happened over that weekend.

Klopp had given his usual press conference at Melwood on the Friday morning, but was taken ill later in the day. He had been diagnosed with a bout of appendicitis and was scheduled for surgery at Aintree Hospital the following day, meaning that he would miss the game.

It was an unexpected spanner in the works, but the backroom team of Buvač, Krawietz and Lijnders were trusted with managing the game in Klopp's absence.

Something else hanging over the game was a threatened mass walkout by fans who had been enraged by the club's announcement that ticket prices in some areas of Anfield would rise to up to £77 the following season, in spite of a new £8bn TV deal coming into effect. Fan groups had strongly suggested that those who wanted to show their disdain get up from their seat and leave on the 77th minute.

Goals from Firmino and Lallana put Liverpool 2-0 up and it seemed that the fans wouldn't miss much by leaving early as the game seemed won. However, two late strikes wiped out that advantage and the Reds had to settle for a 2-2 draw.

It was more points dropped by Liverpool. Jordan Henderson emphasised after the game that the fans walkout had not been the reason for the turnaround in fortunes on the pitch, and that the players had to look at themselves for reasons why they threw what had looked like a comfortable win away.

Another game was to follow just three days later as the Reds needed to travel back to east London to take on West Ham in their FA Cup fourth-round replay. It was assumed that the backroom team would need to take charge of that tie as well, but at the pre-match press conference it was Klopp who appeared, looking as healthy as he had done the Friday before.

'I'm feeling good. I think a lot of people had this before [appendicitis]. I didn't have it before so it was new for me,' he revealed.

'Like always I think, one not too good night, then you get the surgery and everything is okay. I feel good and back in the race.

'I'm back because I feel good, it's pretty easy. If you feel bad you should stay at home maybe but I feel good. I'm very thankful for our doctor [Andy Massey] because he said we should go to hospital – I was not too sure – and then the surgeon was great, a season ticket holder.

'When he told me "we both won't see the game" I was like "okay, sorry". I had the best nurses, everything was okay so I feel really good and that's the only reason I'm here.'

Regarding how he would manage himself during the game, Klopp answered, 'I think I am experienced enough to know that for me it is not a normal coaching game. Of course I cannot jump or things like this because I have a few holes in my body. Hopefully the water stays in, I have to look afterwards! That's all, I know about this. I can't win the games with my emotions outside, I know this.'

As Klopp had put it, he was 'back in the race'. Even his West Ham counterpart Slaven Bilić had predicted that the German would return in his press conference earlier in the day.

'I don't think Klopp will be back because of the pressure. He will be back because he is like that. He is the leader,' Bilić explained.

'He is Jürgen Klopp and is a successful man. He likes to work. For him this is natural and he wants to be back.'

Sturridge was back as well, as was Divock Origi and Philippe Coutinho. All three were named in the squad that travelled to London, though Klopp had stated that he would once again be forced to pick a relatively inexperienced side.

The Hammers again went full strength, and went into the game as favourites. However, it was Liverpool who made the early running, with Benteke coming close with two headers from corners that were batted away by Darren Randolph. Teixeira pulled a shot wide, and then Coutinho struck the post after a nice cutback from Benteke.

At the other end, Mignolet had tipped a Dimitri Payet free kick on to the post, but was unable to do anything about Michail Antonio's volley on the stroke of half-time.

Thankfully for Klopp, their heads didn't go down, and shortly after the restart they were level.

Benteke won a free kick on the edge of the area and Coutinho cheekily slid his effort under the jumping wall and it rolled into the corner.

The game went into extra time, and seemed set for penalties, until Payet swung a viciously accurate free kick into the box. Angelo Ogbonna rose to head the winner and dump Liverpool out of the FA Cup. It was a cruel blow to a young Liverpool side.

Klopp was left sombre-faced after the game, but was still able to look on the positives, 'I thought they [the young players] could play like this so I'm not surprised. But the only reason we were here tonight was to win.

'We changed really offensively and still did well and created chances. It was a big fight. We couldn't use our chances, they got a free kick without a foul and we conceded a goal. Now we go home.

'We don't have to talk about morale, we showed morale and everything is okay with these boys. If you go through the squad tonight, it's a great game.

'We created chances, but we didn't score goals – that's the major mistake you can make in football. But it's better to create chances and to miss than to not create chances.

'If you want, we can see positives. We are Liverpool FC and in this moment it's not the sunniest side – a 2-0 lead [lost against Sunderland], manager in hospital, out of the FA Cup, but tomorrow when we get up, the sun will shine.

'If we want at Liverpool, all together, then we can take a lot of positive things out of this game and make the next step. We can rest a lot of players now because we will have the first matchday when we are not involved.

'We have to use the time, we have to take the time, we have to make steps. That's what we've done until now. We don't like our results too much, to be honest, but it is the difficult way we have to go and in the end, it can be the right way.

'I'm okay, I would have gone to the next round, it didn't work, so let's carry on.'

As Klopp had alluded to, one minor positive to come out of elimination was that for the first time in what seemed like forever, Liverpool would be allowed to go a whole week without a game. The next round of the FA Cup was scheduled for the weekend between the two Europa League ties with Augsburg, which would finally allow the manager some proper time on the training field with his squad.

Ahead of the West Ham game, Klopp also had his say on the ticket price issue, 'It's not what we want. What I know is everyone in the club has a big interest in finding a solution.

'We don't want people to leave the stadium before the game is finished.'

Football fans from across the country had supported Liverpool fans in their actions, as had popular club figures such as Jamie Carragher and Roy Evans.

The day after the West Ham game an agreement was reached. Club owners Fenway Sports Group issued an open letter to fans announcing that ticket prices would be frozen for the next two seasons. It was vindication for the fans and allowed a potentially volatile situation to come to an abrupt and amicable end.

Klopp of all people knew how crucial it would be to have the fans very much onside with the club, as at both Mainz and Dortmund he had led an 'all in this together' attitude, and now that the ticket controversy was out of the way, everyone could get on with recovering the season.

In the wake of the West Ham game, Klopp gave an interview to Sky Deutschland, where he was once again asked about his early experiences at Anfield.

'There were great managers and great players working at Liverpool that have influenced the club's history,' he told reporters.

'Both the Manchester clubs and a few London clubs invest a lot. So if you make a few good decisions that doesn't necessarily mean that you make steps ahead on the Premier League table because these clubs are making the right decisions too.

'I've been here for four months now and I really get the impression that everybody in this club is hungry for success. And despite everybody longing for a very quick success they all are ready to be patient and to invest a certain amount of time that is necessary to gain that success.

'So I feel very comfortable over here. It's a special club, a special place. Anfield is a great stadium and you feel the history in every moment. It's an honour and it's great fun and a great adventure to be here.

'Everywhere you go, all around town you'll find special historic and football-related places.

'And there are the club legends. Every time you speak in public or go to an event you can be sure there are club legends present. The club is important for the city.

'Carragher and [Steve] McManaman are working for television so they are around a lot. And like everyone should have heard by now I'm living in a house that Steven Gerrard built.

'One of our rooms used to be his trophy room. Fortunately he took all the silver with him so I don't have to look at it the whole time. I met him and he is a great guy.

'That's the thing with Liverpool – you can't become someone in this club without being a great person. For everyone in this club, football is important but they want the whole person. Either you are that person or they make you that person, always caring about the club always humble.

'I'm not so much into social media but of course I recognise who tweets or writes something if we win. That passion for the club doesn't end with an expiring contract.'

Klopp went on to say, 'The last thing you should be as a manager is to be a dreamer, because reality will always catch up.

'In the beginning when Liverpool called me and we made the decision to take that offer we realised that it's really the sequel of a great managerial career to coach Liverpool after a great time in Mainz and Dortmund.

'But once you are here it's just going to work in the morning and going home in the evening. And in between you've had a hard day.

'I can't go on about how great it is to be here and to congratulate myself for taking the job. I've just got too much to do and too much to work on.

'But of course you love that especially because I'm doing it in a wonderful environment.'

On paper the next game would be a relatively simple one – a trip to bottom of the table Aston Villa – and it was, as a rampant Liverpool won 6-0 thanks to goals from Sturridge, Milner, Can, Origi, Clyne and even Kolo Touré.

After the game, Klopp hailed it as, 'A result for the soul.' It was the second time since taking over that Klopp's team had scored six goals in an away game, and it was noteworthy that the other game, Southampton in the League Cup, was the only other game that Sturridge had started in for the German. The England striker's influence was obvious.

Liverpool remained nine points off the top four, and qualification for the Champions League via the league was looking unlikely.

The league was to be put on the backburner for a while though, as the next couple of weeks would be dominated by cup football, beginning with the likeliest route into next season's Champions League. The return of the Europa League, and a return to Germany for Klopp.

13

*'If I was allowed to say shit I would
say shit, but I'm not allowed!'*

IN the same week that Klopp would be returning to Germany for
the first time since taking the Liverpool job, he also returned to
sign a player.

Rumours had been circling for weeks that Klopp was interested
in Schalke 04 defender Joel Matip, whose contract was due to expire
at the end of the season.

The day after the Aston Villa win, the club confirmed that an
agreement had been reached with Matip, who would join Liverpool
in the summer on a free transfer.

It was another indication that Klopp was mindful about the lack of
height in his squad. The three players he had signed so far in Caulker,
Grujić and Matip were all taller than Liverpool's current tallest player,
Martin Škrtel.

Klopp was clearly happy that the club had managed to get the
deal over the line, and told the club website, 'He is a top-class centre-
half, very young but experienced. You don't have that too often. To
be honest, when I had my break I thought for the next club, I should
think about Joel, if there was a need.

'He never played for my team, he did the extreme opposite – he
played for their biggest opponent! Maybe that says a lot about his
quality.

'Even when he played for the team you cannot love as Dortmund
manager, you see his quality. Then that's real quality.

'The chance was there and Joel wanted to do something different.
He is and was really close to his club; it's normal, he played there
since he was a youth player. I think there was no chance for another

Bundesliga club in this moment, but Liverpool was the right name and the right club.

'Maybe it was a little advantage that I know him and he knows me. He's still a young player and for a young player, it could help to make the decision when there's a manager from your home country.'

He added, 'He's a real centre-half. He is physically strong, a really tall boy – taller than me! It doesn't happen too often that I have to [looks upwards].

'I know people are saying our defence isn't that good. We have to defend better as a team, first of all. It's not for solving a problem – it's a transfer with a really good perspective for the future, a long-term thing. But he can help immediately and that's really good for us.'

The Cameroonian would be arriving in July, but for now, Klopp's attention was well and truly on another former Bundesliga foe, Augsburg.

It was Klopp's first trip back to Germany since Oktoberfest, and his home country was even more pleased to see him than he was to return. For two days solid, Germany went Klopp-crazy. He was on front of magazines, newspapers, on billboards, on news channels and on the lips of every football fan you spoke to. Augsburg were excited to welcome the world-famous Liverpool to their home, but were more excited to see Klopp as the one leading them.

In his pre-match press conference, Klopp played down the significance of his return.

'I was there [in Germany] for 47 years, it's no problem. I know this country, I will not be surprised. It is more special for other people because there are not too many German managers working in foreign countries,' he said.

'Most of my colleagues are working in Germany so if a German manager works somewhere else and comes back, yes it is possible to be a more interesting story but for us, and for me especially, it is a Europa League game.

'If I wasn't here and Augsburg play against Liverpool, it is still the biggest game in their history,' he added.

'It is not too easy, Bundesliga clubs are never easy to play and especially a club like Augsburg who are a special story in Germany.

'One of the most famous German footballers played there – Bernd Schuster – but it took them a long time to come back to the Bundesliga.

'Now they are there with a really good manager, Markus Weinzierl, who is one of the highest-rated managers in Germany at this moment and a lot of clubs are thinking about him.

'Their manager said it would be better for them if Liverpool had another manager because they would never have been to Augsburg.

'I know a lot more about Augsburg, I've played a lot of times against them and that makes the preparation easier but that is all.

'In the end, they will fight for everything. If it is the biggest game in their history you can imagine how ready they are for this game.

'They have players with big potential and have one of the most physical strikers in Europe – Raúl Bobadilla – who you need a navigation system to drive around! He is a real worker and difficult to defend [against].'

Asked by the German media how it was to be back in his homeland, Klopp replied, 'I've requested pretzels for dinner because you can't really get them in England.'

The game itself was a cagey affair. A typical first leg of a European tie between two teams who know that the first goal can be pivotal.

However, the danger-man for the home side Bobadilla pulled his hamstring just five minutes in. The Paraguay international tried to run it off but he was soon replaced and Augsburg's biggest threat was out of the game before it had really begun.

Chances for either side were few and far between, in spite of the Reds once again being able to play Firmino, Coutinho and Sturridge. None of them were able to penetrate a very organised and concentrated home backline, although Sturridge was presented with a real chance in the second half from a James Milner cross, but he side-footed wide.

The game ended 0-0 to leave the tie in the balance. Liverpool hadn't managed an away goal but knew that any win at Anfield seven days later would see them through.

Klopp wasn't impressed with his team's performance in the WWK Arena, believing that they should have done better.

'We should be realistic about the result, that's okay in a European away game. We could have scored goals but as a performance I am not satisfied.

'We fight for consistency and played like this in the game, but we always let them come back in the game and that's not necessary. I'm not 100 per cent happy about this game.

'My problem is that, with our quality, we should have had more. I have to be patient, but I'm not a patient man.'

However, there was one thing that did put a smile on Klopp's face that night. Before his post-match press conference began, Augsburg officials presented him with a giant pretzel, which he promptly tucked into.

Another thing that will have pleased him was a rare week off for his team. It was unfortunate that this had come about because of their FA Cup exit, but Liverpool would not have a weekend game, which gave them a whole seven days to prepare for the second leg.

Klopp once again went strong at Anfield, with only one change from the first leg, Lucas in for Kolo Touré. It was seen as a slight risk as the Brazilian had only recently played at centre-back for the first time.

The game started well for the hosts, with a fast pace and early minutes of camping in the Augsburg final third showing the benefits that the rest period had given them. The early pressure paid off too.

An outswinging corner was heading for Mamadou Sakho when two Augsburg players collided, with one throwing his arms in the air and handling the ball. The referee pointed to the spot without hesitation.

The visitors felt it harsh, but James Milner didn't mind as he calmly slotted home the penalty to give Liverpool the first goal of the tie.

It would turn out to be the only goal of the tie as the Reds closed the game out 1-0. The draw for the next round came the following day, and almost as if it had been written in the stars, Liverpool's name was pulled out alongside Manchester United.

Just three days later it was the other half of Manchester on their mind as Liverpool readied themselves for their first cup final in three years. They were heading to Wembley Stadium to take on Manchester City in the League Cup Final.

City had been experiencing some rocky form in the league, and were in danger of falling out of the title race altogether with Leicester and Tottenham continuing to pick up wins, but they had comprehensively defeated Dynamo Kyiv away in the first leg of their Champions League last-16 tie the previous Wednesday, and were looking back to their best with their vital spine of Vincent Kompany, Yaya Touré, David Silva and Sergio Agüero fit and firing.

Liverpool were heading into the game as second favourites, but the way they had thrashed City at the Etihad Stadium early in Klopp's reign meant that they were not short of belief either, while the addition of Sturridge to the team only added to the confidence surging among the Reds fans, who travelled en masse to London.

Before the game, Klopp spoke to the *Liverpool Echo* about preparations, and went into detail about how important it was to everyone at the club.

'I am long enough in the business to know I am greedy for success,' he revealed.

'For sure we will go to the final and try and achieve this. It is more important for the club, the crowd and the players.

'Lots of managers work their whole life and never get the chance to win trophies. After a short time we have that chance.

'Of course I would enjoy it with all I have. Everybody will give their all.

'Clubs with a big history like Liverpool, it is always the same problem if they are not successful in the present. With the right decisions and then the right patience you can get back on track.

'With all the big clubs around with a lot of money, we should not go the same way, we have to go our way, how Liverpool always did.

'This win would help. It would help to win the [League] Cup but it is not the only possibility for everyone to believe in this way.

'Sometimes it is the quality of one player who decides the game, but it is more about the performance of the whole team. If you look at big titles in the past, Denmark were European champions [in 1992]. That is the best title I ever heard about.

'They met each other at McDonald's then they heard they had to go to the European Championships and they won the title. That is cool. Greece too. It is not always the best team that should win. Everybody can win if you have the right idea and if you are full of trust.

'Man City are a great team and we will have to give more than a good performance. We have to create the right plan. We have to run maybe more than Man City will run. We have to close the right spaces. We have to keep our nerve, use the pressure and set the level of intensity. If we do that then we can win and they know that.

'The most important thing is to win the final. I don't care how. I care how before the game, but after if we win with a lot of luck 1-0 I wouldn't care.'

The stage was set, the fans were ready, and the time had come for Liverpool to play Manchester City at Wembley to decide the first domestic trophy of the season.

Liverpool started well, pressing City back and almost forcing an early goal when Alberto Moreno fizzed a low cross across the box, but Willy Caballero was able to grab and hold on to it. The Argentinian goalkeeper was a surprise choice to start ahead of regular number one Joe Hart, but Manuel Pellegrini had stuck with him throughout the competition so stayed loyal to the former Málaga stopper.

Klopp had sprung a surprise himself with his selection of Lucas over Touré again. Many had assumed Touré was being rested for the final when he missed out against Augsburg, but Lucas's form had earned him a starting place in the back four.

What had been a bright start from the Reds dimmed a little as Mamadou Sakho and Emre Can went for the same ball. They clashed heads and both were sent sprawling. The German recovered but Sakho looked uneasy. His dizziness was confirmed moments later when Agüero was set loose by Silva, turning away from Lucas and getting past a clearly affected Sakho with ease, before aiming a shot towards the bottom corner. Thankfully for Sakho, Simon Mignolet got down and tipped it on to the post.

Liverpool had survived, but Sakho didn't as the Frenchman was immediately substituted for Touré. Sakho was far from happy but Klopp had to intervene and insist that he come off as it was very likely that he had suffered a concussion.

After some early jitters, Touré and Lucas formed a potent partnership and Liverpool defended with relative ease for the rest of the first half. They weren't able to create much at the other end apart from a wayward shot from Firmino, but they went in level at half-time and had at least held their own.

However, just three minutes into the second half they were behind. Agüero attacked the box and waited for the overlapping run from Fernandinho. Moreno hadn't seen the run and the Brazilian midfielder was given time to shoot from the angle once Agüero had laid it off to him. The ball squirmed under Mignolet's body and City were ahead. It was a sloppy way to undo all the good work that had gone before it, which had largely been the story of Liverpool's season.

The crucial thing was not to crumble and Klopp made sure that didn't happen. He shouted instructions and encouragement to his players and they responded. In the immediate ten minutes after they had gone behind they enjoyed their best moments of the match, dominating the ball and creating dangerous opportunities, but they just couldn't find the final ball to create the shooting chances.

They were nearly caught on the break and were very fortunate not to fall further behind when Raheem Sterling, who had been getting loudly booed by the Reds faithful all game, steered wide from point-blank range when it was easier to score.

Klopp rolled the dice with 20 minutes left as he removed Moreno for Adam Lallana, and moved Milner to left-back. It worked, as suddenly it was Liverpool making all the attacks, drawing fouls in dangerous areas and winning numerous corners. However, they were unable to take advantage from any set piece situation.

Klopp used his final change with ten minutes to go, bringing on Divock Origi for Firmino. It proved to be inspired as the pace and directness of the Belgian opened City up, and within two minutes the scores were level.

Sturridge played in Coutinho on the edge of the box. He squared to Origi, who was brought down. The ball broke to Clyne and he deflected it back into the path of Sturridge, who had continued his run. His ball across the box found Lallana, who hit the post. The ball broke kindly for Coutinho, and he calmly slotted into the net to send the travelling Kop into raptures.

The noise was deafening as Coutinho whipped his shirt off and Klopp tried to contain himself. He released his immense joy by aggressively bear-hugging Firmino on the touchline.

Liverpool had grabbed the equaliser their play had deserved, and it appeared that the game was set for extra time.

City upped their game a few notches though, and before the 90 was up, Mignolet had to save a Yaya Touré header from close range.

The final whistle went and extra time was confirmed. Klopp had used all of his subs and his players had done more of the running. Pellegrini was allowed the luxury of changing his entire right side by bringing Pablo Zabaleta and Jesús Navas on at the start of the additional half an hour, trying to take advantage of a tiring Coutinho and Milner.

It worked to an extent, with City largely dominating the first 15 minutes, and just before half-time, Agüero got in behind and tried to guide the ball past Mignolet, but the Reds keeper was equal to it again and tipped it wide.

Surprisingly in the second half, it was Liverpool who got on top, keeping the ball and putting the pressure on. A cross from Milner found Origi, whose downward header was well saved by Caballero. It was the first save he had made all game, but it wouldn't be the last.

City threatened a few more times before the final whistle, with Agüero lofting over after being accidentally put in by Milner, and Fernandinho heading wide from close range, but nothing was going in and so it would need penalty kicks to decide things.

Liverpool historically had a good record from penalty shoot-outs, and had won two of them in the same League Cup campaign against Carlisle and Stoke. City on the other hand hadn't experienced a shoot-out since the 2008/09 season.

City won the toss and the kicks were to be taken in front of their fans, who were none too happy to see Emre Can score the first one with a cheeky 'Panenka' chip down the middle. They were even less happy when Fernandinho hit the post with his effort.

It was advantage Liverpool early on, and Lucas stepped up with a chance to really pile the pressure on. However, Cabellero saved well, and when Navas bagged his penalty, the scores were back level.

Coutinho came up next, and his weak shot was easily palmed away by Caballero, while Agüero confidently came up to send his penalty into the bottom corner.

Things had turned completely, and all of a sudden it became disastrous as Lallana also saw his penalty saved. It meant that if Yaya Touré scored, City would win. The Ivorian made no mistake and City fans went into delirium.

It was a heartbreaking end to what had been a big effort from all of Klopp's players, and some of them could not be consoled. Sturridge was visibly in tears as he went up to collect his runners-up medal, while Klopp himself couldn't hold back his disappointment in his post-match press conference.

'If I was allowed to say shit I would say shit but I'm not allowed!' he exclaimed.

'It was a great day until the last shot in the penalty shoot-out. Perfect organisation, a perfect atmosphere and a really great experience, but in the end we lost the penalty shoot-out. It's the last possibility to lose. We tried everything.

'I could be proud about a lot of things the players did today, but I expected we could do things like this so it's not too easy to be proud of things you think are normal. But they did well in a lot of moments.

'Before I came to England, everybody told me [the League Cup] is not too important but all the players who were involved today and the players who were not involved today really wanted this cup.

'They all really wanted this, as did all the people in the stadium – it was a great atmosphere. It was really perfect until the last kick.

'Then you have the penalty shoot-out. You need a little bit of luck. Of course, we need to shoot a little bit better than we did. We know how it works but today it was not too difficult for the goalkeeper.

'We were not too lucky as Simon [Mignolet] was really close two or three times. That's how it is and at the end, we have to accept we lost.

'You have to feel a defeat. You cannot say, "I don't care, it's not important." It was important and we lost, so that feels not too good.

'You always have to strike back. We can say all of these things, but you know you can fall down and then you have to stand up. That's the truth, but it's completely normal – only silly idiots stay on the floor and wait for the next defeat.

'Of course we will strike back – 100 per cent. We struck back today in the game. But for this and the next time we are in a final, you have to feel how it is when you lose.

'Not everybody has to learn it like this – I won my first final. It's really not the best moment, but that is all. Tomorrow morning we can change everything, but now we can change nothing. That's the big difference.

'But don't worry, we will go on, we will get better and that's how it is. We have to go the hard way – that's how it is. Nothing is easy in this moment, but we can see if we carry on working really hard then there is new light at the end of the tunnel.

'That's really, really important and that's what we know. We will stay in the race, there is no doubt about this – but tonight we feel rubbish.'

14

*'That was Liverpool as I knew it before
I came here. It was really great.'*

THREE days later they returned to Premier League action
to face Manchester City, again. It was a difficult game for
Liverpool to face just days after their Wembley disappointment.
Not only would they come face-to-face with their tormentors, but they
would be doing so knowing that City were still chasing the Premier
League title coupled with the confidence brought on by winning the
first trophy of the season.

One plus was that it would be at Anfield with a defiant and loud
Kop behind them, determined to make up for Sunday's defeat.

Four years earlier, Liverpool had lost 2-1 to Chelsea in the FA Cup
Final only to play them a few days later in a league game at Anfield.
They hammered them 4-1 in a swift act of retribution.

Klopp made some changes to his line-up, bringing Jon Flanagan in
for Alberto Moreno and moving Nathaniel Clyne to left-back, while
Divock Origi replaced Daniel Sturridge up front. Mamadou Sakho
remained out after his cup final head injury, so former City man Kolo
Touré started alongside Dejan Lovren at the back.

The Reds fans were in good voice and were given every reason to
be early on as Flanagan flattened Sterling with a crunching tackle in
the opening seconds. It set the tone for the entire game.

Liverpool outran, outfought and outplayed City on the night,
with goals from Adam Lallana, James Milner and Roberto Firmino
sealing an impressive 3-0 win.

The most notable thing about the win was in the goals they scored.
All three came after effective and dynamic pressing and counter-
pressing, with Lallana in particular leading the way. It was also the

first time Liverpool had scored three goals at home in a league game under the German.

Klopp was rightly proud of his men after the final whistle, and gave BT Sport a soundbite they would use incessantly in the weeks after the game.

'It was for sure our best home game [since I arrived]. The best word that I can say to describe this is ... boom!'

He added in his post-match press conference how impressed he was with his team's reaction, 'It was very important we showed the reaction.

'The boys did brilliantly. They were very angry in a positive way. The pressing situation was brilliant, the counter-pressing was good and then we had to score goals and we did.

'We lost on Sunday. We had to show a reaction. The most important moment of the season is now. We have to take what we can get. We have to stay angry, to strike back in each game. We have no points to waste in our time. Everything can happen.'

Their work had been spectacular at Anfield, but next up in the league was Crystal Palace, the first team to beat Klopp in England. However, heading into the match, Alan Pardew's side were on a run that had seen them fail to win any of their previous 11 league games, and they had the second worst home record in the league. Revenge was in Liverpool nostrils.

A goalless first half had seen little in the way of quality but shortly after the restart the old curse appeared to be hitting the Reds again. A corner from Palace pinballed around the box and eventually fell to Joe Ledley, and the heavily bearded Welshman cracked the ball into the bottom corner to give the home side the lead. It was a familiar feeling for Liverpool against Palace, and things appeared to be getting worse.

After an attack had broken down, Wilfried Zaha picked the ball up and set off on a counter-attack. Milner lunged in to bring him down, and the subsequent yellow card was his second of the game. Liverpool were down to ten men.

However, this ended up being the start of their best period of the game. From then on Liverpool were rampant, their passing was crisper, their movement was better and their confidence grew. It still took an element of luck for the equaliser to come as Palace keeper Alex McCarthy slipped when trying to clear the ball, which fell straight at the feet of Firmino and he calmly slotted it in for 1-1.

A draw would have been a respectable result in the circumstances, but the introduction of Christian Benteke changed things yet again.

The Belgian came on and played like a man possessed, clearly wanting to make an impact after spending much of his recent time as an unused substitute. Within minutes of coming on he had unleashed two attempts on goal and won several duals with his markers.

With minutes to go, Moreno unleashed a fierce shot from range that crashed against the post and rebounded clear. It felt like Liverpool's spirited fightback would ultimately end in a draw.

That was until the very last minute of stoppage time when Jordan Henderson played a ball down the side of the penalty area for Benteke to chase. Palace defender Damien Delaney went to ground and clipped Benteke's foot with his knee. The striker went down, and after taking time to deliberate with his linesman, the referee pointed to the spot.

Benteke stepped up to take it and coolly slotted home, sending McCarthy the wrong way and the visiting fans into delirium.

Complaints from the home fans, players and manager about the award of the penalty took up most of the post-match media, but the less reported fact was that Liverpool had won three league matches in a row for the first time in 12 months. As well as that, it was the 11th time since Klopp had taken charge that his team had taken something from a game they had been trailing in.

The obvious issue was that they were still falling behind in games, but before Klopp's arrival Liverpool had built an unwanted reputation for never being able to recover when going behind. In the 2014/15 season and the start of 2015/16 under Brendan Rodgers, more or less the same squad had fallen behind in 16 league games, and had only come back to win four points from those encounters. Comparatively, having fallen behind in 11 league games since taking over, Klopp's Liverpool had come back to win 11 points.

Liverpool had been showing much more mental strength and were starting to build a consistency in their performances. This was a crucial part of the season to be finding that consistency as next up it was Manchester United in the Europa League.

The biggest rivalry in English football had never been played out in Europe before, despite near misses in the Champions League in 2002, 2007 and 2008, and although it was to take place in Europe's second competition, it still felt like an epic two-legged clash that would have the world watching.

United had also found a certain amount of consistency, including a 3-2 win over Arsenal, though just after Liverpool's win at Palace, the Red Devils were beaten 1-0 by West Brom.

However, as the old saying goes, the form book goes out the window when these two meet, and the anticipation in the lead up to the match was electric.

The first leg was to take place at Anfield, and well before the game began the ground was full of Liverpool fans creating a noise that would rarely stop through the evening.

Klopp named a strong XI, though Milner missed out due to a virus but Daniel Sturridge was back up front.

The selection from Louis van Gaal was interesting as he kept faith with 18-year-old striker Marcus Rashford, who had burst on to the scene a few weeks prior with four goals in his first two games for United. The Dutchman also picked Marouane Fellaini over Michael Carrick, Bastian Schweinsteiger and Ander Herrera, clearly trying to take advantage of Liverpool's perceived weakness in the air.

A vociferous 'You'll Never Walk Alone' set the tone for the game, and sure enough it was the Reds who started on the front foot. Henderson went into the book early for a high tackle, while Fellaini had already started to throw himself into challenges.

The most meaningful foul in the early stages though came in the 20th minute when Clyne burst through on the right. Memphis Depay put his arm across him to halt his run and the full-back went down, just inside the area. Liverpool had a penalty.

Memphis went into the book and the hosts went into the lead as Sturridge's spot kick managed to evade the clawing right hand of David de Gea.

From then on it was near total domination from Liverpool, with de Gea having to pull off three top-class saves from Coutinho, Sturridge and Lallana to stop the game getting away from United before half-time.

More chances came in the second half as Coutinho fired a shot from the edge of the area that de Gea tipped over.

Then in the 73rd minute, the Kop reached its loudest point of the night. Henderson was sent away down the right-hand side, and his cross fell to Lallana, who cut the ball back to Firmino. The Brazilian calmly side-footed in at the near post and doubled Liverpool's lead.

It had been another excellent performance by Klopp's men, who were left after the game with only one regret, that they hadn't put the tie beyond United with more goals.

The final whistle went and the fans were overjoyed. They had lost their last four meetings with the old enemy, but on this night had not only beaten United, but comfortably outplayed them in every department.

It was widely recognised in the media and among fans as Liverpool's best European performance in over half a decade.

Van Gaal admitted after the game that his side simply could not cope with Liverpool's pressing game.

He said, 'We did not cope with the high pressure of Liverpool. We had expected that and for me it was a surprise we did not cope with it because they did it at their home match this year. That raised the atmosphere in the stadium and they created big chances but we had a very good goalkeeper and because of that we were in the match.

'I don't think we were very creative in the third and fourth phase but it is also the defence of Liverpool and you can give credit for that to Liverpool. We have to improve a lot to create more goals.'

The Liverpool manager on the other hand was delighted with the evening's work, and not just from his players. Sitting in his post-match press conference with a beaming smile he could barely contain, he said regarding the atmosphere, 'It was unbelievable. I want to say thank you to everyone who was involved. It was easy to enjoy from the first to last second.

'That was Liverpool as I knew it before I came here. It was really great.'

Regarding the performance of his players he added, 'It was good, from the first second to last second, with only a few minutes in the second half when we lost control.

'Two-nil is a perfect result. We would have liked to have won by more clearly, but there is nothing to criticise tonight.

'As a human being, I could really celebrate and say it is the best and greatest ever but I don't want to set a limit for them, I don't know how strong they can be.

'We are in a good position now and want to go to the next round but for this, we have to play like this again.'

The next leg was just seven days later at Old Trafford, and as with the previous round, Liverpool had a free weekend in between as the FA Cup quarter-finals were being played out. This meant that United would be playing as they had been drawn to host West Ham, meaning that if Liverpool had still been in the FA Cup, they would be playing van Gaal's men again in that competition.

As a reward for their hard work and flurry of victories, following a recovery day on the Friday, Klopp gave his squad the weekend off. Some went for weekend breaks abroad, while others stayed at home to relax, and by the time they returned to training on the Monday, United had played out a 1-1 draw with West Ham, relying on a late Anthony Martial equaliser to keep them in the competition.

Ahead of the second leg, van Gaal stated that his side were more than capable of turning the deficit around, even if Liverpool were able to grab a goal that would mean United would need to score four in reply, pointing to the fact that they had scored five in the previous round at Old Trafford against FC Midtjylland of Denmark.

Klopp claimed that regardless of his team having a lead to protect, that they would play in exactly the same way they always did, with intensity and looking to attack.

In the days before the first leg at Anfield, the Manchester club had sought special dispensation from UEFA to forgo normal procedure and train at their own Carrington facility the day before, rather than the tradition of training in the opposition's stadium. However, Klopp had decided that he would not be seeking the same treatment.

'I didn't think for one second about it [training and staying in Manchester],' he said.

'When I heard we would play against Manchester United I decided we would come one day early. In a Europa League game it's always like this.

'It's not about feeling comfortable and sleeping at home. We had a few seconds in the hotel before we came here [to Old Trafford] and everything is okay: the room is okay, the bed is okay. The trip was a little different because we usually fly rather than go by coach but the rest is exactly like a normal European game.

'When I played with my former club in European tournaments I always enjoyed it to breathe the stadium and where you will be playing the next night.'

The teams were announced and due to Alberto Moreno picking up an injury, Klopp opted to bring James Milner back into the left-back slot that he had occupied in the latter stages of the League Cup Final.

Liverpool initially struggled to get the ball near the United goal, but eventually worked an opening for Coutinho to hit a hard and low right-footed effort to the bottom corner. However, as he had done in the first leg, David de Gea was looking sharp and got down well to save with a strong hand.

The tie took an interesting turn shortly after as United's chief danger-man, Martial, broke down the left-hand side of the penalty area. Nathaniel Clyne, who had already shown signs of struggling against the Frenchman, stuck his leg out and brought him down. The referee pointed to the spot without hesitation and van Gaal's men had their chance to halve Liverpool's advantage. Martial stepped up to send Mignolet the wrong way and do just that.

All of a sudden the tension was ramped up and it was very much game on. United could smell blood and started to throw more at the visitors, hoping to get the second goal before half-time.

This also opened things up more for Liverpool, and they began to threaten the crucial away goal, with Jordan Henderson side-footing a very presentable chance over the bar.

With seconds left before the break, Emre Can played a ball to Coutinho on the left-hand side. The Brazilian carried it forward, teasing the young full-back Varela, before ghosting past him. He looked into the middle as de Gea began to anticipate the ball across. Then with the impudence of a young boy playing futsal on the concrete pitches of Rio de Janeiro, Coutinho lobbed the ball over the right shoulder of United's unsuspecting keeper and gave Liverpool their away goal.

The travelling fans went crazy, as did Klopp, who raced down the touchline in their direction to punch the air in delight.

The whistle went for half-time straight away and the score on the night was 1-1, meaning that the Red Devils would need three in the second half without reply.

It was never likely as United had been severely struggling for goals throughout the season, especially without the injured Wayne Rooney in the side, and the second half was played out without Mignolet having to do much of anything to keep them at bay. The game ended 1-1, and the tie 3-1 to Liverpool on aggregate.

What had promised to be two legs of fierce competitiveness between two mortal enemies had ended up being a fairly routine passage for Liverpool and Klopp.

'We knew they would show a reaction and it was much more intensive from Manchester United than in the first game,' the boss told his post-match press conference.

'They got the penalty – I think it was a penalty – then Phil had a genius moment. Wonderful. I loved these two minutes before half-time because twice we reacted quicker than the opponent. There was the discussion for the free kick, Hendo played the ball, had a counter-attack but missed the last pass, like we did in the second half a little bit more often. We had to run back but were again quicker in mind.

'Then Phil used the situation – it was a brilliant moment and decided the game tonight.'

Another question that was lingering was the matter of who Liverpool would face in the quarter-finals. In all the excitement at beating the old rival, some had forgotten that it meant that the Reds would advance in a competition that would see them qualify for the Champions League if they went all the way. Inevitably, Klopp was asked whether he would like to be drawn against his former club Borussia Dortmund, who had beaten another English side in Tottenham Hotspur 5-1 on aggregate to go through.

'Dortmund? Of course not. Why should I want the strongest team in the tournament in the next round? I'm not so silly,' he revealed.

The next day, the draw was made in Zurich. Liverpool would play Dortmund.

Three days later saw Klopp return to the setting of one of his best nights as Liverpool manager, to Southampton where he had witnessed his team demolish a Saints side 6-1 in the League Cup.

It would be Liverpool's first league game in two weeks, and with West Ham dropping two points at Chelsea the day before and Manchester United set to play away to rivals Manchester City on the Sunday afternoon, it appeared to be a great opportunity to make a play for the top four in the end-of-season run-in.

Klopp was still without Moreno and had also lost Henderson to illness during the United game. Problems mounted further when Roberto Firmino was ruled out with a hamstring strain.

Klopp selected an attacking side, as he had done in the cup game, with Sturridge and Origi up front as a pair. Somewhat surprisingly, Southampton started with Sadio Mané on the bench, in spite of the fact that the Senegalese had scored against Liverpool in both the cup and reverse league fixture earlier in the season.

Ronald Koeman's side started well, and were unfortunate not to get a penalty when Dejan Lovren barged Shane Long over in the box. It was a warning for Liverpool, and one that duly worked as minutes later Coutinho took aim and fired an accurate shot into the far corner past Fraser Forster.

The Reds had an early lead, and soon doubled it as Origi found Sturridge in the box. The England man shifted the ball on to his left foot before placing it past Forster's dive to make it 2-0.

Both teams made changes at half-time, Klopp deciding not to take any risks with Lovren and replaced the Croat with the returning Martin Škrtel.

Lovren had picked up a booking, nearly conceded a penalty and was playing with a passion probably brought on by the constant booing of him by Southampton fans yet to forgive him for leaving them for Merseyside in 2014.

It was Škrtel's first appearance since the turn of the year, though he had played a couple of games for the under-21 side, including the previous week against West Ham where two reckless challenges saw him sent off. It soon became clear that he hadn't quite gotten the need to foul out of his system.

Koeman had brought Mané on with Victor Wanyama, and the former was given a chance to score very quickly as Graziano Pellè was hauled down in the area by Škrtel within two minutes of the restart. This time the referee did signal for a penalty.

Mané stepped up to take it, but Mignolet dived down to his right and made the save. He had spared his teammate the blushes on that occasion, but it wouldn't last.

Škrtel was caught out of position just after the hour mark and allowed Mané to run at Mamadou Sakho. The Frenchman couldn't stop Mané, who fired past Mignolet to make it 1-2. Then with seven minutes to go, Pellè controlled the ball on the edge of the area, before unleashing a fierce shot past Mignolet and into the net for 2-2.

It had been coming, as had Mané's goal to complete the turnaround just three minutes later. A poor kick out from Mignolet eventually worked its way back to Mané, who calmly slotted into the corner again to make it 3-2 to Southampton and complete Klopp's misery.

What had been a fantastic week for the club had turned sour, and the ecstasy just three days prior was now a distant memory. The fight for the top four had taken a huge blow, made even bigger when United defeated City 1-0 later that day, and now more pressure was being put on the two games with Dortmund if Liverpool wanted to be playing Champions League football in 2016/17.

Many pundits and critics pointed to Klopp's decision to swap Lovren for Škrtel at half-time which, on the surface, appeared to swing the momentum entirely, alongside Koeman's introduction of Mané.

In his post-match press conference, Klopp was surprisingly upbeat, reflecting on how good his side had been in the first half, while acknowledging that they had slipped in the second.

'I saw a lot of good things from my side; I saw a very good first half,' he said.

'We could have scored more. Southampton were not bad in the first half but our goals changed the game, we played really well and could have scored more.

'In the second half, it is like it is – we had this situation twice in the season with the Norwich and Crystal Palace games, with late goals.

'In the second half, Southampton for sure deserved it. But of course we were responsible for the first half and the second half, so we could have done better, but that's how it is in football. You have to use your chances.'

Klopp was asked about whether the players had been suffering from fatigue after their efforts on Thursday in Manchester, but pointed out that his team had actually started energetically.

'Usually after a European game very often you have problems in the first half. I've seen it a lot of times, but in the first half we had absolutely no problems,' he replied.

'We could have done better and there were a few situations where we had to, but it's a football problem and nothing else.

'We can learn from it, of course, and we will – but today it's too late because we lost.'

The final international break of the season gave Klopp a chance to take what was left of his squad on a training camp to Tenerife, believing that getting away from Melwood – and more importantly the weather – would help to get their minds and bodies right for the season run-in.

Families were welcomed as well, as the players not only trained hard in the heat, but were allowed to spend time with their loved ones in the Spanish sun.

Others travelled all over the world to represent their countries, and predictably not all returned unscathed. Belgian duo Origi and Benteke both picked up knocks, with the latter ruled out for a month with a knee problem. However, even if he had stayed fit it was unlikely that he'd have seen much playing time anyway after giving an interview while away with his national side.

Benteke had decided to talk to *Sport/Voetbalmagazine* about how frustrated he was with life under Klopp. He told the Belgian publication, 'Some team-mates have said that I was lucky with the arrival of Klopp because I certainly would play. When your coach says he wanted to take you to Dortmund and a little later you sit at the same club and he ignores you it is hard to understand.

'I was obviously happy [moving to Liverpool], I joined a great club. I knew I could face difficult months but in the long run, it would work.

'I am the first to say that I have not shown enough my worth for a club like Liverpool but, on the other hand, when I arrived under Brendan Rodgers, I knew I would have the opportunity to show my qualities, I was worth all that money [£32m], I deserved to wear the Liverpool shirt. But now ... I knew that the new coach might have a different opinion on me – and that's what happened.'

Regarding the argument that he did not suit the manager's style of play he added, 'I find it bizarre, I do not understand why people say that. I can play pressing and moving a lot. It is not that we play in the Barcelona style.

'I played two full matches in a row since Klopp [arrived]. I went up against Leicester, I scored, I followed up with a game and a goal at Sunderland, and then we lost to West Ham and since then I have been discarded.

'Even my father was annoyed at first by my status as a reservist and told me that I can do nothing. I spoke with Eden [Hazard] and with Marouane [Fellaini], they all gave me the same answer – when a coach does not count on you, you cannot change anything. I never would have signed if I had not been the priority of the coach.'

Klopp played down the significance of the comments, but it was clear that Benteke had been far from his first choice even before the interview. Now with the injury and the big striker's public outburst it seemed likely that he would be moved on at the first opportunity once the summer transfer window opened.

After the international break the Reds welcomed title-chasing Tottenham to Anfield, the same opponents Klopp faced in his very first game in charge of Liverpool. That had ended 0-0 at White Hart Lane, and this match was seen as a good barometer of how far the team had come under his tutelage.

It was noted in the media that Klopp's league record since arriving was identical to the record of the same number of games that ended Brendan Rodgers's reign, but plenty argued that in spite of results not always going their way, the overall performances of the team were significantly more promising.

They were scoring more goals, winning big games against tough opposition and the players were noticeably working a lot harder to improve.

This would be another tough test as Mauricio Pochettino had worked wonders at Spurs. The Argentine coach had found a nice balance with his team, with a solid spine of Hugo Lloris, Toby Alderweireld, Eric Dier, Christian Eriksen, Dele Alli and Harry Kane.

Klopp was still without Roberto Firmino for the game, but otherwise was at full strength, with Origi recovering from his international knock to make the bench.

Both teams showed plenty of quality, and cancelled each other out in a 1-1 draw, with Coutinho's strike being ruled out by Kane's shortly after.

Klopp was perturbed by only claiming a point after leading, but conceded that the fact the team had more than matched a very good Spurs side who were chasing the title suggested that his men were not all that far away from potentially being able to follow suit.

He explained, 'Tottenham are fighting for the title, we fought for the three points. It didn't look like six or seven positions between the two teams. If you want to change the situation, we have to stay in the game. It is about belief. We are not sure we can always beat teams like these.

'You have to learn to become a winner. On this way, we have a few knocks but we are still on a good way. There is not a lot wrong and we can build on this.

'In summary I saw a lot of good things today. A really good sign for us, our future, but on the other side we showed again a little part of our problems.

'But it's much more difficult to show what we showed in our good moments than to finish our problems.

'We will find solutions for them 100 per cent but it's a hard way and on the way we get a few knocks and today we got a knock. We have to accept it and carry on.'

The draw had put a dent in Tottenham's title hopes as Leicester beat Southampton the following day, making the gap at the top seven points.

However, as far as Liverpool were concerned, the league could take a back seat again because next up was perhaps their most intriguing encounter to date since Klopp had taken charge.

He was heading back to Dortmund.

15

'We are not that far on our way to being like they are. We cannot at the moment play like they play, but we can defend and score goals so we can win.'

THERE was a sense of inevitability that Jürgen Klopp would one day return to Dortmund to face his former charges, and the emotion of the reunion would make it a spectacle to behold. However, no one had anticipated that he would be back just ten months later.

Klopp had said ahead of the quarter-final draw that he didn't want to face Dortmund on the basis that they were the strongest team left in the Europa League. However, there was something about the way he said it, and the subsequent awkwardness of his press conferences around the game, where you got the sense that he would also rather not have had the circus of his return come around so quickly; that he wasn't necessarily emotionally ready to go back and see his old friends and take on his old players.

Perhaps he also wanted to do it in the more grand setting of the Champions League, but due to the high-profile nature of the tie, you would have been forgiven for mistaking this for a Champions League clash.

Unsurprisingly, the media around the game was swelled to the max, especially in Germany. The fascination around Klopp had continued even after he'd left his native country to try his hand abroad, which was proven by the amount of coverage he had when returning to face Augsburg earlier in the competition.

Klopp was making every effort he could to keep the attention off himself and on the game. In the pre-match press conference James Milner joked that the players were feeling perfectly relaxed as all the media coverage had been taken up by the manager. Klopp was less light-hearted when informed that one TV station intended to have a 'Klopp-cam', which would just focus on his movements during the entire first leg at Signal Iduna Park. Klopp's response was to threaten to boycott the channel, which worked as the plans were soon dropped.

Klopp mentioned that he had met some old friends at the club and was happily smiling and joking with them, but said that the eve of the game was for that kind of stuff, and that game day would be all about the 90 minutes and his team.

More than 20 television crews, twice as many photographers and about 100 journalists were present to hear him give his press conference.

'A lot has been said ahead of this match but it is easy for me as I just have friends here,' he said. 'It is better to be here than, I don't know, North Korea or something.

'We got here early so I had 20 minutes to catch up with old friends – it would have been daft not to have that chance.

'Tomorrow is different, we are focused on the game. If Dortmund score I won't celebrate for sure but I never plan if I am going to celebrate.'

As well as the German's return to his former club, there was also a lot of focus on the man who replaced him at Dortmund, Thomas Tuchel. The parallels between Klopp and Tuchel were clear, with both having less-than-glamorous playing careers, before stepping into management at Mainz, then after success there, being snapped up by Dortmund.

Tuchel had been brought in to build on what Klopp had done. It was a desire for evolution rather than revolution and had been working well, with Dortmund second only to Pep Guardiola's imperious Bayern Munich side in the Bundesliga, and averaging a remarkable three goals per home game.

Tuchel had built a solid all-round team, but the key to his success had been getting the most out of the star front three of Henrikh Mkhitaryan, Marco Reus and Pierre-Emerick Aubameyang, with the latter having scored an incredible 36 goals heading into the game.

The general consensus from the wider football world was that Dortmund were heavy favourites to go through, and not just because they had a stronger team on paper, but that Klopp's work at Liverpool was still clearly very much in its infancy, while Tuchel merely had to tighten a few nuts and bolts and had his team playing consistently high-quality football for most of his first season.

With the first leg in Germany, Liverpool knew they had to make sure they stayed in the tie for the home leg, ideally grabbing an away goal or two to give themselves a chance when they went back to Anfield seven days later.

Klopp sprung something of a surprise with his selection for the first leg, deciding to leave Daniel Sturridge on the bench and start with Divock Origi as the lone striker; the thought process being that Origi's strength and pace would test the very talented but not too agile defensive pair of Sven Bender and Mats Hummels.

Before kick-off, Signal Iduna Park played host to one of the most remarkable scenes in football. Sixty-five thousand fans from both teams singing 'You'll Never Walk Alone' as one. The stage was set, the fans were ready, the players were ready, the managers were ready.

The decision to start with Origi showed some promise early on as Coutinho played a ball over the top for the Belgian youngster to chase. It rolled through to Roman Weidenfeller, but the intent was clear and it wouldn't be the only time it was utilised.

As predicted, Dortmund enjoyed the vast amount of early possession, and forced Simon Mignolet into a couple of routine saves.

Liverpool then went forward down the left. Alberto Moreno played a ball to Milner, who flicked it on, and Origi was in on goal once again. This time he ran across Łukas Piszczek before steering the ball past Weidenfeller and into the corner, via a small deflection off the full-back. Liverpool had taken the lead against the run of play and had a crucial away goal.

Klopp celebrated, running towards the travelling away fans and punching the air, showing that there was nothing in the way of compromised feelings about this one. He wanted to beat his old team.

Dortmund piled on the pressure for the rest of the first half, but resolute defending from Liverpool's back pairing of Lovren and Sakho kept them at bay.

One sour note before the break was an injury to captain Jordan Henderson. He had damaged his knee in a challenge with Reus, and though he tried to play on, was forced off at half-time to be replaced by Joe Allen. The next day the injury was revealed to be to his lateral cruciate ligament and he was ruled out for up to eight weeks, meaning his season was over and he would be struggling to be fit in time for the summer's European Championships in France.

Origi was played in again right at the end of the half but could only hit Weidenfeller with his effort, but it was a sign that there were potentially more goals in the game for the Reds. Liverpool went in at the break ahead and very pleased with their first half work. However, the second half could not have started in a worse fashion.

Dortmund won a corner on the right, which was taken short to Mkhitaryan, who whipped a cross into the perfect area for Hummels to rise above Adam Lallana and power a header past Mignolet for the equaliser. It was a sloppy goal to concede and had undone a lot of the good work that the visitors had put in. Klopp admitted after the game that the blame was with him as he had told Lallana to occupy that space, not anticipating that the dangerous Hummels would be there as well.

Dortmund continued to dominate the ball but the Reds defended with a maturity that kept the hosts at bay for the vast majority of the game, and it ended 1-1. A better result than many had assumed Liverpool would get, and it gave them something to play for in the return leg.

After the game Klopp was happy enough with what he had seen, 'Dortmund is a pretty good side and everyone could see that, but we had our moments and we could have won the game.

'I'm pretty sure a lot of people thought we would lose 2-0, 3-0 or 4-0. But at some moments we had Dortmund and around our goal we were brilliant.

'We are not that far on our way to being like they are. We cannot at the moment play like they play, but we can defend and score goals so we can win.'

Both teams had to return to domestic duty three days later, and the perception was that Liverpool would have the greater advantage ahead of the second leg as they hosted Stoke City at Anfield, while Dortmund had to travel to fierce rivals Schalke 04 for the Ruhr derby. There was hope among Liverpool fans that Dortmund would exert so much energy in playing their neighbours that they would have less petrol in the tank at Anfield the following Thursday.

Klopp emphasised the importance of his side not losing concentration against Stoke, and a competent performance by a much-changed side saw them dispatch their opponents 4-1, including two more goals for Origi.

The concentration was then set straight back on Dortmund, who controversially fielded a weakened team in their game with Schalke, drawing 2-2 and all but ending their feint Bundesliga title hopes.

The anticipation grew as the week progressed, with most in the media predicting that in spite of the away goal, Dortmund were still the likelier of the two to go through, such was the threat they posed in attack.

Klopp laid down the gauntlet to the fans in his pre-match press conference, saying that the away goal would not be as important as the impact the fans could have. He'd heard all about famous Anfield European nights under the lights, and experienced what he referred to as his first proper one in the victory over Manchester United in the previous round. He wanted this again, but better.

He got it. The team bus arrived to an army of fans, with flares, and flags waving all over the streets. The players took videos of the scenes as the Liverpool faithful set the tone for what was going to be quite an evening.

Inside the stadium, as had occurred the week before, 'You'll Never Walk Alone' was echoing around all four corners of the ground, but then came to a complete silence as everyone in attendance observed a minute's silence for the 27th anniversary of the Hillsborough disaster, where 96 Liverpool fans lost their lives during an FA Cup semi-final.

The volume was then turned back up to the max as the game began. There was an electricity in the air, anticipation that it was going to be a special night and that Dortmund would be overawed by the spectacular home crowd.

After eight minutes of the game, Dortmund were 2-0 up.

Two quickfire efforts from Mkhitaryan and Aubameyang had not only cancelled out Liverpool's away goal, but forced the scenario to one where Liverpool had to win on the night, and that wasn't looking likely.

It was a disastrous start for Klopp, who again had opted for Origi over Sturridge, but had also decided to play the trio of Lallana, Firmino and Coutinho and left out Allen, which appeared to have backfired as Liverpool's midfield was left wide open for both goals, with Coutinho and Firmino guilty of giving the ball away to start fast Dortmund counter-attacks off.

Klopp knew that his team had to at least stem the flow and they calmed the game down with some possession play, even managing to fashion a couple of good chances for Coutinho and Origi, but both were unable to hit the target. Aubameyang was inches away from grabbing a third and putting the tie to bed, but Dortmund still went in at the break with their 2-0 lead, 3-1 on aggregate.

The manager had his work cut out. He hadn't wanted to play Dortmund, and this was why. They were a lethal attacking unit that could punish any minor error, and perhaps his Liverpool team wasn't ready for such a stern test. However, he had to do what he could to convince his men that they weren't done yet.

In his half-time team talk he decided to evoke the spirit of Liverpool's most famous ever comeback, the 2005 Champions League Final in Istanbul where they had recovered from 3-0 down at half-time to draw 3-3, and then won on penalties. He explained how those players believed in themselves and pulled it off against all the odds, and told his players to go out and make their own moments that they could tell their children and their grandchildren about.

It seemed to have the desired effect as within minutes of the restart, some exquisite one-touch passing through the midfield, led by Emre Can, saw the German play Origi in behind. The Belgian kept his cool and slotted home to halve the deficit on the night. Liverpool still needed two more, but it was a start.

However, the excitement was extinguished shortly after as Marco Reus was played through down the left by Hummels and side-footed the ball into the far corner for Dortmund's third. Even the most ardent of optimists was struggling to find hope for Klopp and his team. They were attacking with more threat, but it was clear that Dortmund were capable of scoring every time they went forward. It was a gut punch for Liverpool, but it wasn't the end.

Klopp made a double substitution, taking off Firmino and Lallana for Allen and Sturridge, with almost immediate results. Allen kept possession in the middle, before passing the ball out to Moreno. The full-back found Coutinho, who played a one-two with Milner, before firing low and into the corner for 3-2.

Klopp called for more noise, and he got it. The fans were back onside and all of a sudden Dortmund were reeling. Origi fired a shot from range just over the bar and it started to feel like when, rather than if, Liverpool would equalise.

Dortmund managed to hold the hosts at arm's length for a while, but conceded a corner when Weidenfeller was forced to push a Milner cross behind. Can went down with an ankle injury and was forced to come off. After treatment, the German hobbled away towards the touchline in front of the Kop, but was soon hopping with joy as the resulting corner was headed in by Sakho.

The fans roar nearly took the new roof off the refurbished Main Stand while Klopp raced down the touchline and punched the air repeatedly. It was 3-3. Liverpool needed just one more goal with ten minutes remaining.

Can was replaced by Lucas as Liverpool went after the winner. Dortmund had to regroup, but the calm assuredness they had shown earlier in the game was gone. They were making mistakes and just trying to hold on.

As the board was put up for four minutes of added time, Clyne was fouled near the halfway line. It was a chance for Liverpool to flood the box in a final attempt at improbable victory. An earlier free kick in a similar area found Lovren at the far post, but his audacious left-footed volley sailed into Row Q of the Kop.

However, this time there was an alternative option. Sturridge peeled away and offered Milner an open pass, which he took advantage of. Sturridge struggled to control the ball, but by the time he had, Milner had raced into the penalty area. Sturridge found him with a neat ball and Milner took it out wide, before placing a pinpoint cross to the far post. Lovren was waiting and connected perfectly with his head to send the ball crashing into the net.

They had done it. Needing three goals in the final 33 minutes, Liverpool had scored them. The only figure in the whole ground with a calm exterior was Klopp, who knew the job wasn't done just yet. His team had three more minutes to see out.

The nerves weren't helped when Lucas conceded a free kick on the edge of the Liverpool penalty area with seconds on the clock. İlkay Gündoğan stepped up to take it. Hearts were in mouths briefly as he swept the ball over the wall, but a collective sigh of relief came as it sailed just wide of the post, followed by a joyous roar as the referee subsequently blew for full time.

Klopp had told his players to make their own moments, and they did just that. Progression from a tie that seemed unlikely when the draw was made, and practically impossible when Dortmund led 4-2 on aggregate with half an hour remaining, but the Reds had done it. They had conquered the German side and were into the final four of the Europa League.

At the final whistle Klopp shook hands with the understandably despondent Tuchel, before consoling some of his former players, going to Reus and Hummels and hugging the pair. He then went to celebrate with his players, who were stood in front of the Kop in a line and raising their arms as one. Finally, he went over to the Dortmund fans to give them one final wave goodbye, with a mixed response from the travelling party.

Two days later at his pre-Bournemouth press conference, Klopp was asked about the players raising their arms to the crowd.

He replied, 'I wasn't involved. They did it by themselves. They wanted to say a big thank you to the crowd.

'It was all about the lads and the crowd. What we achieved was only possible because of that special relationship.

'The atmosphere was like I'd heard it could be possible. Before the game it was unbelievable when we drove through the streets. It was a great experience for all the lads.

'On the way to the game it's always silent on the coach but in this moment it was different. They all got out their cellphones to take videos. It was really cool.

'I've seen a lot of Dortmund games this season and I've not seen a game where they were under pressure like this. It was a special story. The fourth goal was brilliant but you need a bit of luck. You can't expect things like this but you have to believe they are possible.

'I don't have a bad word to say about Dejan Lovren. I'm not sure if everyone loved him before I came here but for his relationship with the crowd that will be really important.

'A game like that has influence on everything. Your mood, your attitude and your belief, and on the people around us. It was perfect.'

It had been another epic European night at Anfield to join the annals of the club's rich history, and it was yet more evidence of the effect that Klopp was having on this team, and on the fans.

When his early Liverpool side were 2-1 down against Crystal Palace with ten minutes left, people flooded to the exits. When needing three goals in 33 minutes against Dortmund, not one person intended leaving their seat. Instead they stayed to cheer their team to the unlikeliest of wins.

Doubters were starting to believe.

16

*'My first thought when everyone was
celebrating around me was, "Sorry, this is not
over yet, you still have to come to Anfield, too."
And we will be ready. It will be a completely
different game. It's a holy place.'*

AFTER the adrenaline-fuelled excitement of the Dortmund
victory, there was an 'after the Lord Mayor's show' feel about
the trip to Bournemouth just three days later.

It was an unfamiliar Liverpool line-up. Very little occurred before
Roberto Firmino and Daniel Sturridge both scored just before half-
time.

The England striker was flourishing and finally looking close
to full speed. He hit the woodwork twice in the second half and was
playing with a smile on his face. He was even allowed to play the full
90 minutes for the first time since returning from injury.

The hosts rallied late on and halved the deficit as Joshua King
fired in from the edge of the box as the game headed for injury time,
but the Reds held on for a 2-1 win and left the south coast with all
three points.

Klopp was satisfied with the victory considering the number of
changes, and made clear after the game that he had not been merely
rotating for the sake of prioritising Europe.

He said, 'I had to pick these players because we had no other
chance to win. Sometimes rotation is for resting players for another
tournament, but this is not the case here. Always the most important
tournament will be the Premier League. We only rotated because we
wanted to win the game.'

The win at Bournemouth had been a calming come-down from the Dortmund game, but it was also the hors d'oeuvre for the re-arranged Merseyside derby against Everton three days later.

The concentration of both teams could easily have been on other matters, with Liverpool still in the Europa League and Everton planning for their FA Cup semi-final with Manchester United the following Saturday.

The game was a nice landmark for Klopp. It was to be his first derby as Liverpool boss, to be played exactly 200 days since his appointment and it would also be the reverse fixture of the game that had cost his predecessor his job.

The German was no stranger to fierce derbies. However, his main point in the pre-match press conference was that his players didn't need to resort to hostile stereotypes by getting overly physical. It was pointed out to him that the Merseyside derby had seen more red cards than any other fixture in the Premier League era.

'Maybe one or two fans want to see stuff like this, but it will never help. I understand aggressiveness only in one way, and that is being prepared to hurt yourself, not somebody else,' he said.

'Before I went to Dortmund there were lots of red cards in derbies. I don't want to see this. Not to show "I am the man". The best football is always full of emotion, passion and aggressiveness. It's special because of expectations, that's clear. But to handle emotions and the pressure is one of the big challenges in top-class football.'

The fans were ready for another special night under the lights at Anfield.

Everton boss Roberto Martinez named a surprisingly strong side considering his team were just three days away from a potentially season-defining cup semi-final, but the Spaniard knew that a win in the derby could be just the boost his men needed.

The Toffees had been struggling in the league, though could boast talents such as John Stones, Ross Barkley and Romelu Lukaku. However, on this night they would spectacularly fail to live up to expectations.

Things began fairly evenly, with neither side able to get any passing rhythm going.

The visitors threatened to grab an early goal when Lukaku muscled his way into the penalty area, only to be denied by a spectacular tackle from Mamadou Sakho. The divisive Frenchman had been improving alongside Lovren at the back and was playing with more confidence as the Kop chanted his name.

The game was relatively even for the first 12 minutes, but from that point on Liverpool were dominant, even though it seemed they would go into the break unrewarded. That was until Milner dinked a cross into the box for Origi to attack and the in-form Belgian headed past Robles to give the Reds the lead.

It was no more than Liverpool had deserved and, as they had done at Bournemouth, they quickly made it two before half-time. Milner again provided the cross, this time from the left side, and Sakho was unmarked to power a header into the roof of the net.

The superiority continued into the second half, but then came an incident that would put a dampener on the evening. Everton defender Ramiro Funes Mori fouled Origi with a studs-up challenge that landed on the Belgian's ankle. Funes Mori was shown a straight red card and was booed off the field as he gestured to his badge, seemingly proud of his work. Origi was in clear agony and was stretchered off the pitch.

His replacement was Sturridge, who didn't take long to get his name on the scoresheet. Lucas won the ball high up the field before playing a defence-splitting pass into the path of the substitute, who controlled and finished before Robles knew what was happening. Philippe Coutinho then made it four with a typically accurate finish into the far corner.

A suggestion of how comfortable Klopp felt came late on when a flowing passing move ended with Lucas taking a shot from 25 yards that trickled harmlessly past the post, and the manager could be seen roaring with laughter in the dugout.

The true extent of their dominance was revealed after the game. They had managed 37 shots, with 13 on target. Everton had taken three shots, with none hitting the target. Liverpool had also had 64 touches of the ball in Everton's penalty area, while the visitors managed just three in Liverpool's.

Having not managed to do so all season, Liverpool had now scored four goals in each of their last three home games. However, the victory and nature of it was not the main thing on Klopp's mind after the game.

'We are in a good moment, we played football, we created chances and we could have scored a few more. We did well, but usually after a 4-0 I don't know how to keep my smile off my face, but today it is pretty easy to be honest [after the injury to Origi]. It is like it is, we have to take it, see what happens and in three days we have the next game,' said Klopp.

Klopp as a player for Mainz 05

Former Mainz manager and Klopp's mentor Wolfgang Frank

Klopp as Mainz manager

Klopp with wife Ulla and the Bundesliga trophy following Dortmund title win

Emotional farewell to Dortmund in 2015

Unveiled as Liverpool manager

Klopp in dugout for first game at Tottenham

Klopp with Peter Krawietz (left) and Željko Buvač (right)

Celebrations with players after 3-1 win at Chelsea

Arms and glasses fly in win at Norwich

Disappointed after collecting runners-up medal at the League Cup Final

Klopp comforts former BVB players after beating them with Liverpool

Celebrating second goal against Man Utd in Europa League at Anfield

Klopp leads celebrations after win over Villarreal

Boss and players dejected after Europa League Final in Basel

Past and present. A poster of Klopp overlooks the statue of Bill Shankly

Klopp gives Sadio Mané a piggy back after goal at Arsenal

Celebrates so hard against Leicester his glasses fall off

Klopp v Chelsea screaming 'No one can beat us!' at fourth official

Klopp celebrates v Middlesbrough on final day of 2016/17 season

'It was good for us, good result, clean sheet and four goals. All the other teams in the table above us won too, so nothing has happened, but we can't change this – we have to win as often as possible.'

The following Saturday saw another home game filled with narrative and emotion as former Reds boss Rafa Benitez returned to Anfield with his Newcastle United side.

The Spaniard had won Liverpool an unlikely Champions League in Istanbul in 2005 and was largely revered by the fans for the six years he had spent in the Anfield hotseat, in which time he had turned them into one of the most-feared teams in Europe.

Parallels were drawn with the job that Klopp was now having to do at the club, and that Benitez had also come from a background of winning titles against the odds in another league, having won La Liga twice with Valencia before moving to Merseyside in 2004.

Benitez had started the 2014/15 season as manager of Real Madrid but had been rather harshly dismissed after falling behind Barcelona and Atletico Madrid in the title race in Spain. His desire to once again work in England saw him take on the arduous task of keeping Newcastle in the Premier League after a disastrous campaign under Steve McClaren saw them lodged in the relegation zone.

After some early hiccups, Benitez was starting to see the fruits of his labour as Newcastle had comfortably beaten Swansea and earned a draw with Manchester City in the week leading up to their trip to Anfield.

Predictably, Klopp was asked how he felt about the return of Benitez, and he replied, 'I really like Rafa, we have met a few times.

'From my point of view, if someone wants to celebrate Rafa Benitez in memory of Istanbul or whatever – he is one of the most successful managers at Liverpool – they are very welcome.

'I don't care about that. Be louder than you have ever been, that is absolutely okay. That is how I would say hello to a good old friend, so no one has to ignore this wonderful moment because I am here now.'

Before Klopp's press conference it emerged that Origi would be joining Jordan Henderson on the list of players unlikely to play again before the end of the season. The timing could not have been worse as Origi had been finding some exceptional form and was an ideal foil for Sturridge on the England striker's gradual return from injury.

One other player conspicuous by his absence in the matchday squad was Mamadou Sakho. The Frenchman had not been selected because on the Friday afternoon of Klopp's pre-Newcastle press conference, the club received a letter from UEFA. Sakho had failed a drugs test.

The Frenchman had tested positive for a banned fat-burning substance after the Europa League second leg against Manchester United and would not be officially suspended until the B-sample had been tested a few days later, but the club, the manager and the player all agreed that it would be best for him to sit out of any games in the meantime until the matter was resolved.

It was yet another blow for Klopp heading into the vital Europa League semi-final with Villarreal, and meant that he would have to look elsewhere for defensive cover, just as Lovren and Sakho were showing signs of forming a strong partnership. Kolo Touré was the man chosen for the Newcastle game.

It was a similar story to the home game with Newcastle's rivals Sunderland. Liverpool took a 2-0 lead through Sturridge and Lallana, only to be pegged back in the second half to 2-2.

It was yet another game where Klopp's side had held a two-goal lead and failed to win, the third such occasion in the last ten outings.

It also made 19 points that had been dropped from winning positions, points that if they had been secured would have seen them very much in the title picture.

Benitez was happy with his team's point and had some kind words for his counterpart when asked whether he thought Liverpool would be able to win the Europa League.

'Hopefully it will be the same [as winning in 2005] and we see Liverpool go in the right direction,' the Spaniard said. 'He's got great experience and is a lovely person, someone who the players and the fans will enjoy.'

As Klopp had alluded to, while the Newcastle game had been a disappointment, it was over and done with and the attention now turned fully to the trip to El Madrigal for the first leg of their Europa League semi-final with Villarreal.

The squad travelled to Spain with Christian Benteke, who had recovered from his knee injury. However, Sakho stayed at home. The club had already announced that he wouldn't play as long as disciplinary proceedings were ongoing, but UEFA had made it official by issuing the defender with a 30-day suspension while they looked into the matter further.

It had been an emotional week for the club and the city as a whole. On the Tuesday morning, the verdicts were delivered at the inquests into the Hillsborough disaster, and had come back confirming what the people of Liverpool had been saying since the tragedy had occurred, that the negligence of South Yorkshire Police had led to the unlawful killing of the 96 victims, and that the Liverpool fans who were at Hillsborough on that day played no part whatsoever in the deaths of their fellow supporters.

It concluded 27 years of fighting by the families of the victims, and at two years in duration it was the longest criminal inquest in British justice history.

A momentous week for the city included the away trip to Villarreal, who while considered underdogs, were certainly not going to be a pushover, especially in their own stadium.

The Yellow Submarine were fourth in La Liga, behind only the big three of Barcelona, Real Madrid and Atletico Madrid, and had beaten the latter two at home in the league, while gaining a creditable 2-2 draw with Barca.

They had also beaten Napoli and Bayer Leverkusen in the Europa League, and had only conceded once at home in six games in their campaign.

Klopp raised a few eyebrows with his selection. The back five were understandable, with Touré replacing Sakho, while a midfield three of Lucas, Allen and Milner made sense. However, there was a notable absentee in attack.

Daniel Sturridge started on the bench, with Lallana, Coutinho and Firmino as the front three. Klopp explained his decision before the game. He told BT Sport it was 'a very difficult decision' and added, 'I thought about a lot of things and at the end I decided for a little bit more stability.

'In a 4-3-3 we didn't play with Daniel until now, so we thought for today, this 4-3-3, 4-5-1, sometimes a diamond, this very flexible style, it makes sense that the players played together before and that's why we decided for this line-up.'

It was a calmer atmosphere to the ones experienced in previous rounds in Manchester and Dortmund. The 2,000 travelling Liverpool fans were stuck away in the upper tier, and the home fans held their yellow scarves aloft as The Beatles's rendition of 'Yellow Submarine' blared out. It wasn't quite 'You'll Never Walk Alone', but it still set a tone. It was a typically tentative European semi-final first leg, with neither side committing too much. As three minutes of added time were signalled at the end of the game, thoughts turned to which team would benefit most from a goalless first leg.

Klopp had brought Benteke on for the last few minutes to give his team an out-ball and have someone else to help defend corners, which Villarreal had started to win with regularity.

However, Benteke was being used in attack by his team-mates, who surged forward in search of an away goal. They lost the ball and Villarreal countered. The entire Liverpool midfield was caught on the left side, so the hosts switched it right.

A ball over the top of Touré found the dangerous Denis Suárez, who ran in on goal. He squared it to substitute Adrián López, and he tapped in to make it 1-0.

Manager Marcelino and his backroom team leapt all over the pitch and the players ran to the fans in ecstasy as their team had snatched a goal advantage to take with them to Anfield.

After the game, Klopp had some opinions on the celebrations of his opponents. He said, 'My first thought when everyone was celebrating around me was, "Sorry, this is not over yet, you still have to come to Anfield, too." And we will be ready.

'It will be a completely different game. It's a holy place.

'It happened so we must accept it. It's no reason to be disappointed. If the players want to be angry for ten minutes then do it but we must be ready for Anfield.

'They have to come to Anfield where we know how strong we are. This race is not over.'

17

'I think, especially in 2016, the team has showed a lot of times what they are capable of and what they could be capable of in the future. That's a really good sign. That's more important for me as a manager.'

THE late defeat in Spain had been a real punch to the gut, and the last thing the team needed was a tricky league game in-between the two fixtures.

A trip to an in-form Swansea it was then, and just to make matters worse, it would kick off at midday, just 62 hours after the final whistle had blown in El Madrigal.

Klopp was not happy with the arrangements, saying that in his entire career he'd never been asked to kick off at midday, 'On Sunday all English people will have lunch while we play football. My first time with 12 o'clock kick-off. Who made this decision?'

Due to injury and the need to rest certain players, Klopp was once again forced to name a much-changed line-up. One particularly interesting selection came in the midfield. Kevin Stewart was partnered by 18-year-old Spaniard Pedro Chirivella. The former Valencia youngster had made appearances earlier in the season in some select cup games, but this was his first league start. He was seen as a promising emerging talent, but the lack of experience throughout the team would prove to be a problem as Swansea boss Francisco Guidolin named close to a full-strength team.

It was an awful afternoon in the driving rain for Liverpool, being comfortably beaten 3-1. The defeat all but confirmed that a top four finish would be impossible, and that even top six was looking unlikely, making the return fixture against Villarreal all the more important.

It was now looking like Liverpool would not be qualifying for Europe through their league position, and so would almost certainly have to win the Europa League just to be in European competition the following season.

However, more importantly to Klopp, a trophy was on the line, and it was also a chance for his players to give themselves a reason to celebrate as euphorically as Marcelino and his team had done at the end of the first leg.

At the pre-match press conference the day before the game, Klopp addressed the fans with one last rallying cry, 'I don't have enough words for this. It's one of the things in life you cannot buy. It's most special. These moments when you really know we're all together. Not only the crowd in the stadium – at home [too]. It's a moment, I don't want to make it too big, but it's a moment for the whole Liverpool world. Everyone will watch it.'

If Marcelino was nervous about the return leg, he wasn't showing it, and insisted that the famous Anfield atmosphere would not intimidate his men.

The Spanish coach said, 'This is an occasion to be celebrated. In no way whatsoever will we be affected negatively by the atmosphere, if anything we will be affected positively and galvanised by it.

'We will suffer at moments in the game, we will find it tough but we can cause them trouble. The game will be decided by the team who are more assured at key moments.'

There was a feeling of all or nothing about the game for Liverpool. Win and they would be heading to their first European final in nine years with a chance to win their first trophy under Klopp and qualify for the Champions League. Lose and their season would merely consist of a lost League Cup Final and an underwhelming Premier League finish.

The fans knew the importance of it and had clearly heard the call to arms from Klopp.

In the hours before kick-off, thousands of fans lined the streets around the King Harry pub on Anfield Road. As the coach headed to the ground the fans cheered, waved, sang and lit flares to welcome their heroes. As they had done during their welcome for the Dortmund game, players took videos on their phones, astonished at the scale of the party.

As the fans made their way into the ground, the mood of optimism continued. All week the forums and podcasts had been filled with

Reds fans concerned about the one-goal deficit, being able to score more than once against a very organised Villarreal defence and the danger of conceding an away goal.

However, all those fears disappeared as the fans gathered at Anfield. A mosaic to mark the first home game since the Hillsborough inquest verdict was held aloft by half the stadium.

Klopp had raised a couple of eyebrows with his team selection, this time opting to start Daniel Sturridge, as well as Emre Can, who had made an unlikely recovery from the ankle injury he picked up in the previous round against Dortmund.

The game began and it was the visitors who threatened first, with Cédric Bakambu getting a shot away that deflected off Can but Mignolet parried it to safety. The moment brought some audible tension back into the ground, but that soon evaporated in a wave of cheers.

Can came forward with the ball, played it out right to Clyne whose cross was pushed out by Villarreal keeper Alphonse Areola. However, the Frenchman could only find Firmino, who played the ball back across goal. Sturridge threw himself at the ball and missed it, but the unsuspecting Bruno Soriano could do nothing to stop it bouncing off him and into the net.

It had taken just seven minutes for Liverpool to level the tie, although the threat of the away goal was still looming, so this was merely the beginning of the job.

The game arrived at half-time at 1-0, 1-1 on aggregate, but it had without doubt been a half for the home side.

The first 15 minutes of the second half were more tentative, neither team overly willing to commit too many men forward, but it was still largely Liverpool making the chances.

Sturridge had been on the periphery of the game, but his mere presence was causing a headache for the defensive pairing of Mateo Musacchio and Víctor Ruiz. Eventually though, he got his chance.

After some neat play, Firmino played a reverse pass through the middle of the defence and into Sturridge, who was in behind. He controlled and shot. The ball hit Areola, smacked the inside of the post, rolled across the goal and over the line. The crowd went berserk, as did Sturridge, whose usual trademark 'wriggly-arm' celebration was replaced by an outburst of pure joy, racing away wide-eyed and pumping his fists.

Liverpool were ahead in the tie for the first time, but an away goal would still send them out.

The nerves remained, but were allayed significantly by Ruiz fouling Lallana on the edge of the box and receiving his second yellow card of the night, leaving the visitors needing a goal with just ten men on the field.

The game was put to bed shortly after as Firmino powered past Musacchio down the Liverpool left, before cutting back to Sturridge. The striker mishit his shot, but Lallana pounced to turn the loose ball in and make it 3-0 on the night.

The rest of the game was a procession with Klopp able to bring off Coutinho, Firmino and Sturridge before the end. The final whistle went and Liverpool were in the Europa League Final.

It maintained Klopp's perfect career record in semi-finals and he was visibly ecstatic that his players had come through this one.

He made his way to the centre of the pitch and punched the air to all four sides of the ground, getting a roar from the crowd each time. He had them eating out of the palm of his hand and couldn't wipe the smile from his face. He was, somewhat ironically, criticised by Marcelino for celebrating too much post-game.

It was of no consequence to Klopp though, who had guided his Liverpool team to a second final after just seven months in charge.

He was clearly delighted with his side's performance in the post-match press conference.

He said, 'The problem is I'm not a native speaker so I don't have the right words for this performance. It was nice to watch and nice to be part of it; the whole performance, not from the first second [but] from 6.45pm when we drove through the road again. It's nice.

'The first half-hour ... what power! The will was obvious, I would say. Then for 15 minutes we lost a little bit of patience, that's normal. We tried [to be] a little bit different and it made not too much sense. In the second half, back to the plan – still very emotional plus very smart, wonderful goals, well deserved.

'To go to a final you need a little bit of luck in decisive moments. But most of the time you need outstanding performances. When I came here, the tournament didn't sound too nice for the people – three draws or something like that. It was a difficult group I thought and we came through with a nice game in Russia. That was good.

'We felt really comfortable in this tournament. We liked to go to different countries and adapt to different circumstances and temperatures. I like this in football. The problem was, around these games we had so many other games and so we couldn't really be focused on this. I think, especially in 2016, the team has showed a lot of times what they are capable of and what they could be capable of in the future. That's a really good sign. That's more important for me as a manager.

'But then when you perform in the right moments like we did tonight, or against Dortmund or against United or Augsburg then you want to have more. That's what we try now. Europe is big and a lot of teams want to go to finals, it's not too easy. Now we are there. It's a great opportunity and we will take it as an opportunity.'

Pep Lijnders revealed to me the impact that Klopp had made after the setback of the first leg, and how it was another example of the spirit of the team that saw them through.

'In the moments we need leadership, Jürgen gives direction. For instance, Villarreal away, we lost the game in the last minute, so the players, the staff were really down. The moment Jürgen came back in the dressing room he changed everything in five minutes. We could leave the stadium knowing we were going to attack them at Anfield like they had never been attacked before; we would go and chase them like they have never been chased before.

'Sometimes to influence the next game, the first five minutes directly after the previous one are more important than the five days leading into this next game. Adversity had made us stronger, made us quicker and made us more precise. The German mentality of asking always and believing always a little bit more. The only reason we won the historical game against Dortmund at Anfield came from this mentality.

'We understood from the first minute that good things take time. A hard-working, pressing and counter-pressing team will often make more mistakes because we attempt more and perhaps we will accomplish more in the [near] future.'

The last three league games still needed to be played, but the minds of the fans were already on the final in Basel. Concerns had been raised about the venue of St Jakob-Park, which could only accommodate around 35,000 fans, with the competing teams receiving an allocation of less than 10,000 each.

Klopp had suggested that Liverpool fans head to Switzerland anyway to turn Basel into a sea of red. That was until it was pointed out to him that UEFA were very much against the idea for security reasons, so at his pre-Watford press conference he had to plead with fans to stay at home if they didn't have a ticket.

Watford came to Anfield on a sunny Sunday afternoon with very little to play for. Liverpool had a final to look forward to and not much else they could do in the league, while the Hornets were comfortably safe from relegation.

Another team mostly made up of players that had not featured against Villarreal ran out comfortable 2-0 winners thanks to goals from Joe Allen and Roberto Firmino.

Just a few days later saw the final home game of the season against an out-of-sorts Chelsea. The Blues had been Premier League champions less than 12 months prior, but arrived on Merseyside knowing that the highest they could finish in this campaign was ninth. They did however have a little bit of momentum following a draw with Tottenham that officially denied their London rivals the title and handed it, remarkably, to Leicester City.

Klopp knew that in recent history this had been seen as a big clash, and treated it as such, picking a strong team. He selected the same XI that had started against Villarreal, and it was theorised that he was using the game as a dress rehearsal for the Europa League Final.

Liverpool made a bright start, forcing Asmir Begović into saves and looking really fired up for a big win to end their home campaign. However, Chelsea soon played their way back into things, and took the lead through a mazy run and finish by Eden Hazard. The Belgian had endured a torrid season but had recently rediscovered the form that saw him win the PFA Player of the Year award the season before.

The Reds toiled largely after that, creating some chances, but a goal never seemed to be on its way. It was worrying that the side that was likely to be contesting the final seven days later was struggling to break down a team that had been in such dire straits throughout the season, but right at the death, an unlikely hero emerged.

Substitute Christian Benteke headed home a cross from fellow sub Sheyi Ojo to equalise in the 92nd minute and give the home fans something to cheer. It maintained an unbeaten home record that stretched back to the loss to Manchester United in the January, and made the traditional end-of-season lap of honour at the end of the game a little more cheerful.

Klopp joined his players, their wives, girlfriends and kids as they walked around the pitch to acknowledge the fans for their season of support. He walked over to Coutinho at one point to question him on the trophy he was all of a sudden holding. It was the 'Golden Samba', awarded by the fans to their player of the season (voted for by fan forum *Red All Over The Land*). An Adidas Samba trainer spray-painted gold and attached to a block of wood, and the sentiment was appreciated by both player and manager. Emre Can received the young player award.

This would be the last game played at Anfield before the new Main Stand was put in place and the ground's capacity swelled to over 54,000, but there was still one more league fixture to fulfil.

A trip to West Bromwich Albion would complete Klopp's first Premier League campaign, and feature just one player from the likely final starting line-up in the entire 18, with Simon Mignolet on the bench. The starting XI was made up once again of fringe players and youngsters.

The game didn't start too well as Salomon Rondon fired the opener past Ádám Bogdán at his near post.

On the last day of the previous season Liverpool had been decimated 6-1 at Stoke, and for many fans it was the day when they lost faith in the direction Brendan Rodgers was taking the club. With a strong West Brom team taking an early lead, there were slight fears that something similar might happen at The Hawthorns 12 months on.

Those fears were calmed shortly after though as Jordon Ibe picked up the ball in his own half before driving forward down the right-hand side. He cut across the edge of the penalty area on to his left foot, making use of Benteke's run to pull away defenders, and slotted into the far corner with his left foot to level matters.

Ibe had been a big favourite of Klopp when he first arrived, but his form had dipped in the second half of the season and questions were being raised as to whether he was able to improve under the German. This would prove to be his last appearance for the club before a £15m summer move to Bournemouth.

The rest of the game was played out without much incident, though notable cameo appearances were made by Jordan Henderson and Danny Ings, both back from injury. It was Ings's first appearance since Klopp had arrived having torn his ACL in his very first training session with the new manager.

The game ended 1-1 and Liverpool's domestic season was at an end. Klopp said in his post-match press conference that he was pleased with his much-changed line-up.

Liverpool had finished eighth in the league, their joint-lowest in the Premier League era, but there was a big asterisk next to that placing as they had been playing a lot of youngsters and fringe players in the last few games, and had also included the two months before Klopp arrived.

The league campaign was done. One game to go. On to Basel.

18

'Someday everybody will say Basel was a very decisive moment for the wonderful future of Liverpool FC.'

ADAM Lallana is being interviewed about Liverpool's run to the Europa League Final. All of a sudden, a familiar face appears at the door at the Melwood meeting room, gesturing to be let in.

'What are you doing here?' Jürgen Klopp asks his midfielder.

'Speaking about you!' Lallana replies.

'Ask him if he knows when Spurs start pre-season training?' Klopp jokes in a reference to speculation linking Lallana with the London club.

'Too late, we have already spoken about that,' Lallana responds.

'I asked him and he said 1 July,' Klopp said before descending into laughter.

'I thought you were being serious,' Lallana says.

'Are you crazy?!' Klopp adds before heading back out the door.

Not your typical conversation between a player and his manager, but an indication of the kind of relationship that Klopp had already established with his squad.

His chemistry with Lallana may also have been due to the fact that the pair lived next door to one another in the affluent area of Formby, largely populated by local footballers.

Lallana continues, 'It is nice actually. He has just got a nice family, nice kids and I see him walking the dogs.

'My little boy, when I take him up for a bath, we have the landing and one time he [Klopp] was taking out the bins so I put my lad on the balcony and he was shouting "Klopp" and giving it the fist pump celebration. He just looked at him and gave him a wave.'

Lallana was also reflecting on his own time at Liverpool, and the impact of the German coach since his arrival.

He continued, 'The last seven months have been very important for me. I feel as though I have established myself at Liverpool and I am enjoying it.

'I wouldn't say Jürgen's got inside our heads or he's some kind of psychologist. But it was a fresh start for everyone when he came in.

'He demands hard work. He doesn't do passive. That is a word he uses a lot. He says if you defend passive there is no point in playing.

'You are entitled to make a mistake and he accepts you will have a bad game but he really won't be happy if you are not giving it your all.

'I just feel really appreciated under this manager. That's just how it has worked out.'

Lallana conceded that he himself had been subject to a tongue-lashing from Klopp just the previous week.

He said, 'He was screaming at me during the Chelsea game last week but he screams so much on the day of a game that you've got to take it with a pinch of salt really. You definitely can't take it personally, that's just him. He was shouting at me to be more compact.

'The worst thing you can do in that situation is gesture, "What do you mean?", or dismiss it. The best thing is to just nod your head even if you don't understand what he's saying.

'After the game he will always explain that he was just trying to help you. He is a great character to have around. I really like the way he is and I think his traits bring the best out of a lot of players.

'He doesn't get too angry after a game. Even after a defeat he's more disappointed that we haven't shown our best. He is very structured in what he says.

'He is animated and emotional on match days and that makes him who he is. But when you come away from that he is very affectionate, and has a laugh and a joke.

'People speak about the hugs he seems to give everyone but sometimes that can mean a lot to a player. It can make you feel wanted and shows he appreciates the hard work you have just put into a game.'

Ahead of the League Cup Final against Manchester City at Wembley, Klopp told his players, 'This will be the first of many finals we'll have together.'

'I remember it vividly,' Lallana added.

'The way he said it, you just believed there would be more finals whether it was this year or next year or whenever. It just shows you his confidence and self-belief and I think that rubs off on the lads, subconsciously or not.

'He said we would use the experience whether we won at Wembley or not. We were on the losing side that day but I certainly learned from it and I'm sure the other players did too.'

At his final pre-match press conference of the season, Klopp exuded confidence of a manager who had belief that his players could get the job done.

'I don't feel the pressure, I feel opportunity. I cannot change,' he explained.

'I don't think I've ever felt doubt around me. If that's right, I don't know, but it makes me completely free to make decisions and for my team and myself to be free to develop together. I am really pleased for the boys and that they can be part of the moment with this team.

'I came here because I was really convinced about the qualities of these players and this squad, despite the doubts people had. To see how they have reached this final gives me a really good feeling.

'When I came here, there was a big amount of doubt about these players and now I am really happy they can show how strong they are and it is a big opportunity to make the final step this season and achieve something.

'We have a big chance and winning tomorrow will make it much more easy for you to see it as a success.

'We already know about the desire of our supporters. We know how much they want to win this cup, they showed us in an impressive way, home and away. Travelling around Europe, it was great to see.

'They live all over the world, which shows everything about this club. We would really love to be the team that makes their dreams come true.'

The subject of Klopp's record in finals came up. While his semi-final tally was perfect, he had lost his previous four finals of various competitions, including the Champions League against Bayern Munich and a DFB-Pokal Final against Wolfsburg in his last game in charge at Dortmund.

He reflected, 'Before a final I only think about the performance because I know there are two possible things in a final – you win or you lose. The only thing I can really have an influence on is performance. If you had enough time, maybe you watched the finals before you asked the questions and you will have seen that all the teams I was in finals with always performed really well. They were close games.

'I'm not frustrated about my final record, it could have been a little better that's for sure, but it is like this. When it's over, it's over. I was, for sure, not happy after finals I didn't win but to be honest I don't think about it any more. At home I have a little too many silver medals, that's true, but it's better than having no medals. The longer you don't win anything, the harder you try, the more likely it is it will happen and that's what I believe in.'

He was also asked about his planned stay at Liverpool, with it pointed out that he spent seven years at Mainz, then another seven at Dortmund.

'Seven years in Liverpool hopefully! I don't know if they hope I stay a little bit longer [after the final] but for me it's the only way I can work,' he said.

'When I came here everybody told me the British media are pretty impatient, they are your best friends until they are not your friends. Until now we've had a good relationship to be honest but it's really important that I don't read what they write. I don't feel the pressure, I feel opportunity; I feel pressure of the game and developing players and I don't think I have all the time in the world but I never felt doubt around me in a club.

'Maybe I'm not sensitive enough, I'm not sure, but that makes me completely free for decisions and it gives me and my team time to develop together from the first day. I came here because I was really convinced about the quality of these players but at the start I was the only person. Now that a few more people know about this and see how they deserved this final, it made me feel really good.'

The scene was set, the time had come. Liverpool's season would come down to this. One game in Basel.

The fans gathered in the city, some with tickets, some without, but the peace was kept and the Reds fans that travelled without tickets who were unable to buy them in Switzerland assembled around the fan parks with big screens. Thousands more watched on back in Liverpool, with 9,000 inside the city's Echo Arena to watch the game.

Inside St Jakob-Park, as predicted, around three-quarters of the stadium was filling up with Liverpool fans. Some Sevilla fans had apparently sold their tickets to opposition fans, willing to make a big profit on their allocation. The noise started to get louder as the game approached, with impromptu renditions of 'You'll Never Walk

143

Alone', 'Fields of Anfield Road' and even 'There She Goes' by The La's ringing around.

Barring a slight altercation between fans when the organisers forgot to put a barricade between them, there was little in the way of crowd trouble and on a warm evening in Basel, the 36,000 in attendance were ready to watch the highly anticipated final between Jürgen Klopp's Liverpool and Unai Emery's Sevilla, who had won the Europa League two years running, and four times in the last decade.

Klopp's starting line-up was just as predicted, the same as the one that had put Villarreal to the sword in the semi-final; Mignolet, Clyne, Lovren, Touré, Moreno, Can, Milner, Lallana, Coutinho, Firmino, Sturridge.

Jordan Henderson and Divock Origi had both been passed fit and took their places on the bench.

The two teams came out ready to do battle, and as the whistle went to start the game, the noise levels in the stadium dropped. Nerves had already kicked in.

The Spanish side looked to have more confidence early on, moving the ball about trying to force Liverpool into the press. They had the wild pace of Kévin Gameiro up front to unleash if the Reds came too high at any point, and with 35-year-old Kolo Touré in defence, there was a real fear that the Frenchman could dish out some punishment if given the chance. Gameiro had scored 28 goals in the campaign, but was kept relatively quiet in the early stages.

Though Sevilla had enjoyed a lot of possession, it led to very little. Liverpool conceded a lot of free kicks and throw-ins but nothing had come from them, and all of a sudden they started to play their way back into the game.

Roberto Firmino worked his way to the right of the penalty area, before trying to take the ball past Daniel Carriço. The ball struck Carriço on the arm. The referee waved the appeals away and Liverpool were denied a penalty.

Gameiro had his first effort on goal as he attempted an ambitious overhead kick following a corner, but it flew harmlessly wide.

A game devoid of real chances all of a sudden burst into life as a Liverpool attack saw Coutinho play Sturridge in on the left of the area. A run from Moreno on the outside pulled Sevilla defender Adil Rami out of the way, and in a flash Sturridge hit the ball with the outside of his left foot. It curled perfectly around the despairing dive of goalkeeper David Soria and into the corner of the net. A special goal from Sturridge had broken the deadlock and Liverpool meant business.

They dominated the last ten minutes of the first half, and thought they had doubled the lead four minutes later when Lovren headed in from a corner, but the presence of an offside Sturridge distracting Soria meant the goal was ruled out.

Not to be deterred, Liverpool continued to pile on the pressure, but were unable to find another goal before the break. Sevilla were all of a sudden playing like a punch-drunk boxer, akin to Villarreal at Anfield.

There was little concern from the Reds though as they were in control of the game, had the lead and with an early goal in the second half, could probably close it out with relative ease.

There was indeed an early goal in the second half, and it completely changed the game.

Sevilla kicked off and immediately headed for Liverpool's goal. A long ball was headed away by Moreno, but only as far as the pacy right-back Mariano, who took the ball past Moreno and cut it back into the middle, where Gameiro was waiting to tap in.

It had taken just 17 seconds for Liverpool to go from being in control of the final to losing their lead and being on the back foot. The noise had stopped.

For all of Klopp's pre-match optimism that his team would play with a calm confidence and to react to any setbacks in a positive manner, what followed must have felt like a horror film to the German.

Sevilla attacked relentlessly. Gameiro raced in behind the defence and only a remarkable chase and tackle by Touré, belying his years, kept the Reds level. Shortly after, a header by Steven N'Zonzi found Gameiro unmarked six yards out, but his shot at Mignolet was parried away.

There was a hint that the chances being wasted by Emery's side would allow Liverpool back into the game. That was until a seemingly harmless attack just after the hour mark was turned into a goal as Coke got on to the end of a loose ball and drilled past Mignolet to give Sevilla the lead.

Just six minutes later, the game was done. A double deflection off Clyne and Coutinho fell perfectly to Coke again, who found the far corner despite a hand from Mignolet, and it was 3-1.

Klopp had just brought Origi on for Firmino, and tried something else by introducing Joe Allen for Lallana, but the game was already over. In spite of the spirited fightbacks of previous games, there was no life left in the Liverpool side, shell-shocked by how they'd been torn apart by their opponents in just 29 minutes of the second half.

Klopp tried one last Hail Mary as he brought Benteke on for Touré with seven minutes left, but by then Emery had set his side up to play the game out, and play it out they did. There were no other significant chances to speak of before the final whistle went. Sevilla had won the Europa League for a third year running.

Liverpool had lost another final, and would now not only miss out on a place in the Champions League for the following season, but European football altogether.

The players sat dejected on the field. Milner could be seen mouthing 'I'm really sorry' to his boss as he approached him after the game, but he received a consolatory hug instead of a dressing down.

Emre Can covered his face with his shirt, trying to hide the tears. Clyne was also trying to fight off the emotion of defeat, while Jordan Henderson tried to shoo the cameras away from his distraught team-mates.

Some of the players headed straight down the tunnel after they received their runners-up medals. Others stayed to watch Sevilla collect their trophy, with tears and regret in their eyes.

Klopp attended his post-match press conference with a look on his face that suggested he would rather be anywhere else. However, he had still managed to compose himself enough to analyse the game and what may have been the cause of the second half capitulation.

He said, 'It was obvious the first goal of Sevilla had a big influence on our own game. In this moment we lost faith in our style of play. We changed from passing simply and quickly to complicated. We lost our formation, so it was not compact any more. We've had this situation one or two times before; as I said in the Chelsea game, we were quite happy we had the problem there. That was a good moment to put the finger in and change it.

'The first half was okay and we deserved the 1-0. Sevilla played a lot of long balls to avoid our pressing game. We did okay but not as good as we can.

'In a final, when it's clear it is close, you need a little bit of luck. We didn't. We have no influence on this, but where we have influence on is our game and so now we are disappointed and frustrated, 100 per cent.

'Tomorrow, in a week or whatever we will see it a little bit more clearly and then we will use this experience. That's what we have to do. Now it's clear we are not in a European competition next year, it means no football on a Thursday and it means we have time to train. We will use it and we will come back stronger, that's for sure.

'You saw on the way to the final we had a few moments where we maybe over-performed – we were unbelievable, great and the boys showed what they are capable of, but then to have this consistency you need a little bit more time. They are still young and this was their first big final – unfortunately their second [losing] final of the season, but it was a big final and we will use this experience together.

'Then someday everybody will say Basel was a very decisive moment for the wonderful future of Liverpool FC.'

When asked about his side's second-half performance he added, 'I saw it, so I tried to change it but you could see it was not only the team that was shocked about this situation; maybe the crowd was shocked about the situation. Everything changed in this moment. We had a wonderful atmosphere until it went to 1-1, but then Sevilla took the game and we defended not good.

'For the first goal, usually it's not good to concede a goal immediately after half-time but you have 44 minutes minimum to strike back, so what's the problem? The reaction was the problem. We all have to learn to react better in situations like this. This game, especially in my situation as the manager of the team, all you have to do is self-criticism. Nothing else. It's all about us, it's all about me. It's my job to help the players react better in different situations, so I can improve a lot.'

Klopp was also asked about what this game meant for his team heading into his first full season.

He replied, 'To use the time, to use the experience – that's what we have to do. Time to train. We will still use the break and hopefully they all come back healthy and we have no injury problems from the first day of pre-season.

'It will be a long tournament [Euro 2016] for a lot of my players – the Belgian players, the English players, the German player. They can stay in the tournament for a long time and then have a short break and then they will start again.

'To use the time, that's it. Of course, this team will be a little bit different next year, that's clear. We will do something with transfers, that's clear. But, first of all, we need to use the experience because I am sure we will be in a final again and we will have decisive moments again. And if we have decisive moments then we have to react better, all of us.'

Finally, the inevitable question was raised about it being his fifth consecutive loss in a final, and whether he thinks football has been unfair to him.

'Unfair, I don't know,' he commented. 'There are more important things than football in life. I don't think that God has the plan for me that I can go to the final and then always get a knock. Sometimes the way is a bit harder. I have a lot of luck in my life that I sit here and I am the manager of Liverpool FC. I do not think I am an unlucky person or life was not fair to me.

'Tonight was not too lucky, that's true, and the other finals weren't too lucky, that's true. But we will carry on and I will carry on and there will be another final and you will tell me I lost the last five finals. I will be prepared for this moment. I'm not sure that's a good answer but you can believe that I will try with all I have to reach the next final even when I know you can lose it. It's like this. There are bigger problems in life but in this moment it doesn't feel like this, it's really hard.'

Some believed that Klopp was partly culpable for the defeat, suggesting that he spent more time trying to get the crowd going instead of working on changing tactics or shape. Neil Atkinson and Gareth Roberts of *The Anfield Wrap* don't quite buy fully into that line of thinking.

NA: 'Liverpool were by far the better side first half and the manager deserves credit for that. They then conceded early in the second half and the Reds were all at sea. I think the manager had too much faith that the lads on the pitch were going to sort it and ended up with too many players peripheral to the action while he had options on the bench to try and take 1-1 for 20 minutes. So it became frustrating.

'Liverpool didn't need to chase the game had they shut it down with Joe Allen or Lucas Leiva. However, the manager could have made that change and still conceded. The late changes seemed like gambles, just throwing the dice, getting forwards on the pitch.'

GR: 'I think this gets overplayed among the conversations about Klopp, particularly the criticisms regarding his attempts to rev up the Liverpool supporters at the game. Could he have reacted quicker from a tactical point of view second half? Very possibly. Was the fact he didn't down to him waving his arms around a bit? Absolutely not. We can pick apart performances with hindsight but Liverpool – with clear deficiencies in strength of squad depth and quality – did well to reach two finals. Once there, well one goes to a penalty shoot-out, the other Liverpool take the lead, should have had a penalty, and then ...'

Later on in their Basel hotel, Klopp had one final thing to say. Not to the media, not to the fans, but just to his players, who were gathered in the hotel bar feeling morose into the early hours of the morning. Klopp saw the despondency among the group and realised it was up to him to lift his men.

'Two hours ago you all felt shit, but now we are back here and hopefully you all feel better. This is just the start for us. We will play in many more finals.'

Klopp then led his team in a rousing rendition of one of the Kop's favourite chants.

'We are Liverpool, tra-la-la-la-la!

'We are Liverpool, traa-la-la-la-la-la!

'We are Liverpool, tra-la-la-la-la!

'We're the best football team in the land, YES WE ARE!'

19

'We are very much at the beginning of our journey, but to already have the connection we have with this very special place is incredible.'

IT was a long summer between the Europa League Final and the first day of the new season, feeling all the longer after the events in Basel.

Staff and players went their separate ways, either on holiday or off with their national sides for the Copa América or European Championships. Klopp and his family went to the US for a post-season break, though he still could not tear himself away from football entirely. He was spotted attending the Copa América Final in California between Argentina and Chile.

The presence of Klopp did not go unnoticed. Photos of the Reds boss taking in the game were soon circulating on social media, as were rumours of the man he was sitting next to, with many claiming it to be the brother and agent of hotshot Argentine striker Gonzalo Higuaín. This sent social media into meltdown as 'Higuaín to Liverpool' rumours started running rampant. That was until it was pointed out that the man pictured was not Higuaín's brother, but was in fact Klopp's son.

Something Klopp was going to have to get used to as Liverpool boss was transfer talk. At Dortmund he could mostly leave that side of things to sporting director Michael Zorc, but with less certainty and more scrutiny on player incomings at Anfield, rumours would be abound all summer of who would be joining Klopp's Liverpool revolution.

One of those rumours involved former Dortmund starlet Mario Götze. The German had been brought through by Klopp at Signal

Iduna Park and was a regular in a title-winning team at the tender age of 18. However, he controversially left the club in 2013 to join rivals Bayern Munich. Klopp described the move at the time as one that broke his heart.

Three years later and Götze was struggling for game time at Bayern, unable to force his way into the team on a regular basis under Pep Guardiola, and now that Carlo Ancelotti was coming into the Allianz Arena, Götze's future was even less certain. That led to stories in the media that Klopp would look to bring him to England for a reunion, with Bayern reportedly willing to part with the 23-year-old for a fee in the region of £20m.

The story would not go away, but a transfer never seemed to progress. Germany manager Joachim Löw had said before Euro 2016 that he did not want his players to be involved in transfer talk during the tournament, and so once the first game had been played in France, it seemed that any deal would be off the table until mid-July.

There had only been one Liverpool representative at the Copa América in Philippe Coutinho, who had scored a hat-trick in a group game against Haiti, but there were plenty of Reds in France at the Euros, in fact the most of any club.

Several of those were with England, who were eliminated at the first knockout stage, which was quite good news for Klopp as he'd be getting them back for pre-season earlier than perhaps he had anticipated.

Joe Allen and Emre Can both reached the semi-final stage with Wales and Germany respectively, but only one would make a return to the club following the tournament.

Before the Euros had ended and Portugal had held the trophy aloft after beating the hosts in the final, clubs returned to start the hard work of pre-season training. There would be few, if any, training grounds where the work would be harder than at Melwood.

Klopp's insistence during his first season that having a full pre-season with his players would make the world of difference would now be put to the test, 'It's triple training sessions, of course. I'm really looking forward to pre-season. The problem with pre-season is that for the first three weeks we have 15 players who will have been away at the European Championship and we also have to see how the squad is changing.

'On another planet we would have six weeks together where we train because in this league it is the only time when you can only train. In all of the [pre-season] games we will play we will play out full training. So if we play our best in pre-season then I've done something completely wrong. It's another session, it's not about beating our opponents. I don't care about how big the opponent is we will say nothing about the situation.

'We have to do a lot to create a base for one year. We stop pre-season in the middle of August – maybe with the players who come back from the Euros it will be difficult so we might have to make their pre-season two weeks longer so that it goes into the season. That might mean they do not play at that stage or they are only allowed to play so many minutes.

'Football is about training and all that we have done is because of the work we've done together. We have a special plan of what we want to do with the boys. They cannot go home now when they are off. Nearly all of them have national team games now so you cannot have six weeks off, you have something like four weeks and in four weeks you cannot sleep for the whole time, so you have two weeks completely off and you have a plan and you have to do it.

'That means when you come back you are not at nil, you are at 60–70 per cent and then you can start training. That's how it works.

'Everything you do is based around physical potential and what you create in pre-season is key to that.'

As well as implementing a strict regime on the training field, Klopp made some alterations to his staff that would be overseeing the sessions, with Andreas Kornmayer being brought in from Bayern Munich as fitness coach. The 41-year-old was highly thought of in Germany, but after several years at Bayern he chose to try a new challenge with Liverpool and it was the influence of Klopp that persuaded him to join the backroom team.

Kornmayer told the club website, '[Klopp] was my first contact. He called me and asked me; we talked about everything.

'To be honest, I didn't have to think about it for too long. I was really impressed with what he said to me and impressed that the club wants to have me.'

There was also the slightly amusing fact that Kornmayer bears an uncanny resemblance to Klopp, with blonde hair, thick stubble and glasses. Rumours were spread that Klopp had merely brought Kornmayer in as a body-double in case he ever got sent to the stands.

Also arriving from Bayern was nutritionist Mona Nemmer, who had a reputation as one of the leading nutritionists in world football having spent time working for Bayern and the German national team.

Klopp's staff were in place ready to welcome the players back and to get them as prepared as possible ahead of what was going to be a crucial campaign.

The club had lined up nine friendlies for the pre-season. These would be chances for the fans to get a first glimpse of the new players that had come through the door during the break. As well as January signing Marko Grujić, Joel Matip also completed his free transfer from Schalke 04.

Klopp moved to tie up one summer deal very quickly, with goalkeeper Loris Karius signing from Mainz 05. It was unclear whether the young German would displace Simon Mignolet as number one, but his signing increased competition that was badly needed.

As time went on it emerged that Klopp had decided against bringing Götze to Liverpool, as it appeared that the lack of European football was making the attacker have second thoughts about a move to England, and so he headed back to Dortmund. Klopp only wanted players who didn't have any doubts about moving to his Liverpool.

'There are a lot of players who will only join a club when it is in the Champions League. I don't understand that but it is like it is,' Klopp said during a press conference on the US tour.

'I know about these players so I don't ask them. I look for other players, the ones who have the quality and ability to play in the Champions League but are ready to qualify together.

'Maybe there is only one year when they don't play Champions League but that is maybe the most important part of their thoughts. I never understand it.'

With money to spend, Klopp decided to go with two new players who would not only add attributes that his team currently didn't have, but he would add it in the form of two players from English football who had shown that they could perform to the levels required in the Premier League, and had done so particularly against Liverpool.

Sadio Mané had terrorised the Reds across the past couple of years, particularly in the 3-2 win for Southampton the previous season when Klopp's men had been 2-0 up at St Mary's. However, after a successful £34m bid from Liverpool, he would now be a weapon that Klopp could use against other teams.

The other big-money signing to arrive was Giorginio 'Gini' Wijnaldum from Newcastle. The north-east side had been relegated to the Championship, despite Wijnaldum's 11 goals for them from midfield. The Dutchman didn't fancy a season in the second tier and so once Liverpool had agreed a fee of £25m with Newcastle, he joined up with Klopp's squad to add a goal threat that the Reds midfield had somewhat lacked previously.

A lower-profile signing was centre-back Ragnar Klavan from Augsburg. The 30-year-old Estonian had also played against Liverpool the previous season in the Europa League, and his performances in those games had convinced Klopp – who was already aware of the player's qualities from his time in the Bundesliga – that Klavan would make a good experienced option for his defence.

These incomings meant that outgoings were needed, especially as a smaller squad would be required due to a lack of European football. Klopp did not waste time when it came to shipping some of his players out.

Joe Allen, Jordon Ibe, Martin Škrtel, Kolo Touré and Brad Smith were among the first-team players to be moved on, while youngsters Jordan Rossiter, Jerome Sinclair and Sergi Canós chose to leave rather than sign new deals.

The biggest sale of the summer though was Christian Benteke, who after a protracted negotiation between the clubs, eventually signed for Crystal Palace for a fee of around the £32m he had joined for a year prior. It meant that the club would actually be in profit after their summer dealings once Benteke's move was confirmed in mid-August.

The new season would bring new possibilities, but also new challenges. Klopp's former Bundesliga rival Pep Guardiola arrived to take the reins at Manchester City, while José Mourinho returned to the Premier League to take over at Manchester United. Antonio Conte left his role as Italy manager to go to Chelsea, and Ronald Koeman became Klopp's new foe for Merseyside derbies as he swapped Southampton for Everton.

There were also new levels of big money being spent by rivals on new players. Guardiola signed the likes of John Stones and Leroy Sané for a combined £85m, while Chelsea picked up Michy Batshuayi for £33m and re-signed David Luiz for £38m. Arsenal bought Granit Xhaka and Shkodran Mustafi at £35m apiece. However, no one could match the levels of spending at Old Trafford as Mourinho signed Eric Bailly, Henrikh Mkhitaryan, Zlatan Ibrahimović and Paul Pogba for United.

Pogba was the headline act for Mourinho as United broke the world transfer record with a £90m bid to bring the Frenchman back to Manchester, having sold him to Juventus for less than a million pounds just four years earlier.

Mkhitaryan was not the only former player that Klopp had managed at Dortmund to make the move to the Premier League in the summer. İlkay Gündoğan joined Manchester City for £25m, in spite of an injury. Despite rumours to the contrary, Klopp had decided against bringing any of his former players to Anfield, deciding to go forward in his Liverpool career with a squad of completely new players at his disposal.

'I had that player [Mkhitaryan]. If you have had players, you know more about them. You want to learn about other players. That's how it is,' he said.

'I knew quite early that he was going this way [to Manchester United]. There was absolutely no reason for me to jump in there. That isn't how we work.

'We didn't look for players we had already worked with. If you do that, you know their good, their bad and you wonder whether you will do it again.

'It's not boring but you know everything about each other so how can you develop? Where is the next step? Where is the next push for development?'

The first pre-season game would be one of four games arranged with local sides to make sure the team were well prepared before they went off for a tour of the US. Tranmere, Fleetwood, Wigan and Huddersfield would provide the opposition, with Prenton Park just across the Mersey the first port of call.

Ahead of the game, as if fans weren't excited enough about seeing their team in action again, the club released some significant news. Klopp and his backroom staff had signed new contracts that would see them committed to the club for the next six years.

It was not only a show of belief from the owners in Klopp and his staff, but also a commitment from Klopp to stay at Anfield for the foreseeable future.

A statement from the owners on the club website read:

'When you have an individual of Jürgen's quality in the building it makes perfect sense to secure that person for the long term. To not do so would be irresponsible.

'The overriding motivation behind this decision is Jürgen's commitment to overall improvement and development. In Jürgen we have someone who is always looking ahead, always looking beyond his own wants and needs and putting the club first.

'The ideas and plans he has for the football infrastructure excite us and we believe it benefits the organisation to have Jürgen committed to

Liverpool for a sustained period, to make sure he is here to oversee this development. By making this commitment to him, we are taking away any future distractions or doubt. We will move forward in partnership together, with confidence in each other and with the club's future at the forefront of every decision.

'He is a world-class managerial talent and his leadership will be critical to everything we hope to achieve in the years ahead.'

Klopp seemed equally pleased with the deal, stating, 'It's hard to express in words how honoured myself, Željko and Peter feel by the commitment shown in us by the ownership and the club in general.

'We are very much at the beginning of our journey, but to already have the connection we have with this very special place is incredible.

'I am the first to recognise that with this great commitment comes a great responsibility. All of our coaching careers we have looked to make teams and clubs better, with the ultimate goal of making the supporters proud and happy.

'To do this we have to make sure we always put player and team development at the heart of every major decision. It is my job to lead that and ensure every element of the LFC football environment reflects the best practices in the game. It is fantastic that the club's ownership is just as committed to this as we are.

'There is much to do and much to achieve and we look to do this by being the most completely together group anywhere in the world. That's everyone and we all have responsibility for it – all of us who are part of this LFC family: players, staff, ownership and of course the supporters.

'By being together at all times, we will be stronger, better and our successes sweeter.'

Tranmere provided a stern test though and kept the score at just 1-0 to the Premier League side, with Danny Ings providing the only goal of the game in the second half. Ings was back from a serious knee injury that had cut short his first season at the club after moving from Burnley the previous summer.

The next game against Fleetwood was a much more impressive outing from Liverpool, scoring five without reply, including a first goal for Grujić, as well as strikes from teenager Ben Woodburn, Lucas Leiva and two from Firmino.

Sixteen-year-old Woodburn had played well against Tranmere and shown even more promise at Fleetwood. His performances, along with those of fellow youngsters Ovie Ejaria and Trent Alexander-Arnold, had excited supporters and shown that Klopp was indeed taking a good look at some of the talent coming through the youth ranks.

A few days later the Reds visited former Premier League side Wigan Athletic, a friendly which included a return to action for Philippe Coutinho. The Brazilian soon set about causing problems for the hosts, hitting the woodwork with two separate efforts. It took until the second half for goals from Ings and Woodburn to settle the game.

The last of the four domestic friendlies came at Huddersfield, which was significant for two reasons. First of all the two teams would be contesting the 'Shankly Cup' in recognition of the role that the great Bill Shankly played in managing both clubs during his career. It was therefore appropriate that the current managers of both teams also shared a connection, with Klopp going up against his former Borussia Dortmund colleague and best friend, David Wagner.

Grujić hit another well taken goal to give Klopp's men the lead, and Mané almost had his first goal for the club but his strike was ruled out for offside. The game was made safe late in the second half as Alberto Moreno put away a penalty to make it 2-0.

One negative of the game was losing Lucas to a hamstring injury. The Brazilian pulled up in the second half after Klopp had subbed on all of his outfield players, so the fans were treated to a cameo from youth-team goalkeeper Shamal George, who was brought on and played as a striker. The 6ft 5in teenager was very nearly played in on goal by Lazar Marković, but the Huddersfield keeper and his lack of a sense of humour rushed out to deny him.

After the game, thoughts turned to the tour of the US. The squad flew out on the Thursday morning and before long were making public appearances, having open training sessions and going on excursions.

One such outing saw Klopp and his players visit Alcatraz Island. They Touréd the famous penitentiary, with one highlight on the club website being Mamadou Sakho wandering around with a GoPro camera, interviewing his team-mates.

It had been a distressing summer for Sakho. Having been banned for taking an illegal substance towards the end of the previous season, meaning that he missed the latter stages of the Europa League run as well as Euro 2016 in his home country, it emerged after an investigation that he would in fact not be serving a further ban, in spite of being threatened with one of up to two years initially. To make matters worse he picked up an Achilles injury that would rule him out of the start of the season.

However, he had no one else to blame for the next incident that befell him.

Just days after arriving in the US, Klopp sent him back to the UK. The manager indicated that this was due to the Frenchman not acting in a manner befitting a professional footballer, citing incidents such as almost missing the flight out, being late for a team meal and missing a recovery session. Klopp stressed that this was not a signal that Sakho would be moved on, but that he needed to improve his attitude if he wanted to be involved in the first team.

That was the only incident of controversy during the trip. Klopp and his squad got down to business, starting with a game against Premier League rivals Chelsea in Pasadena, California.

It was Antonio Conte's first game in charge of the Blues. The Italian was known for organised efficiency during his time in Italy, and it appeared that he had already set about getting more of the same out of Chelsea as his team ceded the ball to Liverpool for the majority of the game. However, a first-half header from Gary Cahill had given the London side the lead and they were able to hold on to the end, giving Liverpool their first defeat of the pre-season.

Another blow was an injury picked up by new boy Karius. The German goalkeeper had gone to punch a cross away and only managed to connect with the head of Dejan Lovren. It was announced the next day that Karius had broken his hand and would be out of action for up to two months, meaning that regardless of who his true first choice was, Klopp would be forced to start with Simon Mignolet in goal for the opening few games of the season.

The next game was much more positive as a dominant Liverpool saw off Milan 2-0 in San Francisco. However, a few days later they played another Italian side, AS Roma, in St Louis, where a timid performance that was unrecognisable from the one against Milan saw the Reds lose 2-1.

It was a disappointing way to end the US tour, but valuable hours had been done on the training ground and lessons had been learned.

There was also something to look forward to when the squad returned to England as next on the fixture list was a glamour friendly with Barcelona at Wembley Stadium. Almost 90,000 Reds fans turned up to see Klopp's men in action against one of the best teams in Europe, with Andrés Iniesta, Lionel Messi and former Liverpool icon Luis Suárez in their ranks.

The sun was shining, the fans were loud and they were treated to a performance that matched the occasion.

Liverpool were imperious, executing Klopp's gameplan to perfection. There was organised movement, pressing, counter-pressing, solid defending and lethal finishing. This was all summed up in the move that gave them the lead as a loose Barca pass was intercepted by Adam Lallana, who carried the ball forward. He played the ball into Firmino, who worked it back to the Englishman once he'd broken into the area. Lallana threaded the ball through the legs of a defender to find Mané, who took one touch and then slammed the ball past Marc-André ter Stegen.

Despite some Barca pressure that saw Messi hit the post and Mignolet forced into a good save from Suárez, Liverpool led at the break.

The Reds manager made some half-time substitutions and was rewarded straight away as a Mané cross and Henderson slide forced another former Liverpool player, Javier Mascherano, into an own goal. Then just seconds later, a high press, tackle and pass from Kevin Stewart released Origi, who ran through and slotted a third. Within minutes of the restart Liverpool had made it 3-0 and taken the game away from Barca.

The rest of the game was played at more of a casual pace, but right at the death just to put an exclamation point on the performance, another high press and tackle from Henderson released Origi. The defence blocked him, but Marković ran on to the loose ball and crossed for Grujić to place a looping header over Claudio Bravo to make it 4-0.

Liverpool had decimated Barcelona just a week before the start of the season, and the fans all of a sudden had something tangible to get them excited about what could be achieved in the upcoming campaign.

Klopp was of course delighted with the performance and the win, but not completely satisfied.

He said, 'I could be sitting here today when we had lost 4-0. Life would have not been that nice as it is at the moment, but [it would be] useful too because of the things you can learn. But it was Barca, it was a friendly and a lot of things can happen. If they start playing then it's pretty difficult to defend. But of course when you win 4-0 you have to use it. It was wonderful today, special – 90,000 people here for a friendly game and they could enjoy the game. I would say 98 per cent of what happened today was really great.

'Barcelona were not bad, are never bad. I think we did really well around the goals especially, and in one or two situations we needed a little bit of luck to defend, it's clear. Barcelona start one week later in the season, that's a difference in pre-season always.

'Obviously, for us, it was a more important game because 90,000 were here because of us – and Suárez and maybe Messi – but they were here because of my team. So we had a little bit more pressure but maybe we were a little bit more motivated. It's a friendly game and I don't want to overestimate this game but it's still good for us. We didn't think before the game we are one level with Barca and we don't think after the game we are on a higher level than Barca – we are not crazy.

'But the only job to do today was to play football as good as possible and we did it, and I've no idea how good Barca can be but I'm pretty sure better than today.'

It had been a great day at Wembley, but as with the US tour, a positive was swiftly followed by a negative.

The club had arranged its final friendly against Mainz 05, in Germany, less than 24 hours after the Barca win. Klopp fielded a very different side, and it was a very different outcome. A haggard and disjointed Liverpool were on the wrong end of a 4-0 hammering this time to end what had been quite a bizarre weekend.

Klopp said after the defeat, 'We came here at 2am and it's not perfect, but they are only things to explain the circumstances. We created a very tough situation. Of course, we should not lose 4-0 but it happened and we can work with it.

'Yesterday we could not stop smiling but that was not right, and today if we cannot stop being disappointed that's not right either. It's not between these two poles, if you want.

'We are in a good way, 100 per cent. And if we have a proper line-up, which we can have of course for next week, then we will be strong.'

There were seven days between Mainz and the first game of the season, which would be a trip to Arsenal.

The pre-season was over. The work had been done. It was now time to see how much fruit it could bear. It was time for Klopp's first full season in charge of Liverpool Football Club.

20

*'I love this game because it is a team game.
Trust, faith and togetherness.'*

IT could not have been a harder start for Liverpool. The fixture computer had pitted them against the previous season's top three of Arsenal, Tottenham and Leicester in their first four games, with the fifth game being a trip to Chelsea, who were being widely tipped to be back among the title challengers.

The first of their three early visits to London was to face Arsenal on the opening weekend of the season. Arsène Wenger's men had pipped rivals Spurs to second place in 2015/16, but many were still doubting their ability to be genuine title challengers this time around. The Emirates Stadium was a ground where the Reds struggled in past seasons and it was the first time Klopp had taken his Liverpool side there, though he did have previous experience with Dortmund from the Champions League.

He named an attacking looking line-up, particularly notable for the fact that he put Roberto Firmino in the false-nine role. The first side of the season was Mignolet, Clyne, Lovren, Klavan, Moreno, Henderson, Wijnaldum, Lallana, Coutinho, Mané and Firmino.

Three new players started, but it was an older one who was centre of attention early on. Liverpool had struggled to get a foothold in the game, and Alberto Moreno was finding himself unable to contain Theo Walcott down the Arsenal right.

A sloppy attempt at a tackle from the Spaniard saw the referee point to the spot. Much to Moreno's relief, Mignolet saved Walcott's penalty, but moments later the ire of the away fans was again on Moreno as Walcott snuck in behind him to take aim again and this time give Arsenal the lead.

Klopp's men had been poor and deserved to be a goal down, but eventually managed to stem the tide and get some more of the ball after the goal. With seconds to go before the break, they won a free kick.

It was a long way from goal but Coutinho fancied it, and in spite of the imposing figure of Petr Čech between the sticks, the Brazilian whipped the ball over the wall and right into the top corner to give Liverpool a sensational equaliser.

It was an ideal time to strike back as it caught Arsenal completely by surprise, which may explain their start to the second half.

Four minutes after the restart the visitors went on an attack that saw several players rush to the box. Wijnaldum picked the ball up on the left before lifting it towards the edge of the penalty area. Lallana ran on to it, took it wide and slotted his effort past Čech to put Liverpool in front.

The Reds had gone from being on the back foot to being confident enough to flood the opposition box. This increase in confidence was apparent again minutes later as a 19-pass move ended with Clyne fizzing the ball across the box and Coutinho putting in his second and Liverpool's third.

Arsenal were on the ropes and like a punch-drunk boxer, looked helpless to stop this onslaught of relentless attacking. Then Mané dealt what appeared to be a knockout blow. The Senegalese picked up the ball on the right and ran, and ran, then cut inside, and ran some more, before slamming the ball into the top corner with his left foot to make it 4-1.

However, it was far from game over as the Gunners managed to pull one back through Alex Oxlade-Chamberlain. The mood changed slightly as Liverpool sat off a bit not wanting to throw their hard-earned lead away. Then when Calum Chambers headed in another to make it 4-3, all of a sudden it looked like the game would swing back in the hosts' favour.

There were still 15 minutes plus stoppage time to play, but after having their character tested severely, Klopp's men were able to hold on and play out the remaining time.

It had been a heart-stopping encounter, but crucially the Reds had won, and at the home of a rival. It was a statement of intent to kick off the campaign, though some of the much-talked about defensive frailties had appeared too often for comfort.

In typical fashion, Klopp blamed himself for the near capitulation of his side after the fourth goal, suggesting that his involvement in the celebrations was a sign to his players that the game was over when it wasn't.

'I played a big part in the excitement of the last half-hour, because it's not allowed to celebrate the fourth goal like this with 35 minutes to go,' he told BBC Sport.

'At this moment, we switched off the machines. The game was not over. Arsenal lost, but we gave them a path back into the game.

'Nothing is sure until the final whistle. Over the whole of the 90 minutes it was a deserved win.

'We can always score goals and we can defend much better. It's the Premier League and nothing should be easy in this league. Nothing is easy.'

The German had no idea how prophetic those words would be as his side went into their second game of the season. In their opening five encounters in the league, this would on paper be their simplest one.

They had originally been scheduled to host newly promoted Burnley at Anfield, but due to the slight delays in the rebuilding of the Main Stand, they requested that the game be reversed, which the Clarets and the Premier League accepted, so they instead visited Turf Moor.

It was an awful afternoon for Liverpool, limply losing 2-0 to the Lancashire side. After beating the previous year's runners-up in the first game, they had lost the very next week to a team expected to be fighting relegation. It felt like the same old story.

Liverpool came away from the game with 81 per cent possession and 26 shots on goal, but the score never looked like being any different. The 19 per cent possession that Burnley had was the lowest ever recorded by Opta for a winning side in the Premier League.

Klopp was clear post-game that he was disappointed with how his team had played, but that at least he knew why they had failed and could learn lessons.

'Our decision making was not good. We'd put in a good cross but there were no bodies in the box and then when we had bodies in the box we ended up shooting,' he said.

'The lesson here is don't give the ball away like we did twice today. We will work on it 100 per cent. We need to have a plan for deep defending teams. We have a few things to do – that is clear.'

The result had not gone according to plan but there had been two interesting selections in the side that played at Burnley. Daniel Sturridge started the game in place of Mané, who had picked up a knock in training, and James Milner came in to replace Moreno.

The Spanish left-back had never really recovered from his mistakes in the Europa League Final, certainly in the eyes of the fans who had clearly lost patience with his errors. Questions had been asked as to why the club had not sought to sign a new left-back in the summer, but Klopp maintained that the answer to every problem is not always to sign players, and that work on the training field would be more beneficial.

Moreno had been taken out of the firing line though and replaced by Milner, who though he had filled in at right-back during points of his career and filled in at left-back in emergencies the previous season, had played predominantly as a midfielder. This was a relatively new position for him, but one that Klopp was sure he could manage.

The Burnley loss had hurt Liverpool but they had a chance to get back on track just a few days later as they travelled to Burton Albion for the second round of the League Cup. After agonisingly missing out on the trophy following the penalty shoot-out loss to Manchester City the previous season, this was a chance for the Reds to start another campaign that they hoped would end with redemption at Wembley in February.

A comprehensive 5-0 win against Burton was the perfect way to blow off the cobwebs, but the next league game would be a slightly tougher affair; a trip to Tottenham.

The north London side had been well in the title race up until the last couple of weeks of the previous campaign, and a slight collapse had seen rivals Arsenal overtake them on the last day, but a third-place finish was still very impressive and a sign of the good work Mauricio Pochettino was doing at White Hart Lane.

The visitors took the initiative and started outplaying Spurs, who had been forced to name their back-up keeper Michel Vorm in place of the injured Hugo Lloris in the starting line-up. The Dutch stopper was playing well though, making a vital early save from Coutinho and rushing off his line twice to thwart Mané.

He was given little chance to stop Liverpool from scoring when they did though after Firmino was felled by Kyle Walker in the box. Milner stepped up and sent Vorm the wrong way to give the Reds the lead from the penalty spot just before half-time.

In the second half came the inevitable fight back from Tottenham, but Liverpool looked strong and were able to keep them largely at bay. However, eventually a mistake from Milner allowed a ball to come into the box from the right and an unmarked Danny Rose fired in the equaliser.

Both teams had chances to win it late on but overall a draw was fair and a draw was the final outcome. Klopp had claimed a point from the trip, as he had done in his first Liverpool game, but the performance was certainly an improved one against a better Tottenham. Klopp's men had gotten more shots away than Spurs and, notably, had enjoyed more possession, which was practically unheard of against a Mauricio Pochettino side.

The German was pleased with the performance and felt his team could have gotten more from it.

'I still feel a little bit disappointed ... When we played like this then I think we could have won the game, but it is like it is.

'We made one mistake in and around their goal and they also had a header from [Toby] Alderweireld and a wonderful save from Simon. There were not plenty more chances for a home game for a football-playing team, a good side like Tottenham. This says a lot about our defending.

'This game showed again what we can do, how we can play. It was not only about pressing and things like this, although we did it really well. We were really flexible in offensive defending and then played football.

'Yes, I wish we would have won it but now we have to accept the point and that's no problem because it's Tottenham. They scored a goal and they could have won the game too. If they had scored the header, it was the same game but with two goals for Tottenham, so we have to accept it. We showed again we can be really good and that's what we have to show in each game. Then everything will be good.'

There was an international break next that allowed Klopp to review his team's start to the season, but in the immediate aftermath of the Spurs game was also the end of the transfer window. As they had been in January, Liverpool fans had been vocal on forums and social media that they felt the squad was not yet as strong as it could be, and seeing rivals spending ludicrous sums on star players while the club had actually made a profit on their summer deals didn't help matters. However, Klopp maintained that he was happy with what he had and didn't want to be drawn into buying players for the sake of it or just to appease supporters.

It was Klopp's faith in the abilities of his current players, and in his and his backroom staff's capability of improving them that meant he was happy to wait on potential deals for the future rather than find lesser options for the present.

During the international break, Klopp gave an interview to Martin Samuel for the *Daily Mail* in which he put to bed certain myths about his character.

Samuel writes that, during the interview, Klopp pointed to a Metallica CD on a shelf in his office, *Master of Puppets*, sent by a fan who took his heavy metal analogy at face value. It was still in its original wrapping.

Klopp said, 'It was a joke. I'm not into heavy metal. I mean, I used to like Kiss when I was young.'

There were also a number of psychology books on the same shelf. 'In Germany, they all thought I was a bit mental, very emotional,' he adds. 'So they were convinced this is what I am interested in. In Germany, each psychologist will send me a letter, those who coach the mentality of sport, all that stuff. It's not for me.'

Samuel also asked Klopp about his famous facial expressions during games, often seen gritting his teeth with wide eyes.

'That is my face for sport,' Klopp explained. 'When I was a kid, when I played tennis, that's how I was. I don't like it, but I have to accept it. I cannot change my face in this situation. People want me to change it. They tell me, "Jürgen, you have to, it's not good."

'I try with everything I have, but it doesn't work. I'm that kind of person, I think. I sleep like that. If I see a little baby I make the same face.'

Moving on to more serious matters, Klopp then gave Samuel his opinions on how people view football, and how annoying it can be for a manager.

'This is a crazy time where football is, for some people, the most serious thing in the world, but no one really cares about it. Look at the transfers: all everyone wants to know is what happens. They never want to know what it means behind, for this team, for that team.

'It's just, "Come on – give me the next big signing." To be cool enough to stay out of this colourful world around football, that is what I do. I'm not part of that, I'm not there, I don't enjoy it.

'My car knows only one way, home to here, here to home. There are more exciting lives around. The day I step back, I will never miss any of the world around football.

'Without being the most confident person in the world, I think I am the right person for Liverpool.

'I can't score goals and I can't make saves. I am not saying I am the best manager in the world, either. But I'm quite good and I am one of those managers who is really interested in structure.

'I don't sleep too long. Here is a moment when the club needs consistency in this chair – they need the right person and I am the right person, because most of the time I am really serious, but normal.

'I am not saying there was no one else around. The club would have found another manager, and I would have found another job – maybe an easier job. But I liked this club before I came here.

'It wasn't a big decision for me. It was the only club that could have broken up my holiday. I had enough offers, I was saying, "No, no, sorry, not now," and then came Liverpool. And I know how this sounds, and what people will say, but I fell in love.

'I felt responsible really quickly. It's like if you are in my inner circle, my family, my friends. I felt Liverpool was both: family and friends.'

Liverpool's travelling in the early stages of the season was over for now. Their next game would finally see them entertain at Anfield under the new Main Stand, which had been completed to add an extra 8,500 seats to the famous ground. The impressive structure dwarfed the Kop, and Klopp insisted that his players train in front of it the night before the game to make sure they weren't distracted by its impressive size on the day.

Appropriately, the first home game would be against the champions, Leicester City. Claudio Ranieri's remarkable achievements with the Foxes the previous season had captured the imagination of the whole football world, with their ruthless counter-attacking style and the threat of star players Riyad Mahrez and Jamie Vardy.

The pre-match rendition of 'You'll Never Walk Alone' seemed louder than usual, which may have been due to the extra fans, or just a sign of the enthusiasm and optimism that the fans had of the season ahead.

It took Liverpool a few minutes to get into the game but once they got on top, they stayed there. After some recent rumblings in the media of whether Daniel Sturridge was surplus to requirements under Klopp, who seemed to favour Firmino as a front man, the England striker started this game and made an unselfish run to draw defenders out of the way of the Brazilian, who was played in by Milner and slotted home the opener.

Then it was Sturridge again who this time ran on to a ball over the top from Henderson, before spotting the inside run of Mané. A cheeky back-heel from Sturridge found the Senegalese and he lofted his shot over the onrushing Kasper Schmeichel to make it 2-0.

The Reds were running rings around the champions and but for some wayward finishing and good saves from Schmeichel the game could have been done by half-time.

However, an error from Lucas handed the ball to Vardy at point-blank range and he halved the deficit to change the atmosphere from euphoric to nervy.

The home fans need not have worried though as their team came out in the second half and set about tearing Leicester to shreds again with goals from Lallana and Firmino sealing a 4-1 victory and a stellar performance in front of the new stand.

Klopp said after the game how pleased he was with the character shown by his team, especially after it went to 2-1.

He explained, 'It's a really exciting moment. We were here Thursday night for training because I thought it made sense that we show the new Main Stand to the boys earlier so we didn't come in and be shocked because it's really so different, it's so nice, so big. We're all football players and we all love wonderful stadiums. It was really good but we knew we had a job to do today and that's what we did, against a strong opponent.

'It was a deserved win, we were physically strong, we were clear, we were hard, flexible, quick, creative – all that stuff. We scored wonderful goals ... and conceded a not-too-wonderful goal! We had a few minutes when you saw what can happen in a football game – West Ham were 2-0 up today and lost 4-2 so that sort of thing can happen, not only here. At half-time I told the boys, "This is our challenge," because when we are good we are really good.'

However, it wasn't all positive from the manager. He was not too happy with the fans' decision to chant his name when the score went to 3-1, suggesting that it allowed the players to think the game was over. Moments after Lallana's goal, Vardy had got in behind the defence but was denied by Mignolet. Klopp ran towards the Kop and pleaded with them to sing anything else.

'I have to say, because I don't know how else I can say this, please don't sing my name before the game is decided!' he continued.

'Immediately when the Kop started singing "Jürgen Klopp la la la" they were clear on Simon Mignolet. 'It's like celebrating a penalty before you have scored!

'I don't play! It's nice, I like all the players, but please don't sing my name before the game is decided.

'It was the same against Arsenal. It's nice, but it's not necessary. It would be really nice if you could stop please!

'I wanted to say this, because [at the time] nobody could understand me. I know it doesn't sound too smart, but sorry. That's me. It's very nice, thank you very much. But I've heard it often now!'

The fans were too pleased with the performance to take offence and all of a sudden the negativity that had been around after the Burnley defeat had been replaced by an optimism that something was occurring at Anfield; that Klopp had really put together a good team during his first pre-season that was maybe ready to achieve more than people gave it credit for weeks earlier.

As if there hadn't been enough tests for Liverpool in the early weeks, next up was a trip to Stamford Bridge to play Chelsea.

The fixture had marked Klopp's first league win in England the previous season as the Reds ran out 3-1 victors, but that was against a Chelsea in crisis under José Mourinho. This Blues side was led by Antonio Conte, who had made a promising start to his own English adventure.

The former Italy international enjoyed incredible success as manager of Juventus, and had performed admirably as Italian national coach at the summer's European Championships in France, being harshly eliminated by Germany on penalties in the quarter-finals.

He also had an impressive home record that was widely reported before the game, showing the size of the task that Klopp and his side would have. Across his time with Juve, Italy and his early days at Chelsea, his previous 30 home games had seen 28 wins and two draws.

The game took place on a Friday night, a new thing for the English Premier League as television tried to stretch the football weekend even further, but it was something that Klopp welcomed, being used to such things in Germany.

When asked at his pre-match press conference about what he thought of Conte's touchline expressiveness, which had been compared to his own high energy nature, he admitted, 'I don't know Antonio well enough to say why [he celebrates enthusiastically] but he looks quite emotional when they don't score!

'Obviously he's involved in the game, but that's not the most important thing. The most important thing is that he's a great manager, a successful manager, something like the Pep Guardiola of Turin if you like – he created [Juventus's] special style of play and had a very successful time there.

'Stamford Bridge is a good place to play football, Friday night is one of the best moments to play football. Let's go for it.'

Liverpool did go for it. From the first whistle they got in Chelsea's faces, pressing relentlessly and winning the ball back with regularity. They held most of the ball in the early moments, with Sturridge forcing an early save from Courtois, and had it not been for heavy rain in the capital during the day the ball may have squirmed over the line after it slipped under the Belgian.

The hosts had given David Luiz his second debut for the club after he had re-joined on deadline day. The Brazilian's first outing for the club years earlier had also come at home to Liverpool, a game in which the Reds won 1-0. He and his team-mates were hoping history didn't repeat itself.

However, they did themselves no favours on 17 minutes as a ball in from Coutinho found a completely unmarked Lovren at the back post and the defender calmly side-footed in to give Liverpool the lead.

It was no less than Klopp's men deserved and all of a sudden Conte was under pressure to respond. They were struggling to find a way through though, with Matip dealing well with the physical Diego Costa, while Eden Hazard and Willian were kept relatively quiet by Clyne and Milner. The Liverpool bench was anything but quiet on 36 minutes though as the ball broke to Henderson 30 yards from goal. The captain curled an inch-perfect strike over and round Courtois and into the far corner of the net. The bench celebrated, but Marko Grujić just stood there open-mouthed, unable to comprehend what he had just seen.

The second half brought inevitable pressure from the hosts, and on the hour mark they managed to get back into things as Costa prodded home following a good run from Nemanja Matić, but for everything Chelsea threw at Liverpool after that, the visitors had an answer to it. Klopp brought Lucas and Kevin Stewart on to shore things up late in the game and his team managed to see out another impressive win.

They had beaten yet another team that was expected to be challenging for the title come the season's end and looked imperious doing it.

Klopp was more than happy after the game and told the BBC, 'It was a satisfying win of course. From the first second we had unbelievably good movement. We were quick in mind. We did really well. We deserved the lead at half-time.

'We have to learn how to manage the game plan. So often this season Chelsea scored in the last few seconds with a direct style. But I can't remember too many chances from them. We had a few moments where we weren't so good but that's normal against a good team.

'We played football like hell. It was really nice to watch. In the second half it was a bit more difficult. After their goal, we managed it well.'

All of a sudden articles were popping up on mainstream sport media websites asking whether Liverpool were equipped to challenge for the Premier League title, with the general consensus being that if these levels of performance were sustainable then there was no reason why not.

Belief was growing everywhere.

21

'It's a year, I'm a year older and all this shit, but everything else is good. Not perfect, but in a good way. That's what we hoped, that's what we said.'

THE first signing of the summer for Klopp had been in the goalkeeping department, bringing in promising stopper Loris Karius from Mainz 05. It had been widely expected that Karius would become first choice at Anfield ahead of Simon Mignolet, but an unfortunate hand injury picked up in pre-season meant that he had to wait to make his Reds debut.

That wait came to an end in the League Cup third-round trip to Derby County.

It was a straightforward victory for Liverpool as a first goal in England for Ragnar Klavan was followed in the second half by strikes from Philippe Coutinho and Divock Origi. Such was the ease with which Klopp's men won that the manager felt comfortable bringing 18-year-old Ovie Ejaria on for the last 15 minutes for his debut experience of competitive first team football.

Karius may as well have sat next to Mignolet on the bench such was the lack of action he saw, though there was one moment in the first half where he raced out of his area to deny Darren Bent an opportunity when the former England striker was through on goal. That along with elements of his calmness with the ball at his feet gave hints at the attributes Klopp had seen in him.

He would get another chance just days later as Liverpool hosted Hull City at Anfield. It was Karius's Premier League and home debut, and it would be another 90 minutes of very little to do. There was a moment in the first half when a carrier bag blew on to the pitch, which arguably caused the German more problems than the opposition did.

Klopp's side were sensational, with quick passing, strong pressing and counter-pressing, and clinical finishing.

This was a truer test of Klopp's Liverpool than any of the tougher clashes that had preceded it. Liverpool were able to raise their game for big matches, but it was when they came up against the more defensive teams that they often struggled. A decent start to the season for Hull had placed them in the role of a 'tricky opponent' who might be able to frustrate the hosts, but no such worries were necessary.

Goals from Adam Lallana, James Milner (penalty) and Sadio Mané made it 3-0 before half-time.

However, no Liverpool performance seemed complete without at least one defensive lapse and that came early in the second half as a Hull corner was not dealt with and fell to the feet of David Meyler, who smashed past Karius from point-blank range. The visiting fans optimistically set off a flare in celebration and perhaps in hope of a dramatic comeback. Before the flare could even start to extinguish, Coutinho slammed in a swift response at the other end from all of 30 yards.

A further Milner penalty rounded off a dominant afternoon for the Reds, dispatching their Yorkshire opponents 5-1 to record their second big home win in a row.

It wasn't just the goals, but the overall energy and flow of the team that was clearly starting to become second nature to them and was appearing to be incredibly effective, even against teams who had turned up with an intent to disrupt them.

There had been numerous occasions during the game when the intensity of the pressing had caused Hull players to get visibly flustered and boot the ball out of play just for a chance to get their heads straight and back into formation.

Hull's captain Curtis Davies said after the game that it was the most exhausting 90 minutes he could remember playing. 'They didn't give us a chance to breathe,' he said.

The Tigers had been beaten 4-1 by Arsenal the previous week, but Davies was more impressed by Liverpool's demolition.

'Arsenal are a very good passing team, but a lot of their stuff is in front of you,' he continued. 'Nice little passes. Liverpool have that mix of nice little passes and then people who will run and run at you and beat you as well, like Mané and Coutinho.

'They weren't satisfied with 3-0. They wanted six, seven, eight. That is the difference. It is hard to lay a glove on anyone. When there is so much interchanging you cannot put your mark on one person. It is tough to make a tackle. One second Mané will be in that hole, then Lallana and then Coutinho. There is a lot of interchange, quick football and with the full-backs playing like wingers it becomes very difficult because you end up with backs against the wall.

'They play with Henderson and the two centre-halves at the back and the rest can go wherever they want. That is not an ill-disciplined thing. That is organised.'

Klopp was duly impressed with his men. He told the BBC, 'It was a world-class performance in counter-pressing. We didn't give Hull the opportunity to create confidence. It was wonderful to watch. All in all, really good.

'I was a little angry we conceded. It would be nice to have a clean sheet one time in the season. Maybe we will work on this. It was a professional second half from the players. I am not interested in statements now, just collecting points.'

In his post-match press conference the subject of the title was brought up, and Klopp predictably dismissed it due to the fact only six games had been played.

'We are far away from Christmas now and after Christmas there's January, February, March, April, May and then it stops, so it's a long, long, long race and I never saw in any race that, if you have to run 20km, that after 5km you are like this [hands in the air celebrating]. I know there's a lot of work to do still,' he said.

'The big difference between us and the rest of the people in the Liverpool world was that everyone thought we should change a lot of the team.

'We changed a few things but not a lot. Most of the players who performed most of the time last year are still here. That's what we want to build on. We brought a few things in, that's true. A few new skills. But it's all about the base that we already had.'

Those who enjoyed listening to Klopp talk about the game will have been delighted to learn that he was booked for a guest appearance on *Monday Night Football*, joining Liverpool legend Jamie Carragher for an hour before the Sky Sports coverage of Burnley v Watford.

Klopp's popularity in Germany had skyrocketed after his television punditry during the 2006 World Cup so it was a scenario he was used to, and he didn't disappoint.

'I have no problem with this [being on television]. I'm here for the first time and I see you're already working on it. I only don't like when people don't think before they speak,' he explained.

'I'm far away from being the "wise person" in football, so I listen to a lot of people. As long as you are really involved mentally, that you really care about what happens, then it's all good. If you only sit back and say "they should have done more, they should have done better, why didn't they score this goal?" Then I have no time to listen because that's a waste of time for me.'

Klopp was asked about his team, and in particular the apparent weakness at defending set pieces.

'It's not so much of an issue this year because we've done much better already, but it doesn't feel too good when you are really good in a game like the Hull match when they had no chances, and we give a goal away,' he replied.

'Most of the goals we gave away in the early stage of the season when I came here, we had to change a few things, change a few formations, but we always played against specialists in set pieces. When you play against West Brom, Crystal Palace, West Ham, they are unbelievably strong at this and we had to change. But it's not about a formation, it's more about how we react in the moment.'

Klopp then moved on to talk about the specifics of his team, and touched on the way his own ideas of roles within the team have altered over time.

He said, 'A Jürgen Klopp full-back has changed in the last few years, but this kind of full-back in the team now, it's much more like a midfield player. They have to play in the half-spaces, they have to play really high, they are the wingers or central midfielders sometimes. The rule is be an option to get the pass or be protection for all the players.

'I don't think about us having a false nine or no nine or whatever. These players are all responsible for being in the opposition box in all situations they can be.

'Of course, not the centre-halves, I would like to have them only around at set pieces and, as always, we have one holding player, which can be a full-back or a midfielder.

'But all the rest, let's not hear them say, "Well I couldn't score, somebody told me." It is all about being flexible.

'You want a playmaker in a position where he can make a genius pass and counter-pressing [creates similar situations].

'We win the ball back high on the pitch so you are close to the goal. You then are only one pass away from a really good opportunity most of the time, and it's why I said no playmaker in the world can be as good as a counter-pressing situation.'

He then gave an overview of things, again refusing to get carried away with the form of his team while acknowledging the advancements that were being made.

'It is as good as it should be. We are a good football side but we have to improve. Not just in set pieces, but at a lot of things. We did well against Hull, and now Swansea is the next challenge and it is a big challenge. It feels good at the moment, it is better that we are optimistic, but nothing has happened really.'

Swansea was indeed the next challenge, and a challenge it would be if the previous season was anything to go by.

The Reds had been deservedly beaten 3-1 on a wet day in Wales in-between the two legs of their Europa League semi-final with Villarreal, but had fielded a largely changed line-up. This time they were able to go full strength and it paid off as they ran out 2-1 winners. They had started poorly and fell behind to a Leroy Fer goal, but a second-half header from Roberto Firmino and another Milner penalty meant the three points had been won, which made it five wins from five since the international break.

Klopp was pleased with the outcome, even if not with the way his team had struggled to begin with, 'I thought we could have done better in the first half. Our body language was not good, we were static and it was easy to defend against us. We were not as good as we should have been.

'You have to show why we are here. We showed a reaction, were more organised, clear in all situations and we deserved to win. Of course I am happy we have had two or three brilliant games in a row.

'If Milner is our top scorer at end of the season with penalties, I have no problem with it. All is good. The performance was not perfect but it was good enough.'

It was time for another international break, meaning that there were more than two weeks before the next game, which would be hosting Manchester United at Anfield.

During the break, Klopp reached the milestone of his first full year in charge at Liverpool, which led to many reflecting on what he had achieved in that time, but Klopp was only looking ahead.

'I have no time, and I am not in the mood for reflection, to be honest,' he told *The Guardian*. 'It's a year, I'm a year older and all this shit, but everything else is good. Not perfect, but in a good way. That's what we hoped, that's what we said.

'After one year standing here, we can talk like this. There was doubt, there was a lot of rumour around me. People said "obviously he was a good coach at Dortmund but a German managing here doesn't work", things like this. That's better now.

'The thing is, I'm not here for a year, I'm here hopefully for the long term, and it means that we have to use all the information we have until now and learn from it.

'That's how life works, collecting experience, learning from it and being ready for the next challenge. We will not celebrate [the anniversary], I can tell you that! Hopefully nobody brings me a cake!'

He added, 'We have to create hope, dreams, whatever. The only problem is that we cannot hope and we cannot dream!

'Everyone else is allowed [to dream]. So far this season it's a very positive thing to talk about but we have to go out and do it.

'I liked the club before I was here, but when you are in it, it is so different.

'This club has a lot of work to do, it's not about enjoying the history, it's about being part of it. And being a part of it is nice.

'It was such a positive week. Interview here, interview there, "the manager is brilliant", "everyone is enjoying themselves".

'And then at the end of the week, Swansea is waiting with the knife between the teeth, and you have to go and perform again!

'That's what I mean. We have to get used to it. To be a successful team you need to be a challenger in each game, challenging for three points in every game.

'I'm happy with the performance from the stands, it was great! We didn't make it too easy for them, but you saw that they took each good moment from us to help us back in the game. That was nice.'

It was not just in England that Klopp's influence was being noticed. A former student of Klopp who arguably improved as much as any of his players while at Dortmund had some positive things to say about his former manager's start to life in England.

Robert Lewandowski left Klopp's Dortmund for rivals Bayern Munich and Pep Guardiola in 2014, but not before scoring the goals that brought them so much success during his time at Signal Iduna Park, and he told reporters, 'Under Klopp I think they [Liverpool] will be fighting for the title this season.

'Pep and Manchester City will not make it easy for anybody to win the title, but Liverpool have a real chance.

'I have watched some Liverpool games since the arrival of Klopp, and you can see that the players are enjoying playing for him.

'As a player you know that he totally has your back, he is like a father figure and, because you have that trust in him as a player, it makes you totally open to his methods and his ideas which, in the long term, you always see are for the benefit of your game and for the team.'

Lewandowski scored big goals in big games for Klopp in Germany, and next up for Liverpool was a very big game as they hosted Manchester United in the Monday night football. Dubbed 'Red Monday' by Sky Sports, it would be the first game under the lights at the newly renovated Anfield and the occasion was set up for quite a spectacle. As it turned out, it was anything but.

The build-up to the game had actually been surprisingly low-key from the managers. Klopp was looking forward to it like any other game, while José Mourinho decided only to comment on the referee, and how it was unfair of the Premier League to appoint Greater Manchester-based official Anthony Taylor.

The media were far from low-key though, building up to it as if it were the game to end all games. There was some justification in that as the clash had always been seen as the biggest historical rivalry in English football, as the two most successful teams in England by a distance. However, historically speaking, their times on top of the English game had rarely crossed. When Liverpool were winning things, United were well behind, and vice-versa.

However, on this rare occasion, albeit very early in the season, both teams were being touted as genuine title contenders. The old adage was dusted off and used relentlessly that you cannot win a title in October, but you can lose it.

United had already been beaten by Manchester City a few weeks earlier and Mourinho knew that losing to both rivals in the first two months of his tenure at Old Trafford would have been disastrous, which may explain why he set up in the way he did.

In 2014 he had denied Liverpool the Premier League title by coming to Anfield with his Chelsea team and parking the proverbial bus. His impeccable ability to organise his team defensively denied and frustrated Brendan Rodgers's side. He went a similar route against Klopp's team.

The best opportunity of the night came in the second half when Emre Can played the ball in to Coutinho. With one touch he managed to flick the ball perfectly through to the run of Firmino, who was bearing down on goal. However, just as he was about to finish, Antonio Valencia got back to perform a heroic tackle to prevent what looked to be a certain goal.

The game petered out to a goalless draw and it was the visitors who left the happier of the two.

Despite the disappointment of two points dropped, Klopp and his team could take solace in the fact that the great Manchester United had come to Anfield, played ultra-defensively and been happy to leave with a point. When Klopp took over, the Reds were struggling to beat anyone at home. Now, following 4-1 and 5-1 wins, they had United and Mourinho fearing them.

It was an unspoken compliment from the Portuguese to Klopp, who said after the game, 'I'm pretty sure the last thing José Mourinho wanted to do was pay a compliment to my team. He thought about his line-up, you saw the line-up. It was clear there would be a lot of high balls in the game, so we needed to make pressure high because of Smalling, Blind, whoever, Bailly. When they play the long balls, it's difficult, and Fellaini is immediately in our last row and Ibrahimović is there and Pogba is there. It's really difficult to defend, but we did it really well.

'We lost patience much too early, that was the first problem, and then our passing game was not good any more. We had 65 per cent possession, but you have to do better things with it when you have the ball. I didn't expect we would have 10 or 15 chances before the game, but in the first half we could have had – with two better passes – two 100 per cent chances, which we didn't. Second half, we had them but de Gea was finally warm and made brilliant saves. They had their chance with Ibrahimović, which he would usually [finish] I would say.

'The second half, maybe we would have deserved the win but in the end, the best news tonight is we have one point more and a clean sheet – nothing else. We can do much better, we have to do much better and you have to learn in a game like this – when an opponent creates an atmosphere on the pitch like this, you need to stay cool.'

Eight games into the season, Liverpool had 17 points and were just two points from the top of the Premier League. Not only that but their start had included five away games and they had already faced Arsenal, Tottenham, Leicester, Chelsea and Manchester United. They arguably only had one more potential title rival to face in the first half of the season, Manchester City on New Year's Eve.

Until then they would face a much simpler-looking fixture list. However, the cliché of there being no easy games in the Premier League would be tested as their next three league matches were against West Brom, Crystal Palace and Watford, three teams that took points off Klopp the previous season.

West Brom in particular had annoyed Klopp. In one of his first games in charge he had faced Tony Pulis's side at Anfield and experienced perhaps the most extreme example of the physical and direct style of English football. A late Divock Origi goal had salvaged a 2-2 draw in that game, which saw the German refuse to shake Pulis's hand following a hot-blooded affair.

Lallana came back in from the start and Sturridge dropped back to the bench as Klopp decided that his in-form front three would be able to break through the Baggies's backline.

It was the right decision as Liverpool dominated, albeit having to navigate a tricky final few minutes to secure a 2-1 win. Early goals from Coutinho and Mané set them on their way, but another goal conceded from a corner meant a nervy ending. It was testament to the progression of the team that they had been happy with a point the previous season, but were now slightly disappointed that they had only just won the game. Klopp didn't mind too much though.

He said, 'In dreamland then you always win four- or five-nil and then the crowd can go a little earlier and do something more serious. This game tonight created one of the best atmospheres we've had because it was exciting until the end, with the chances we created and with the chances we didn't use. Actually, in this moment it feels better that we only won 2-1 than three- or four-nil, which would have been possible – but all good.'

When asked about continuing defensive frailties, Klopp added, 'Obviously not having a clean sheet is part of our game, I don't know! It's not a big problem. I think defending, first of all, is not to let them [the opposition] create a lot of chances and I cannot remember a lot of chances in the last few games. All of them were under pressure with a lucky cross or something or a set piece. It's part of the game, I know this and we are improving in this.'

He had a point. In spite of Liverpool's difficulties with set pieces, their defensive record was not as bad as was being made out. In open play they were largely keeping the opposition at bay. This made it five games since his side had conceded a goal from open play.

One slight mark on the game was the fact that a two-goal margin of victory would have seen Liverpool go top of the league after Arsenal could only draw at home to Middlesbrough. The team that did end the weekend top, Manchester City, also dropped points, drawing 1-1 at home to Southampton, while Manchester United had lost 4-0 at Chelsea. Aside from the three points for the Blues, it had been a very good weekend for Liverpool.

It was back to League Cup action next as Tottenham came to Anfield in the fourth round. As Mauricio Pochettino's men had Champions League commitments, it was not much of a surprise that the Argentine named a largely second-string team for the game. However, Klopp also used the opportunity to rotate.

Full first-team debuts were handed to promising youngsters Trent Alexander-Arnold and Ovie Ejaria, while Mignolet came back in goal for Karius.

It was a different line-up but a very recognisable Liverpool as some effective pressing from Marko Grujić forced an error at the back from Spurs. The Serbian's shot deflected into the path of Sturridge, whose lightning-quick reactions saw him prod the ball over Michel Vorm and into the net for 1-0.

Sturridge grabbed another in the second half, but a Vincent Janssen penalty made for an anxious finale yet again. However, the Reds managed to get through it with relative ease and book their place in the quarter-finals.

When asked after the game if it should have been more comfortable, Klopp said, 'Yes, when you see our chances and see the chances of Tottenham. The penalty made it a little bit closer – that was the only really difficult situation for us. After this, with 10 or 12 minutes to go, it is like it is – it's a game-changer. But we had the opportunities, we had the chances, we could have scored two, three or four [more] times.

'But we don't live in dreamland and it's not that you can think about closing the game at 3-0 or 4-0 early enough that everybody knows we go to the quarter-final. No, we had to do the job. We didn't score in the moments when we could have. They scored the penalty. 2-1 is close but now it is not interesting any more because we are in the next round.'

On the performances of the younger players he added, 'I don't know what it says exactly, but it's something good and that was clear. I made the line-up then I saw it on paper and thought, "Oh, still really good!"

'There are a few more to come, a little bit younger than the guys who made their debuts tonight – in under-23s, under-18s and even under-15 already. There are good boys and that's good news for Liverpool. We can talk about it, but after tonight we should not talk about it too much because they [will go] back in the academy, train hard and come again when there is a game when we need them. That's how it is.'

Back to the league and it was another potential banana skin for Klopp and his men, which was ironic as they chose to wear their bright yellow away kit for the trip to Crystal Palace. Selhurst Park had actually been the setting for a Reds triumph the previous season, but only after an injury-time penalty won and scored by Christian Benteke, who would now be turning out for the opposition.

Wijnaldum was not considered fit enough to start so Can retained his place, but a more notable selection was that of Alberto Moreno, who kept his place following a good display against Tottenham, but also due to the fact that James Milner was suffering from illness. The much-maligned Spanish left-back would be given the hard task of looking after mercurial winger Wilfried Zaha, but it was at the other end that he would impress in the early stages.

An overlapping run was found by a deft lob from Coutinho. Moreno played the ball into the path of Can who ran on to it and poked home via a deflection. It was another early lead for Liverpool and should have helped to settle any pre-match nerves.

However, those nerves were shredded when a simple-looking header from Joel Matip was inexplicably skewed up in the air by Dejan Lovren, which allowed James McArthur to run on to it and head over Karius to equalise. As with their previous games, Liverpool had been on top when from nothing, they conceded.

The mental fragility that had consumed them, and Lovren in particular, during recent seasons was tested, but the Croat quite literally rose to the challenge as he headed home a Coutinho corner to make amends and restore the visitors' lead.

Normality was restored, for a short while, until Zaha picked up the ball and crossed for McArthur to head in his second. The not-particularly-tall Scot now had two headed goals, when all of the talk before the game was of the aerial threat posed by Benteke.

Liverpool's efforts to get back in front were eventually rewarded, and again from a corner as this time Matip rose to head emphatically past Steve Mandanda to make it 3-2.

The game was put to bed in the second half as Firmino ran into a gap created by Lallana's run and waited for Henderson to play the ball through to him. With one glance up, Firmino dinked the ball over the advancing Mandanda and whipped his shirt off before the ball had even crossed the line.

As was becoming a common occurrence, the opposition manager and players were quick to praise Klopp's men post-game. Alan Pardew, who had caused controversy the previous season by shoving his hand in the direction of Klopp's face after a disagreement on the touchline, was quick to lavish praise on the Reds.

'It's very difficult to play against them,' Pardew said. 'The speed, the runners, they're coming from every angle. They've got some fantastic players.

'Firmino plays that striker's role really clever, you don't really know where he is and it's unnatural for centre-halves. He pulls you around, pops up in midfield, then when he's in midfield, someone else replaces him. It's like a piston in an engine working there.'

Palace's double-goalscorer James McArthur added to the kudos, 'They're a very good side. I'd say that's the best side we've played this year as a team performance. The front six, the way they press the ball and rotate, they are a really strong contender this year in my opinion.'

Philippe Coutinho in particular had stood out at Selhurst Park. His early season form was starting to earn rave reviews, and Klopp was just as pleased with the little Brazilian's contribution.

He enthused, 'What can I say? Phil is a good football player, everybody knew that before, I think. For him, he is now 24, his work-rate is outstanding and that's important for the team. You cannot change this because you cannot be a genius every day, but then you have to be kind of a proper football player still. All good. That's how the boys are.'

After ten games Liverpool found themselves in the thick of the early running in the title race, level on 23 points with Man City and Arsenal, with Chelsea one point further back.

Things were moving well on the field, and off it the club were ensuring they didn't stand still either. Ahead of the next game with Watford, Liverpool announced the appointment of a new sporting director, Michael Edwards.

Klopp had worked under a sporting director at both Mainz and Dortmund – his successful professional relationship with Michael Zorc in Dortmund was well documented – but he had so far just worked alongside the numerous members of the so-called transfer committee since arriving on Merseyside, which had included Edwards.

The 37-year-old had previously filled the role of technical director, having been promoted from head of performance and analysis, but the key difference in his new role would be that he would take charge of talks with players and agents on new contracts and transfers.

Giving his reaction to the appointment, Klopp told the club website, 'This decision is hugely positive for us and it will make us better and stronger in managing the process of building and retaining playing talent at all age groups. Development is so important and it makes sense to have a position, within the football structure specifically, that focuses on where we can improve.

'It's no secret I like the concept of a sporting director and having worked under this model previously I have found it to be nothing but positive and forward-thinking.

'Michael is absolutely the right person for this. He has the knowledge, expertise and personality to flourish in the role and I was delighted when he told me he would be accepting the position.

'If somebody is not happy with whatever and you ask, "Is that your player or his player?" 'It's always my player. I can't blame anyone for anything. I can take the pressure. In this business, the manager is not allowed to be a one-man show. I'm a specialist in football things, I know a lot, but not everything like finances. I like to have the best people around me and Michael is for sure one of the best I have met.

'What we try to create is a structure for LFC. This wonderful club changed philosophy three or four times in the last 10 to 15 years because different managers came in and say, "Let's do this, let's change that." That's the English way of doing of things – a new manager comes in and you have to change everything. Football managers get sacked because results are not good but a lot of things around them could have been good. We have tried to create a situation where everything around is perfect. If the manager changes in the future, this club will have a good base.'

As if the feel-good factor around the club wasn't already high enough, there was an added boost for Klopp on the Saturday when league leaders Manchester City, fresh from dismantling Barcelona in the Champions League, were held to an unexpected 1-1 draw at home to Middlesbrough. This meant that a win for Liverpool the following day would see them leapfrog City in the table.

As a bonus, the north London derby between Arsenal and Tottenham also ended 1-1, and so a Liverpool win over Watford meant they would go top of the Premier League table for the first time under Klopp.

The home side started slowly, happy to knock the ball about but not attacking with the verve and pace that had perhaps been expected of a team chasing the summit of the league.

Watford were being led by new manager Walter Mazzarri. The well-respected Italian had taken over from Quique Sánchez Flores in the summer and had made a good start to life in England. Watford went into that weekend in seventh place, ahead of Manchester United, and had not conceded a goal in their previous three games.

However, their sheet was not only dirtied, but well and truly defecated on by Liverpool. Goals from Mané (2), Coutinho, Can, Firmino and Wijnaldum sent the Reds top with a 6-1 demolition. They had 17 shots on target, the most in a Premier League game since Opta stats had begun in 2003. Wijnaldum had become the 13th different scorer of the season, and it was only early November.

Klopp said, 'I'm really happy actually. It was a good performance, absolutely, against a difficult opponent. In the last few games they had three clean sheets and not lucky clean sheets. We knew about the challenge and we tried to do the right things in training and prepare the team for this. Obviously it worked, together with the confidence we obviously have, and the skills and the attitude of the players. So it worked out today.

'It was a good performance on the pitch and on the stands, so it was a really nice afternoon.'

On being top of the league, he again tried to dampen expectations, 'If somebody thinks being one point ahead after 11 matchdays is a big sign for the rest of the season, I can't help this person. Sorry! We stay cool, nothing happened.

'We didn't speak one word before the game – we knew already that Arsenal drew against Tottenham – but we didn't speak one word about the possibility of being top of the table. The only thing you can do is to work and stay concentrated, because a lot of different things could happen in the next few weeks and months. How positive they are is up to us, actually.

'There's no pressure after 11 matchdays – absolutely no pressure. We saw Chelsea playing yesterday, quite impressive. We saw City playing Barcelona, quite impressive. Man United, never write them off. Tottenham, a good side ... there are a lot of really good teams around and you can play a really good season, but when they are better – which is possible because they're really not bad – then you could be fifth or sixth and nobody would be really happy. So, stay cool, take the things like they are, playing your best football and win football games – that's the only thing we can do.

'When I came here, I asked for time, patience, belief and a lot of things. Now after 11 matchdays, everyone is asking for guarantees but they are not there. There are no guarantees. The only thing we have is a pretty good football team, so let's try to use it.

'We have to [play better]. I know how it sounds, it's not that we have to score more goals or something. I'm really happy that we didn't score more because what would this have meant? We could've scored more. But different moments – you saw when we lost a little bit of concentration, that's normal with this kind of result.

'Keeping the ball is the best defending, we gave the ball a little bit too easy away and had to run a lot to get the ball back. There was one situation with three midfield players around the 18-yard box, losing the ball and we needed three minutes to get the ball back. That's a waste of energy, but you don't have it too often when you're 5-0 in the lead, so how can you be prepared for this? We could've done better in these moments, but of course there's not a lot of things to criticise. Good, all good.'

Following in the theme of admiration post-match from opposing managers, Walter Mazzarri was quick to praise the side that had just torn his one apart. He told Sky Sports, 'Congratulations to Liverpool because they were much better than us. They are a great team, not only tactically and technically, but they are athletic and their performance along with everything else was very, very strong.'

The former Napoli and Inter boss later added, 'No doubt of the teams we have played, Liverpool are the team I'm most impressed by. If they continue to play like this, they are number one for winning the Premier League.'

22

'I played in Germany against Bayern Munich and Dortmund, I played against Manchester City in the Champions League, but I must say this is maybe the best team I have ever played against.' Pierre-Emile Højbjerg

KLOPP was impressing people with how he had his Liverpool team playing. Friends, foes and the media were all falling over themselves to heap praise on him and his players.

I was fortunate enough to speak to Rory Smith, chief football correspondent for the *New York Times* and author of the award-winning book *Mister: The Men Who Gave The World The Game*, about Klopp as a man, a manager and what he had achieved at Liverpool.

He said, 'I think what he's done really well is that he's energised the club. I think for a while Liverpool were drifting, there was no real certainty about where they were going. If you take it back to Rafa Benitez's last season and the whole Hicks and Gillett thing I think that's where the chaos started, then there was Hodgson who was a pragmatic choice, similar with Kenny [Dalglish] where I think they hoped he could just repeat the same trick, then Brendan [Rodgers], which was all a bit muddled. One minute they wanted a sporting director, then Rodgers said he wouldn't work under one so they had a transfer committee. I remember doing a piece I got slaughtered for on FSG and how they seem to just go with whatever the latest fad is.

'That amazing season under Rodgers [2013/14] disguised that to an extent, but though you can't take all credit away from him a large part of that season was that they happened to have the best striker in the world playing for them [Luis Suárez]. Then it fell apart again the following year when they finished seventh.

'There's been a sense of endemic drift about Liverpool. They had potential and certain finances but never really had any idea of what they wanted to do or what they wanted to be. Then Klopp came in and fixed that almost immediately.

'Things have improved this year and I think that even if from here they end up finishing fifth, I think people would still look at it and say there has been progress made. They now have an identity and a style.'

In terms of Klopp's suitability for Liverpool, Smith added, 'They could have hired managers who could have achieved the same or perhaps done even better, but in terms of the character of someone, Liverpool more than most have this need for a saviour and needed someone with charisma who could be the focal point.

'He was also a massive coup. He'd only been in a Champions League Final two years prior, had won two Bundesliga titles, while Liverpool had finished in the top four once in the last seven years, and that was quite important in terms of giving the club a boost.

'I think one of his biggest successes has been instilling in those players a sense that they are good enough, and in Liverpool as a club, a sense that it is good enough.'

On the subject of Klopp's style of play and the idea that he's all about 'gegenpressing', Smith isn't so sure the widely held belief that he's got one way of playing is entirely justified.

He continued, 'There's a misconception that it's this innovative way of playing. It's basically closing people down, which is something that's always happened, just in a more organised, more angled, more scientific way, and I think there's a much more layered approach that I believe comes from his final year at Dortmund where he just couldn't find a way of playing.

'A lot of the teams in Germany were doing counter-pressing as well, but also figured out that the way to counter Dortmund was to let them have the ball. If they had the ball then they couldn't hurt you as much as they could without the ball, and that was a criticism that was levelled at him a lot in that last season in Germany. He tried to find a way around it and tried to mature Dortmund's style of play but it never really worked. I don't know if in the time he had off [after he left Dortmund] whether that gave him the chance to figure out how to make his style more multi-layered.

'Dortmund now under Tuchel are a possession team, but if need be can resort back to counter-attacking. I think that's what he [Klopp] wants his Liverpool team to be much more than an echo of what his Dortmund side was years ago, because football moves so fast that one trick doesn't work for very long. Liverpool are better with the ball than people would have thought a Klopp side could be.'

Smith believes that Klopp's ability to improve players has been in strong evidence since he came to Liverpool, and that no one has exemplified that improvement more than Adam Lallana.

He explained, 'I think that was always likely because Lallana had that background in that style of play under Pochettino [at Southampton]. I also think he's improved Henderson in a more subtle way, and also Firmino, though I'm not sure if that's improving Firmino or just allowing him to find the levels he reached at Hoffenheim. Coutinho seems to be more consistent, I think Lovren has benefitted immensely, and Origi as well.

'When he arrived he looked very raw but Klopp seems to have enabled him to make use of the obvious abilities he has. I don't think Origi knew quite what to do with the qualities he had but I think he's made a huge improvement, and the other you have to say is Milner. He's taught Milner how to be a left-back, which is incredible.

'Everyone talked at the start of the season about how this was the "season of the coach" and that's what we're seeing. Antonio Conte has shifted Chelsea to a three-man backline and it's worked, that's good coaching, Pep Guardiola has enabled Raheem Sterling to become a decent footballer again, that's good coaching, Klopp has turned James Milner into a left-back and Jordan Henderson into a holding midfielder! That's what coaches should be doing.

'This is only a theory, but Klopp came from a tradition in Germany that started with [Ralf] Rangnick, of managers who wore smart casual clothes on the touchline. They looked like they were going to work at an advertising agency rather than as an accountant, and that to me says something about the way they were looking at the game.

'It was a little bit more creative, it wasn't "this is our uniform because this is what is always done", it was more "things are a bit more relaxed now, we need to be more original, more innovative" and I think Klopp is more from that tradition than someone like José Mourinho.'

I also asked Rory whether he thought Klopp could bring sustainable success to Liverpool, and what that might reasonably look like.

He replied, 'What would represent success now for me over the next five years would be being in the Champions League more than they're not in the Champions League. If they finished third three times in five years I think that would have to be taken as success because the margins in the Premier League are so fine and so vast.

'Whether Klopp can win the league or not, I think you have to remember that Liverpool are still underdogs compared to other teams, they don't have the money that other teams have, they don't have the squad depth of other teams and there's a lot of other teams that are doing stuff well. I do think though that if, when he comes to the end of his contract, the club can say "we were a lot closer to winning the league than before he came" then it can be considered a success.'

Another international break allowed Liverpool to stay top of the league for an extra week, but it would not be an ideal return to action when they resumed Premier League duty. A trip to Southampton awaited.

This was a game that Klopp's side had badly thrown away the previous season, on a day they were taken apart by Sadio Mané, who this time would be lining up on their side.

Mané, along with fellow members of Liverpool's devastating front three Firmino and Coutinho, would cover several thousand miles during the international break to compete in World Cup qualifiers. Such was the desperation for the club to get the Brazilians back to England as soon as possible that they chipped in on the cost of a private jet for them plus some other Brazilian team-mates playing at Chelsea, Manchester City and Paris Saint-Germain.

It meant that all three lined up to face Southampton at St Mary's, but one key player who wouldn't was Adam Lallana. The former Saint picked up a groin injury during England's draw with Spain, and would go on to miss the Reds's next three games.

Having gone to battle with Ronald Koeman in his first experiences with Southampton, Klopp now faced Frenchman Claude Puel, who had taken to his first job in England fairly well, in spite of recent setbacks against Chelsea and Hull. His Saints team had beaten Inter in the Europa League just a few weeks earlier and had shown a fresh dynamism after losing Koeman to Everton in the summer.

Puel had been seen as a nearly man in his highest profile job at Lyon, but had worked wonders at Nice the previous season and was now trying to replicate similar success on the English south coast.

They were largely frustrated in the first half by a solid Southampton defence. The pair of Virgil van Dijk and José Fonte had formed a potent partnership in front of Fraser Forster in goal.

The second half saw Liverpool's rhythm return and their dominance start to show in spades, and yet the goal still eluded them.

They were able to carve out some clear-cut chances, with Coutinho slicing wide after being played in, Firmino firing wide when in a glorious position after a flowing move and then Nathaniel Clyne heading wide after a cross from substitute Sturridge. It wasn't to be and Klopp was made to settle for a point.

Southampton's players came off red-faced and gasping for air. They knew they had been in a contest and seemed very pleased with their well-earned point.

Striker Charlie Austin had missed their one opening, directing a header wide of Karius's far post, but that was one of only three efforts the hosts managed all game. They had not had a single shot on target in a game for the first time since they were promoted back to the top flight in 2012.

Klopp was, as ever, philosophical about his team's point, 'Not bad first half, much better second half. It was a really good performance against a difficult-to-play side – Southampton are one of the best organised teams in the league. I think they adapted their style a little bit to our strength. We had enough chances to win the game, especially in the second half. The reaction in the second half was really good; the body language was better.

'First half, you could see we thought, "It's really difficult." We were prepared for a difficult game but then in the game it feels different, obviously. I'm fine with the performance, absolutely. We could have scored and maybe we should have scored – but that's how football is. And very often in my life, I lost games like these, when we were so much better and had many more chances.

'We didn't because we stayed concentrated and that's very important, maybe the most important thing for us. Everybody could see already this season that on a very good day, we are able to score fantastic goals. But today it was much more difficult because of different reasons. Even then, to stay in the game is the best news we can get. I'm not happy, but I'm fine.'

In the aftermath, as was becoming a game-by-game occurrence, Puel and his players were lining up to praise the quality of their opposition.

Puel said, 'We played against a good team, with good players. It was difficult for us to develop our game today and to have possession. But it was important that we kept good discipline, good organisation and that we played well in defence.

'It's very difficult to play against this team, because they love the ball, and they have a very good transition to recover the ball.'

The Frenchman was also asked about his side having just 35 per cent possession, and sitting back for large portions of the game in spite of having the home advantage.

'It was not our tactic, it's just that we played against a very good team,' he said.

'In the first half for example, we didn't have the composure to keep the ball. We lost it too quickly. It was difficult for us to keep the ball.

'They are a good team, they are physical but technical also, with a good spirit. You can see that they love the ball and work very hard. They are very difficult to play against.

'Sometimes you have to defend. We would like to play football all the time, and keep possession and control of the game, but that was not possible today.'

If those words of praise weren't enough, Southampton midfielder Pierre-Emile Højbjerg went one further and paid Liverpool the ultimate compliment after the match.

The Dane told the official Southampton website, 'I played in Germany against Bayern Munich and Dortmund, I played against Manchester City in the Champions League, but I must say this is maybe the best team I have ever played against.

'It's unbelievable how they move, how they stand, how they work together – it's like a symphony.

'It's not only that they move the ball quickly. They also have fast players, and with the ball they are very good one against one.

'As always, the best is to win, but against a fantastic team like Liverpool you have to realise that a point is a fantastic result.'

The mood of the weekend was soured by results elsewhere. Manchester United and Arsenal had drawn 1-1 at Old Trafford, which was a positive, but Manchester City, Chelsea and Tottenham all secured wins, with Spurs fighting back from 2-1 down in the 88th minute to win 3-2 against West Ham.

Chelsea's 1-0 win at Middlesbrough took them above Liverpool, who moved down the second. There was going to be a lot of movement around the top of the table heading into the Christmas period.

Given how rampant the Reds had been in the opening months of the season, especially at Anfield, a 2-0 home win in their next game with Sunderland was most welcome.

It took a while to make the breakthrough but a Divock Origi goal and late Milner penalty was enough.

However, Klopp's men did not come through entirely unscathed. Coutinho's attempt at firing the ball across goal caused him to kick the foot of Didier Ndong, and the Brazilian went down in a heap. He was in trouble and immediately signalled that he needed attention. He was stretchered off the field.

While Liverpool had been largely sharing the wealth when it had come to quality performances, goals and assists, there was no doubt that Coutinho had been the shining light that had stood out in the opening weeks of the campaign, and losing him for a significant amount of time would be a major blow.

Among the fans in attendance was Steven Gerrard. The club legend had officially announced his retirement from playing just days earlier and had been strongly linked with a return to his boyhood club in a coaching role. On this day though he was watching as a fan, and was also witness to the league debut of Ben Woodburn. The youngster had barely turned 17 but was sufficiently trusted by Klopp to make his first league bow, coming on for the last few moments.

Klopp was eager to praise the teenager in his post-match comments, while also trying to dampen any expectations and pressure that might come on him after making his first-team debut.

He revealed, 'Ben is a wonderful boy, but I am not sure [if he is ready for more first-team football]. A lot of signs are very positive signs, not only with him. That's good to have and we can all speak a lot of times about opportunities for the young boys in our squad and all that stuff – and sometimes we have to show it.

'I thought it was a good moment, not only for Ben but to show it for all the other boys in the academy. There is really always a way, even when the first team is a really strong side. There is a way, especially for you, whoever you are, as long as you are here and train hard and work hard, everything can be possible.'

He also addressed his dressing down of the crowd, admitting that this was just something he did if he felt it necessary, 'I did it a few times in my life, things like this happen and I've spoken about it. That's not too big a thing. My opinion is during the 90–95 minutes, plus warming up, plus all the stuff, we all who are interested in Liverpool FC and want to be successful together need to do a job, that's how it is. Everybody who cannot play because they're not on the pitch has still to do a job.

'I have to do a job and the crowd have to do a job. That's all and I am sure they know, that's what they want, that's what we all want. It is much nicer to watch a football game in a great atmosphere than in a silent room. Sometimes you need reminders in life, I need reminders too. That was my job in this moment to remind and it was obviously quite easy because everybody was ready in a second and, as everybody could see, it helped a lot.'

Some bad news from the game was the confirmation that, while there was no break, Coutinho had suffered ankle ligament damage that would see him miss the busy December period, and up to seven games. This was far from ideal with Sturridge also out, Lallana still to return from his international break injury and Danny Ings ruled out for the season.

Liverpool had overcome a difficult test against Sunderland, and had another one shortly over the horizon, hosting Leeds United in the League Cup quarter-finals.

Liverpool and Leeds had been a great rivalry in years gone by, but the fall of the Yorkshire outfit after over a decade of issues off the field had meant that they had not faced each other at Anfield in 13 years.

Garry Monk brought his improving Leeds team to face an as expected much-changed Reds side. Fringe players who had played against Tottenham in the previous round returned, including youngsters Trent Alexander-Arnold and Ovie Ejaria. Woodburn made the bench once again.

As with the Sunderland game, Liverpool struggled to find the opening goal. As the game went on, Leeds grew in confidence, and a sharp save from Mignolet denied them from taking a shock lead.

However, a second-half ball whipped in from the right by Alexander-Arnold was perfectly placed for Origi to stick out his boot and guide it home, and again the sighs of relief could be heard all around L4.

Woodburn was brought on to play off the left of the front three, and his moment would come in the dying minutes of the game. Mané broke down the right, back-heeled the ball to Origi, who laid it into the path of Wijnaldum. He managed to turn and divert the ball towards Woodburn, who lashed the ball hard and true into the roof of the net to put the result beyond doubt. He wheeled away with the look of a young man whose dreams had all come true at once.

There had been a significant lack of homegrown talent coming through the ranks in recent years, but Klopp was more than willing to give them their chance to shine, as long as they continued to work hard for it. The image of Alexander-Arnold and Woodburn leaving the field laughing and smiling with one another was a sight to behold as their collective efforts had put Liverpool into the hat for the semi-finals.

Klopp was again effusive in his praise, but also aware that the last thing Woodburn needed was endless publicity.

He said, 'We know what Ben is capable of and what he is already able to do. My first job is to help these boys so that they can be the best. In this case, Ben Woodburn. There's a lot of things to do, especially to keep the public away as long as possible. That's quite a difficult thing to do. But on the other hand, we only bring him in because we want to use him. So that means when he's on the pitch he's absolutely allowed to score goals, to prepare situations, to make crosses – how Trent did, for example. So, all good. I'm really happy for him.

'The only problem is I'm a little bit afraid about you [the media]. That's why I'm so quiet on this. Think and do what you want, but don't write anything – only "Goalscorer, Ben Woodburn." Done. Quite a challenge!'

When asked generally about the feel-good vibe around the club in that moment, he explained, 'I have the same feeling, but it's difficult to feel it because we're not too often in the city. Most of the time we're at the training ground and then at the stadium! We want enthusiasm in the stadium. It's a good moment for LFC, but it's difficult too because there's a lot of work to do and a lot of games to play.

'Four weeks ago we had no clean sheets, now we start getting clean sheets but we don't any more score six goals in a game and all that stuff. We have problems, we have injuries, we have strong opponents, but we have wonderful people around us, we have a wonderful crowd, a wonderful stadium, wonderful away supporters.

'We go now to Bournemouth – small stadium, but very intense, good team. We are in a good moment until now, but we have to carry on and that's how it is. We feel good in the moment and we have to carry on. Hopefully it stays like this.'

That feeling was to be sorely tested in the trip to Bournemouth.

Eddie Howe's team had impressed since overcoming the odds to make it to the Premier League, staying up with relative ease in their first season and enjoying some impressive wins in this campaign, including a 6-1 drubbing of Hull.

Klopp needed to shuffle his pack after the injuries to his attackers, and there was another headache for him to deal with after Matip was ruled out of the game at the Vitality Stadium, with Lucas Leiva coming in as his replacement.

This didn't seem to affect Liverpool too much in the first half as they dominated the Cherries from first minute to last. Origi missed a sitter early on, but this was soon forgotten about as a long ball from

Can found Mané, and he prodded the ball past Artur Boruc to give the away side the lead.

This was soon doubled as a counter-attack led to Henderson playing a through ball for Origi, and he rounded Boruc and guided the ball in from an unlikely angle to make it 2-0. Klopp's men were cruising, for now.

The second half did not get off to the best of starts as a poor header from Lovren gave the ball to substitute Ryan Fraser, who was brought down by Milner for a penalty, which Calum Wilson dispatched. After being completely dominated, the hosts were somehow back in the game.

Liverpool appeared to have put the game to bed again though as Mané laid the ball off to Can, and the German expertly sent the ball into the top corner to restore the two-goal cushion. There was yet more drama to unfold though.

A Bournemouth break down the right saw the ball inexplicably make its way to Fraser in the centre and he slotted into the corner to make it 3-2. Then just moments later, a loose ball in the box was controlled and fired in by Steven Cook for 3-3.

Somehow after being in complete control, Liverpool's heads had gone and they had thrown their lead away. At 3-1 Milner had taken a corner that appeared to go straight in, but goal-line technology showed that Boruc had stopped the ball on the line by barely a couple of millimetres. That proved to be the turning point as the hosts then laid siege to the Reds's goal and got themselves level.

Liverpool had one more chance to win it as Origi controlled and turned on the ball in the box, but his effort looped narrowly over the bar. There was beginning to be a sense of the inevitable with the way the game was going, and so it proved.

A Bournemouth corner led to Cook firing a hard low shot from the edge of the area that Karius spilled, only for Nathan Aké to tap in to win it for Howe's men.

It was a dramatic collapse from Liverpool, the type that they hoped had become a thing of the past. In spite of a public perception that the backline was weak, there had been plenty of examples of Klopp's side needing to see a game out when one goal ahead, and they had largely managed to do so against better teams than Bournemouth. They had also dominated the game for the vast majority, limiting their opponents to barely half-chances until the 75th minute.

Klopp tried to hide his disappointment in his post-match press conference, but there was no denying that this was a huge blow.

'What can I say? In all our good moments it was pretty clear who was the better side today. I think it was obvious Bournemouth wanted to press high and early, and had no chance for it. We played really good football and were quicker in all our decisions,' he surmised.

'We had Divock Origi up front and Sadio Mané, who we can use in these situations – which we did twice very well. Two-nil up but then already we didn't play too well and I didn't like it too much. I told the boys at half-time that the first half was perfect preparation for the second half because we already showed that at 2-0 the game is not done.

'We were too static in our passing, kept the ball too long in the wrong moments and then passing too late, [so] the guy who concedes the pass is under pressure. Everything changed – not because the boys wanted [it to] only because they did it because they lost a little bit of concentration. But still, 2-0 at half-time, it was clear something can happen.

'The penalty, of course, changed the game a little bit. We scored the third one, a wonderful goal, and then it happened quite quickly again. We opened the door, but Bournemouth had to run through and they did it.

'Of course I'm not happy with the result. There were not a lot of moments where Bournemouth could get confidence, but when there was the moment they were immediately there. The atmosphere was really good. Eddie was on fire – even after 3-3 he pushed the boys up. We had our chance and then they scored the goal.

'It's a wonderful story if you're not on the wrong side. Today we were on the wrong side. That's what we have to accept. We have to learn from it and we will do, for sure. Then everything will be good again. But in this moment it doesn't feel like this, of course.

'I'm not angry. During the game, I was angry a few times, when I still had influence on it. I saw in the moment that it's not that you really want to do the wrong thing – I know my boys well enough – only you do it and it's a little bit too late and you lose the momentum in the game. It's not too simple to come back. That's why you have to keep the momentum all the time or as long as you can. That's where I tried to help. But now it has happened, I cannot change it any more so why should I be angry?

'I would say you know about the problems in life, it's easier to handle them – I knew that it could happen, now it has happened and now we have to deal with it.'

The bubble had burst spectacularly on the south coast, and it was up to Klopp to ensure that it didn't derail what had been looking like a very promising campaign.

23

*'We wouldn't have had that success
with another coach in Dortmund, no way.'*
Mats Hummels

FORMER charges of Klopp's were never shy about declaring their love and admiration for the man they had worked with. Dominic King of the *Daily Mail* sat down with one of Klopp's former captains, Bayern Munich centre-back Mats Hummels.

The big German admitted in the interview that without Klopp he likely would never have reached the heights in his career that he has; winning the World Cup, two Bundesliga titles (he would win a third at the end of the season), playing in the Champions League Final and earning a big-money move to Bayern, from whom Klopp had signed Hummels for relative peanuts in 2008.

'We wouldn't have had that success with another coach in Dortmund, no way. He is very emotional. All the time, on the training pitch. He can't settle down,' Hummels explained.

'How intense? Every day? 100 per cent! The important thing is that when he thinks he made [a mistake], he can really apologise to a player – whether that is alone or in front of the whole team. If he says something inappropriate, he realises it afterwards. He doesn't take things personally.

'We had two big opinions, two big egos. Sometimes you can get into a fight but you know everything the next day will be okay. We could always talk about it. He was never like, "I will never forgive you for this!" The relationship I had with him was really important. He would be like "Mats, this happened to me too". That was the biggest thing.

'I can't say I am a Liverpool fan. I don't have a club in England. I just want Klopp to win. If he was coach of another team, I would support them. I cheer for Klopp.'

Hummels will have been disappointed to see what happened to his former boss at Bournemouth, and the best way to blow off steam after that shock defeat for Liverpool would have been to put the next team to the sword.

West Ham arrived for their game at Anfield on the back of a 5-1 home defeat to Arsenal, which had been another stumble in a torrid start to the campaign and despite positivity brought on by moving into their new stadium and a successful previous season under Slaven Bilić, they came into this clash just one place above the relegation zone.

Klopp was without Emre Can, who had picked up a slight injury, but was able to line up with the previously favoured midfield trio of Jordan Henderson, Adam Lallana and Gini Wijnaldum.

It appeared to be normal service resumed as an early Liverpool attack saw Divock Origi play Sadio Mané in down the left. His ball in found its way to Lallana, who managed to turn and steer the ball into the far corner.

It was an ideal start for the Reds, but the feelings of unease reared their head again as Lallana conceded a free kick just outside the area. Dimitri Payet had built a reputation as the deadliest set-piece taker in the Premier League, and sure enough he sent his effort into the corner to equalise for the Hammers.

In spite of Payet's accuracy, attention came on Loris Karius for his positioning, appearing to be too far over, and then not being able to get a stronger hand on it to keep it out.

Liverpool were all over the place and it wasn't long before they fell behind. A ball over the top was deflected over Joel Matip's head by Lallana, which allowed Michail Antonio a one-on-one situation. Karius was reluctant to rush out, and Antonio prodded his shot past the keeper to give the visitors the lead.

It was starting to feel like the poor end to the Bournemouth game was perhaps not just a blip, but that there was a more inherent issue with the team, whether it was injuries, individual errors or just that oppositions had figured out how to counter Klopp's system.

That fear was calmed slightly when Origi took advantage of a Darren Randolph handling error to make it 2-2 shortly after the start of the second half, but Liverpool's inability after that to break down a West Ham defence that had surrendered so readily to Arsenal just a week earlier was concerning and they had to settle for a point.

It wouldn't have been so worrying had Chelsea not picked up another three points against West Brom to record their ninth consecutive victory and pull away further at the top of the table.

There was understandable frustration after the game. West Ham had performed well, but it was a game the Reds should have won, and the ire of the media and fans turned quickly to young Karius. The new goalkeeper had endured a mixed start to life in England, but had indeed been culpable for some of the six goals that had gone past him in the past two games.

He received particular criticism from Sky pundits Jamie Carragher and Gary Neville after the Bournemouth loss, and had actually responded to that criticism in an interview during the week, appearing to take a shot at Neville for his failure during his 'short time' as manager at Valencia.

Karius's mistakes against West Ham opened him up to more of the same and Carragher and Neville didn't hold back, with the former suggesting Karius should 'shut up and do his job'. Neville's brother Phil was one of the pundits on *Match of the Day* and after the game condemned Karius not just for his performances, but for doing the interview and criticising his sibling.

It was starting to become a bit of a circus, which is exactly what Liverpool didn't need at this stage of the season.

Klopp did the only thing he could in that situation. He came out in the media in stern defence of his goalkeeper, also questioning Neville's authority to comment given his past in management.

'He showed he struggled with the job to judge players so why do we let him talk about players on TV?' Klopp said.

'The pundits, former players most of them, have forgotten completely how it felt when they got criticised.

'Especially the Neville brothers; the one who was the manager, he obviously should know that too much criticism never helps.

'But he is not interested in helping a Liverpool player I can imagine, but that makes things he says not make more sense.

'I don't listen to them. I am pretty sure Jamie Carragher doesn't speak too positively about Manchester United players.

'Obviously the Neville brothers don't like Liverpool. By the way, you can tell him I am not on Twitter so if he wants to tell me something Twitter doesn't help.'

It was a defence of his goalkeeper, but he had stopped short of suggesting Karius wasn't playing badly. He was left with a hard choice, and he made that hard choice in his selection for the trip to

Middlesbrough. Simon Mignolet came back in for his first league outing since the win at Chelsea in September.

Boro had been struggling for goals since their promotion back to the top flight. Heading into the game they were the lowest scorers in the league, but also had the joint fourth best defence.

However, that defence was breached just before the half-hour mark as a cross from Nathaniel Clyne found the onrushing Lallana, who headed in past Victor Valdés to give the visitors the lead.

In the second half they stepped it up a few more gears. Having not looked as fluid without Coutinho, the front three of Mané, Firmino and Origi shone in the second 45, causing Boro all kinds of problems, and further goals from Origi and Lallana sealed the win.

After the game the players went over to the fans and started handing their shirts out, with James Milner giving his to a young boy who had been in with the home fans but had still loudly and bravely cheered for Milner whenever he got the ball.

Klopp was delighted in his post-match press conference, in particular with the way his team had stepped up their level of performance as the match went on, 'Thrilled? Yes, with the result for sure – and the performance was, of course, really good. The nice thing is when you even have something to improve in a good game – and we had things to do better in the second half. You could really see how the boys took the information and did it.'

After an inevitable question regarding the goalkeeper situation, Klopp was predictably effusive in his praise of both of his players.

'The situation is LFC is a long-term project. We really want to improve the club. We know we have to be successful as soon as possible, but on the other hand we all feel comfortable in the situation with each other – the goalkeepers included. I know how strong Loris Karius is, but unfortunately he couldn't show it in the last one, two, three games – I'm not sure, that's not too important,' he commented.

'I am absolutely not interested in public pressure, but I am interested in the boy and there is no reason to push him through this situation. In the end, everything is one little mistake – which can happen to each goalkeeper in the world. So after one little mistake, should I say, "Okay, that's it, final judgement – I don't want to see him anymore?"

'There's absolutely no reason, especially when you have a goalkeeper like Simon Mignolet in training, on the bench, in character … a great footballer, a really, really good goalkeeper. He played really well at the beginning of the season, so there is no reason to push Loris through, that's why we made this change quite early and that's all, nothing else. We are fine and good.'

Boro boss Aitor Karanka joined the ever-growing list of opposition managers who were labelling Klopp's team as the toughest they had played. The former Real Madrid defender told Sky Sports after the game, 'It was difficult because we played against the best team we've played against this season. It was impossible to stop them.

'The second half, with two new players we tried to pressure higher, but it was difficult because they showed they were a really good team. And today they can say and admit that they were much, much better than us.

'Always we have competed against every single team, but today it was impossible. I can't say anything bad about my players because the fight on the pitch was amazing.

'It was difficult to go forward when you don't have the ball.'

The win took Liverpool back up to second place after Arsenal had lost 2-1 at Everton the night before. This was of course a positive result in terms of the title race, but came with a side issue. The next game was the derby.

In spite of a poor run of form before their win against Arsenal, Everton had gone nine months unbeaten at Goodison Park, and under manager Ronald Koeman, were aiming for their first derby win in six years.

On a Monday night under the lights at Goodison Park, the stage was set for a derby that would not just give local bragging rights to the red or blue half of Merseyside, but have a potentially massive effect on the title race as Chelsea had once again sealed a one-goal win, this time at Crystal Palace, to make it 11 wins in a row and reach 43 points after just 17 games. Even a win for the Reds would still leave them six points off the pace, so any other result wasn't worth contemplating.

Matip had not recovered in time so Lovren and Klavan would be asked to look after Romelu Lukaku, but better news for Klopp was that Emre Can and Daniel Sturridge were fit enough to make the bench.

In spite of the early dominance from Koeman's side, they were struggling to create anything. Lovren and Klavan were dealing comfortably with any threat that got close to Lukaku and, inevitably, Everton soon tired and Liverpool were able to come into the game.

Whether it was down to an improvement in Liverpool or a decline in Everton, it was the Reds who dominated the second half, but for all their ball possession, it looked like they would have to settle for a draw.

It had been a relatively well-behaved derby up until Ross Barkley lunged in on Henderson and clattered his studs into his England teammate's shin. The Liverpool captain was down in agony as Barkley protested his innocence and was relieved to see only a yellow card produced. The incident ramped up the atmosphere though and all of a sudden it felt like a derby.

Klopp would not be satisfied with a single point, especially as Everton weren't showing much threat at the other end, and so looked to his bench and called for Can and Sturridge.

As the board went up for eight added minutes, a roar went up from both sets of fans for their team to go for the win, and one of them did.

After Barkley had mishit a cross out for a goal kick, Liverpool went up the other end, with Wijnaldum sending a cross-field ball to Clyne, who laid it inside for Sturridge. The returning striker dribbled across the edge of the Everton penalty area looking for a chance to shoot. He took his chance and the ball rolled past Robles and struck the post.

The first on the scene as the ball rebounded was the alert Mané and he slammed the ball into the open net to win the derby for Liverpool.

The away fans jumped up and down, threw flares on to the pitch and generally went bananas as the players followed suit.

Klopp sent Lucas on to see out the remaining minutes and secured a vital three points to go back to second in the table and back to just six points off Chelsea.

The manager hugged all his players, his subs, his staff and pumped his fist in triumph at the away fans, knowing that a win at Goodison in the derby meant more to them than just three points.

After the game he was asked what he had said to the players at half-time to change things.

He replied, 'You cannot be 100 per cent sure what the opponent is going to do. We had an idea of course, and it was pretty much like what Everton did; making a wide game of it, starting like they finished [the Arsenal game] – pretty wild and intense, with man-orientated defending. We did it in training to cope with this, but it is different when you have it on the pitch.

'The first touch in a game that each player has is very important because you open your passing options or you close your passing options. We didn't play simply and quick enough in the first half.

'So, we spoke about football at half-time – and obviously it worked. The boys are more used to it, but obviously not enough otherwise we could have done it in the first half already.

'It is very important in a game like this, even when it's a little bit wild as it was in the first half, that you don't give a chance away – and we didn't give chances away, I cannot really remember [any]. We didn't have a lot actually, we had our moments and in the second half we had more, [we're] much better and could have scored earlier.

'Then Daniel came, hit the post and Sadio finished the situation, so it was great, intense, how a derby should be, not the best football in the world, but you cannot ignore the intensity, you cannot ignore the importance of a game like this, you have to take it like it is. In the second half we took it like it should be.'

Liverpool spent Christmas Day in second place in the Premier League table, only the fourth time they had done so, and had amassed their second-highest number of points in the Premier League era after 17 games (37). After the blips against Bournemouth and West Ham, it appeared that things were back on track for Klopp and his men.

The trip to Everton was their tenth on the road, meaning they had just nine away trips left and 12 home games due to the fact they had started the season with three away fixtures.

Those figures would even out before the New Year though as the next two games would both be at Anfield, with Stoke City the first visitors.

The Potters were the last visiting team to win at Anfield, having beaten Liverpool 1-0 in their League Cup semi-final second leg in January, although the Reds ultimately progressed to Wembley on penalties.

As he had done that night, Mark Hughes came with a very obvious game plan as he started with Jonathan Walters and Peter Crouch up front. Long balls and second balls would be the name of the game for Hughes, and initially it worked as Stoke took the lead through Walters.

However, once Lallana equalised it was all Liverpool. They dominated from there on and further goals from Firmino, an own goal and Sturridge confirmed a 4-1 win.

Sturridge's goal was also a landmark one as it was the 100th scored by Liverpool in league games since Klopp had taken over. The tally had taken just 48 games to reach, which was the joint-fastest ever alongside Kenny Dalglish's first reign.

It was noted during the game that Manchester City boss Pep Guardiola was in attendance. Not an unusual thing as he would be bringing his team to Anfield just four days later, but Klopp was still asked about it in his post-match press conference.

'Unusual, I don't know,' he reasoned. 'I did it a lot in the past, but obviously it's not too easy any more because it's more a signing hour than you can watch a game. Maybe he saw nothing. Hopefully we had no security and Pep had to write all the autographs! The game is on 31 December and whatever I say tonight can't win it. But maybe I could say a few things that would make it a bit more difficult for us to win it, so it's probably best I shut my mouth!'

Yet again the game with City would come after Chelsea had played, and sure enough the league leaders took their remarkable winning run to 13 games as they also managed to overcome Stoke, despite a slight scare as they were pegged back to 2-2, but ran out 4-2 winners. It meant that Liverpool would have to beat City just to stay within touching distance and cut Chelsea's lead back to six points.

City had got their momentum going again in recent games, beating Arsenal at the Etihad and coming off a 3-0 victory away to Hull on Boxing Day. They also had the plus of having Sergio Agüero back after a four-game suspension.

The build-up acknowledged the renewed rivalry of Klopp and Guardiola, who had battled previously as Borussia Dortmund and Bayern Munich managers in the Bundesliga just a couple of seasons before.

When asked about Klopp's style of football ahead of the game, the former Barcelona boss suggested that his opposite number was perhaps the best in the world at creating attacking sides.

He said, 'Our styles are not similar but I like a lot the way they play. Maybe Klopp is the best manager in the world at creating teams who attack the back four with so many players, from almost anywhere on the pitch. They have an intensity with the ball and without the ball, and it is not easy to do that. They attack wide sometimes with Clyne and Milner but they especially like to attack from inside, through the middle. I don't think there is another team in the world attacking in this way with so many players capable of launching moves in an instant.

'I learned a lot in Germany the first time I played his team. I was new and it was "wow, what a good lesson". We lost 4-2. Afterwards in the league I learned a bit more about how to control those situations but it was never easy. When Klopp speaks about his football being heavy metal, I understand completely. It is so aggressive. For the fans it is really good.'

Klopp had also been complimentary to his opponent in the build-up to the game on New Year's Eve.

'He [Guardiola] came here with open eyes. He could have had easier jobs in easier leagues, that is for sure. He could have gone everywhere. He wanted to come here. He was probably aware 100 per cent of the big challenge.

'He knew he had a wonderful squad at Barcelona and a wonderful squad at Bayern but he had big influence on the way they played football. If you go to Barcelona as a new manager they will tell you, "By the way, don't forget, we play like Pep Guardiola played." That's the biggest influence you can have. Bayern loved the years he was there. He is a fantastic manager.

'Johan Cruyff started "Total Football", but Pep made it perfect. He's an outstanding manager, 100 per cent. He's very influential.'

It was sure to be a fascinating tactical battle, with the added element that defeat for either would leave the gap between them and Chelsea looking like a chasm at the halfway point of the season.

Klopp made one notable change to the team that beat Stoke, replacing Origi with Emre Can, whom Guardiola had managed for a short while at Bayern. This meant Firmino playing as the false nine.

The Anfield crowd was ready to cheer their team on to a win on the last day of 2016, but had to negotiate some nervous moments in the early minutes as Raheem Sterling tested out the pace of Milner, and City won a couple of free kicks around the Reds penalty area, one of which led to Klavan receiving an early booking.

However, one free kick was sloppily given away by Yaya Touré, and that set Liverpool off on a counter-attack. Lallana was released down the left and he played in an early cross with his left foot. The ball arced perfectly for the onrushing Wijnaldum and he powered his header into the corner of the net past Claudio Bravo to give Liverpool an eighth-minute lead.

An early goal suggested that the pre-match predictions of a high-scoring encounter appeared to be coming true, but it didn't play out that way. Liverpool remained on top for the rest of the first half.

In the second half City found their rhythm. They dominated the ball and kept Liverpool in their own half for large periods, but struggled to create any meaningful chances, with Agüero and David Silva resorting to hopeful left-footed shots from range.

Klopp's men remained patient and showed the tactical maturity that they hadn't against Bournemouth and West Ham, and in the end ran out relatively comfortable 1-0 winners.

It was a perfect end to what had been a very good 2016 for Klopp and Liverpool, in spite of some bumps along the way, and it meant they would end the year four points clear in second place, still six behind Chelsea. Some had suggested that it must be demoralising for Liverpool to be winning so many games but unable to catch Antonio Conte's relentless winning machine at Stamford Bridge, but Klopp, as ever, had another way of looking at it.

He said, 'As I've said before, we cannot have a look at Chelsea; they obviously are unbelievably strong, of course, and they are in an outstanding run and have won 13 games in a row already – not bad – but can you imagine how annoying it is when you've won 13 games in a row and there's still one team only six points behind? I am pretty sure they don't think about this, so why should we?'

In terms of the game itself, Klopp was just as happy as the fans at the outcome, and again praised his team for their tactical discipline, but wasn't entirely satisfied with how his team had passed the ball.

'It was a difficult game, of course. City are a good side, a really good side. It was clear we needed to be very compact today because if you are not compact against City then you don't have to play. We did well, I cannot remember a lot of chances for City, which is maybe the biggest compliment for my team. The problem we had tonight was that we were not as good as we could have been in our own possession.

'We lost the ball too easily and, because of that, the game was so intense for us – then we had to close the spaces with the highest intensity, the highest passion level and all that. It was really hard work tonight, but it was not that we were expecting something different. Against Man City, you have to work for three points. If you are good enough, you can get them – and we are good enough and that's cool.'

Just over four hours later the bells rang to welcome in the New Year, but there would be no celebrations for Klopp and his team as less than 48 hours later they would be playing again.

24

'The world can change and that's the reason you should create your own values. On the money side and the attitude side: what do you really want? What do you stand for?'

THE thorny issue of fixture congestion had come up before, and Klopp had made his feelings quite clear that it was something he could do without. Due to the fact that Christmas Day and New Year's Day had fallen on a Sunday, there weren't quite as many strange fixture patterns as there usually is in England around the end of the year, but there was one anomaly in particular that rankled.

The game with Manchester City had been moved back for TV, which meant that the clash at Sunderland would kick off less than 44 hours after the final whistle had blown at Anfield. The club had requested that the Sunderland match be pushed back but were denied by the Premier League, in spite of the fact that Burnley had made a similar request for their fixture at Tottenham a few weeks earlier in spite of a much longer break and had it granted.

To make matters worse, Chelsea's schedule had been far more favourable, having a seven-day break between their three encounters over the period, while Liverpool had just four. For the first time in weeks Liverpool were kicking off before Chelsea, but it was the one time they'd have rather not done so, with Conte's side having an extra two days to prepare for their crucial trip to Tottenham. Ahead of the game, Klopp said he would pick whoever he could for the game, but added that it was no excuse for a below-par performance at the Stadium of Light.

'I will make a line-up when the medical department gives me the opportunity to,' he said. 'If I have no choice, then the players which are fit will play. That's how it is. No excuses for anybody. We have to deliver, and we will deliver.'

As it turned out, Klopp ended up making just one change to the team that had beaten City, with Sturridge coming in for Jordan Henderson, who had picked up a slight problem during the win. This meant Emre Can filling in the deep-lying midfielder role while Lallana dropped back to his previous midfield job.

David Moyes had been struggling at Sunderland, who were ensconced in the relegation zone. They had also been comfortably beaten 4-1 by Burnley on New Year's Eve.

However, in spite of his poor record against Liverpool down the years in terms of beating them, Moyes had often managed to find a way to stifle them and take a draw.

His approach paid off again in this one as his side managed to come back from a goal down twice to draw 2-2. Sturridge and Mané had both given the Reds the lead but two Jermain Defoe penalties denied them all three points, including one that had been awarded after a Mané handball. It would be the Senegalese's last contribution before heading off to the African Cup of Nations.

It was far from the ideal start to 2017 for Klopp's side, and the German manager was clearly irked by the outcome, unsure whether or not the lack of time in-between games had been the crucial factor.

'For me, it's completely difficult to assume [anything about] the game, because I have no experience – in situations like this, I have no idea what I could have expected from the performance side,' he said.

'I thought we started really well and then we lost concentration. That's not usual for us. But, of course, it happened before. It could be because of the fixtures, I'm not sure.

'Second half, we again dominated the game. Usually I would say we could have done better, but I don't know exactly if we could have done better because I was not in the boots. We scored the second goal – felt good, felt deserved. Then, I would say no foul, but a free kick [given]. I saw it again – no contact. Then handball, 2-2. That's how it is.

'In this moment, it is really hard for me to accept, but I am professional so I have to. Obviously, [the title race] is not finally done. Maybe I look like not the best loser in the world, I have no problem with this – today two penalties feels not good. I usually like to talk about football, but it's difficult today.

'I know what I can expect when I say [to the players] "that was not enough" or "that was enough" but today if I said "that was not enough" I have no idea if they could have done more. That's my lack of experience.'

It was a disappointment, but there was some good news on the horizon as Chelsea were finally beaten two days later to end their 13-game winning streak and meant Liverpool had cut their lead at the top to five points. The bad news was that it was Tottenham who had beaten them, 2-0 at White Hart Lane thanks to a brace from Dele Alli.

The win for Spurs meant they now also had to be taken seriously as title contenders. The top six in the league were pulling away from the rest, and by this stage it appeared that any of them were capable of finishing anywhere between first and sixth.

The league would have to wait for a couple of weeks though as the next two encounters were cup ties. First up, Plymouth at home in the FA Cup third round.

Klopp named the youngest starting-XI in Liverpool's history, with an average age of just 21. This average age was made all the more impressive by the inclusion of Lucas as captain, soon to turn 30. Loris Karius returned in goal, teenagers Trent Alexander-Arnold, Ovie Ejaria and Ben Woodburn all started, as did Sheyi Ojo returning from injury.

Another injury return was the first appearance under Klopp of Joe Gomez. The young defender was seen as an exciting prospect when he was brought in from Charlton Athletic under Brendan Rodgers, and even started a handful of games under the Irishman. However, he picked up a horrible cruciate knee ligament injury on international duty just days after Klopp was announced as Liverpool manager, and hadn't been able to play since. He lined up at centre-back alongside Lucas, but as it turned out, it would be a very quiet return.

Understandably given the obvious gap in stature, Plymouth decided to sit deep and pretty much forgo any intent to attack, or even cross the halfway line. A terrible game stumbled to a 0-0 draw.

As Exeter had done in 2016, the plucky League Two underdogs earned a draw against the mighty Liverpool, but it was made all the more impressive that they had done it at Anfield, becoming only the third side in a 12-month period to prevent the Reds from scoring at home, albeit against a very second-string line-up. It meant a money-spinning replay for Plymouth, which was the last thing that Klopp needed. Another game to fit into an already packed January schedule. It meant that, assuming Liverpool won the replay, they would play nine games in the first month of 2017.

Klopp did not show his annoyance at the extra game or at his team's failure to put away a team three divisions below them, but conceded that there were plenty of things they could have done better.

The inevitable question came up about whether it was a mistake to pick the side he did, making ten changes from the team that drew at Sunderland.

He replied, 'I don't think the line-up was a mistake, but you can see it like this if you want. We made mistakes in the game and always with the boys, the good things they are responsible for and the bad things I am responsible for. If you want to see it in a bad way then I am 100 per cent responsible, I have no problem with that.

'I always choose line-ups to win the game and I accept that it was not to see in all situations today, but in a lot of them it was. It's really important for us, having games like this where we really have to fight for the result with a different line-up. There is a long season still to go and we need to change. If you make that many changes, it doesn't make it easier for the boys – I know this – but they need this experience and now they have it so we can go on.'

The result was frustrating but it was a pertinent point that Klopp had again entrusted the youngsters to get the job done, even if they hadn't quite managed it.

On the morning of the Plymouth game the *Sunday Times* published an interview by Jonathan Northcroft with Klopp and Pep Lijnders that specifically touched on Klopp's ideas regarding youth development.

Northcroft asked Klopp about his first managerial job with Eintracht Frankfurt as head coach of their under-ten team. He said, 'I loved it. I wasn't sure I wanted to do something like [coaching] but I needed the money actually. I got 400 marks and a winter jacket. And a season ticket.' Klopp was just 21 years old at the time and explained his first realisation that he wanted to coach more than procure, 'I never had a philosophy or something but I had this team. After the first season the club asked, "For next year how many new players do you want?" I said I don't need new players.

'"But every year we change …" I said, "Well, this year don't." My first decision in coaching … to keep exactly the same squad for the following year. I was 21 years old.'

When reminded that he took Dortmund to the Champions League Final in 2013 with three academy products and seven players signed by Klopp before they turned 21, the German said, 'I would say the biggest stories are written by local players. If it's Barcelona, if it's Ajax, if it's Manchester United, if it's Liverpool I don't know how long ago.

'Dortmund was like this. The "Boys of 88". A special year, because my son was born then and a lot of those guys were born in 1988 too. It's maybe not the most important thing in football, but it is nice [those Dortmund players] are friends for life.

'First you should try to be successful. At Liverpool we need to be successful, but you should try to be a little bit more independent of the money. Because in a world of money it looks like everybody in football has more than they need. Each club can buy who they want, this player at that moment, blah, blah, blah, but in the end it is always short-term thinking.

'The world can change and that's the reason you should create your own values. On the money side and the attitude side: what do you really want? What do you stand for?

'And I think Liverpool have always [had] a special identity. That's why I loved this club even before I was here. My first responsibility is to use it, to keep it and, if possible, make it more special. Not all old things are bad things.

'We try to do it differently here,' he added. 'We try not because it's about being different, but because it's what we believe in.

'I think that's what life should be: that you make your own experience and if it's good or bad you share it. That's how I think football should work too. The problem in this world is everything is so quick. Everybody wants everything in this moment. Nobody gives you time to develop.'

When asked whatever happened to the Eintracht Frankfurt under-tens he said, 'The goalkeeper made it, had a decent career actually – third division in Germany. One or two played in Turkey. But I missed contact with them, it was 27 years ago, 28 … Good boys.'

His new set of good boys had another cup game up next, the first leg of their League Cup semi-final against Southampton. Klopp was aiming to maintain his career record of having never been beaten in a semi-final, and tongues were already wagging about a potential final against José Mourinho and Manchester United.

The first leg took place at St Mary's where Liverpool had drawn 0-0 a couple of months earlier, a result that was disappointing in the league but would be seen as a good outcome in the cup.

Klopp promised in his pre-match press conference that he would bring his first-team players back in for this one, in spite of a crucial away clash with United scheduled just four days later. Karius kept his place, as did Lucas and Can, while the frontline was made up of Lallana, Firmino and Sturridge.

As they had done in the league game, Liverpool dominated the ball in the opening minutes. It appeared that Claude Puel was happy for his team to survive, almost as Plymouth had done. The atmosphere was flat as the Saints fans seemed bemused as to why they weren't going for a first-leg advantage.

Then from nowhere the home side broke down the right. A cross found Nathan Redmond unmarked at the far post. He got his shot away but was closed down well by Karius, who blocked. The young goalkeeper didn't have long to celebrate the save though as it came straight back down the pitch. Ragnar Klavan missed his clearance and the ball fell kindly for the hosts. Redmond was played in again and this time made no mistake. St Mary's cheered vociferously and against the run of play, Southampton were ahead.

The run of play stayed in that direction as it was Puel's men who threatened a second, Karius again called into making a fine save from Redmond. The second half wasn't much better for Klopp as his players just couldn't get anything going.

One big plus came on the hour mark as Wijnaldum was replaced by the returning Coutinho, the little Brazilian making his first appearance since his injury against Sunderland a month earlier.

In spite of his return, the game ended 1-0 and the Reds suffered just their third defeat of the season.

The most concerning aspect of the game was that they had been second best for most of the night. It was really the first time in the season they had lost and deserved to, whereas they had dominated Burnley without firepower and been on top for 70 minutes at Bournemouth before their capitulation.

'The start was good – the start was really good,' Klopp said after the game. 'If we played like this for 90 minutes, then it would have been very difficult for Southampton to cope with it. But after, we conceded one goal and obviously the game changed. Even if I would try to explain it, it's not easy because I'm not actually used to a reaction like this from my boys. But we have to accept it, tonight it was not good. We were again dominant second half, all that stuff, they had one or two counter-attacks, that's how it is, it's not a big problem.'

He was able to take one positive from the night. After the recent criticism of his performances, Loris Karius had put in his best display in a Liverpool shirt to keep his team in the tie. Klopp said, '[He was] good. If we lose 3-0 or 4-0 then it could be much more difficult for the second game so yes, he kept us in the game, that's how it is. That's his job and I'm not too surprised that he was able to do it. But actually, if your goalkeeper has to make saves like this then something else is wrong in the game and that was our problem tonight.'

However, Karius would be one of the few players who would not be lining up in the next game, a trip to Manchester United.

The Red Devils had been on a nine-match winning streak, finding form under José Mourinho and working their way back into the title reckoning.

Preparations were not ideal for Klopp, who had already lost Mané to the African Cup of Nations and Coutinho was not yet ready to start such an encounter. It also emerged that Nathaniel Clyne had picked up a rib injury against Southampton so Trent Alexander-Arnold came into the starting line-up at Old Trafford. It would be the 18-year-old's first league start for the club, and he was up against Anthony Martial.

However, there was one absence from the team that was a little less straightforward. Joel Matip had been missing for most of the previous month with an ankle problem, but was now fit and raring to go, only he couldn't.

Liverpool released a statement ahead of the match explaining that due to FIFA and the Cameroon Football Association failing to confirm his eligibility while the African Cup of Nations was happening, they would not be able to risk selecting him. Matip had not played for his country since 2015 and had made it known that, as far as he was concerned, he had retired from internationals. However, Cameroon still called him up to their provisional 35-man squad.

Matip refused to be included in the final squad, but due to a rule that says players cannot play club football without their nation's permission during their time in the tournament, the club could have risked a heavy fine and points deduction if he had been selected, and with FIFA refusing to step in and address the situation, Klopp's hands were tied.

That meant that Lovren and Klavan continued in the centre of defence, while Mignolet returned in goal and Jordan Henderson was able to make his first start of 2017.

Sky Sports had built the game up as part of their 'Merseyside vs Manchester' Sunday coverage, with Everton playing Manchester City earlier the same day.

Absolutely no one from Merseyside or Manchester saw it that way, and were only concerned about the other match in terms of what it would do to the title race. With Everton thrashing City 4-0, it meant that a win for either side at Old Trafford would give them a significant advantage not only over the other, but over Pep Guardiola's team as well.

There was an interesting tactical move from Klopp as the game kicked off, with the German opting for a 4-4-2 diamond formation. It meant that Firmino would return to a more central role while Origi was asked to drift wider than usual. It also meant that Alexander-Arnold wouldn't get quite as much protection, and he was targeted early on by United. He was able to largely hold his own as he and the rest of the defence limited the hosts to just half-chances in the opening stages.

The only moment to set the hearts racing came as a weak Lovren backpass was closed down by Zlatan Ibrahimović. Mignolet came to clear but only hit the ball against the big Swede. Fortunately for the Reds goalkeeper it looped back just over the bar.

The first real chance for United came as Klopp's former charge Henrikh Mkhitaryan set up Paul Pogba, but the Frenchman could only skew his shot wide when in space.

Pogba was influencing the game again just a few minutes later. The world's most expensive player had been at the centre of the pre-match hype, even getting his own Twitter emoji every time someone posted #Pogba on the social media platform.

This was on display on all the advertising boards around the pitch, and was all over social media, especially in the 26th minute when he handled the ball from a Liverpool corner and conceded a penalty. The 23-year-old had been struggling to contain Lovren from set pieces and took his eye off the ball as it came down and struck him on the arm. James Milner stepped up and comfortably dispatched his shot past David de Gea to give the visitors the lead.

Pogba was determined to make amends and aggressively threw Henderson to the floor when attacking a corner at the other end. Fortunately for him the referee did not see it, but he did see Origi commit a foul on the edge of the area. Ibrahimović stepped up and slammed the free kick towards the corner of the net, but Mignolet parried it away well. The Belgian was then also alert to deny Mkhitaryan after a mistake by Klavan.

Liverpool's shape and pressing had been working well, especially the deliberate tactic to hurry Michael Carrick and Ander Herrera in the midfield into quick decisions and poor passes. Carrick was so uncharacteristically flustered that he was taken off at half-time and replaced by Wayne Rooney.

The pre-match coverage that hadn't been about Pogba had been about Rooney and the fact that he needed just one more goal to become

United's all-time record scorer. The script almost seemed written that the former Evertonian would score the crucial goal against his fiercest rival, but his early influence on the game was minimal.

Klopp turned to Coutinho on the hour mark, with the Brazilian replacing Origi, and the effect was immediate as a clever reverse pass from the new arrival found Firmino in space, but his shot from an angle was straight at de Gea.

Then the moment looked like it might come for Rooney but his shot was closed down by Milner.

Wijnaldum had a chance to put the game to bed after a well-worked move ended in a cross to the Dutchman, but he could only send his header high and wide. It would prove to be a costly miss.

With five minutes remaining, a ball in from Rooney was headed goalwards by another substitute, Marouane Fellaini. It struck the post and rolled to Antonio Valencia, who crossed back to Ibrahimovic, and his looping header evaded Mignolet and crossed the line. It was frustrating after holding on for so long and with so few minutes left, and that frustration grew further when replays showed that Valencia had been offside in the build-up.

Another late chance for Wijnaldum was tamely hit straight at de Gea and the score ended 1-1. It was a point that many Liverpool fans conceded they would have been happy with at the start of the game, but it felt like too little after an impressive performance and almost an hour of being in the lead. It also meant dropping two further behind leaders Chelsea, who had beaten Leicester 3-0 the day before.

They had though stopped United's winning streak, and as Mourinho's side were now 12 points off the top, it was widely thought that despite initial elation at grabbing a late draw it was probably the end of their faint hopes at a title charge.

Klopp was frustrated after the game, especially as the goal conceded should not have stood, but he also saw a lot of positives in a performance that had been exponentially better than the one at Southampton just days earlier.

He commented, 'I'm fine with the performance. I always have to think about two things after games – number one is the performance. And, of course, the result too. When you see the line-ups and see the circumstances, you would say, "A point at Old Trafford, come on, take it, go home and don't think about it, well done." Unfortunately, it doesn't feel exactly like this and that's because of the performance of my boys.

'Over the whole game, we were the better side. But then they came with the long ball, Fellaini on the pitch and that's difficult after

75 minutes of dominating the game, and then having all the balls bouncing around the 18-yard box. We made this mistake – I have no idea how it exactly happened, but we could have cleared the situation already and then it comes back from the post.

'They were then more awake and used the situation. Then we had again two unbelievable chances and before that we had Roberto's big chance, when Phil came on the pitch. Of course, I'm used to it, I can easily accept a draw at Manchester United, that's not a problem. But I think, over the whole 98 minutes or whatever, we would have deserved the win.

'That's absolutely not interesting for anybody but it's important for me to know about the attitude and character of my boys, because they played with a lot of little problems. We don't make big things of it, but we had a few issues, smaller or bigger. And the boys did really well, so I'm happy.'

He was also happy with the performance of Alexander-Arnold, who after a few early jitters had established himself well in the game.

When asked directly about the youngster's showing, Klopp said, 'Nice, eh? It was clear in the beginning. Then you see Martial, one of the quickest players in the Premier League, in the first two situations it was difficult and he needed a little bit of time to adapt. But then he did brilliantly. All the boys like him and so they wanted to help him.

'The decision was not that easy. The first impulse if Clyney can't play is Millie on the right and Alberto [Moreno] left – but I didn't want to change two positions because of one injury. I knew, with a new system, with a diamond which we played, to change both full-backs, I didn't feel too well [about]. We didn't have to be too brave to bring him, we thought he was ready for it and he proved it.'

In his post-match comments, Mourinho indicated that he wanted the media to point out that Liverpool had come to Old Trafford and been 'the team that defended', referencing the criticism he and his players had been subject to after their defensive display at Anfield in the reverse fixture.

While United had certainly been more attacking in this game than they had on Merseyside, Mourinho's point was not especially valid as Liverpool had still managed more shots than his team (13-9). It was disappointing for Klopp to concede the late goal, but a draw at Old Trafford was not a bad result, and his team put in a level of performance that showed signs they were heading back into form, which made what happened next all the more bewildering.

25

'We stay together, we stay positive, we come out and we punch back hard.'

AFTER a tough run of fixtures Liverpool returned to Anfield for what appeared to be a straightforward game with struggling Swansea. The Welsh side were lodged in the relegation zone having recently sacked Bob Bradley, their second managerial dismissal of the season, and in his place they appointed Carlo Ancelotti's number two at Bayern Munich, Paul Clement.

The English coach's immediate impact had been minimal, losing 2-0 to Hull in the FA Cup and 4-0 at home to Arsenal in the league the previous week. The Reds were yet to win a league game in 2017 but were confident ahead of this one, especially after the farcical situation with Joel Matip was finally resolved.

Unfortunately for Klopp, the decision from FIFA that Matip could indeed play while the African Cup of Nations were taking place didn't arrive until late on the Friday night, so the defender had been unable to be a part of the pre-match preparations just in case the news had been negative. Klopp had prepped the team with Dejan Lovren and Ragnar Klavan once again at the back, while there were returns to the team for Nathaniel Clyne and Philippe Coutinho, making his first league start since his injury.

The Brazilian had played an hour of the FA Cup replay at Plymouth three days earlier and come through unscathed, as had Liverpool after the unlikely source of Lucas had scored the only goal of a drab game on a cold Devon evening.

Swansea were expected to sit deep, but they had spent the season failing even the very basics of defending. It was therefore with some surprise that in the first half they appeared to be incredibly well organised, well drilled and full of hard work. It was very unlike what had been seen as recently as a week earlier from Swansea and Liverpool were unable to create much in the way of chances.

They were not moving the ball fast enough, and were clearly missing the pace of Mané, with the skilful but comparatively slow trio of Coutinho, Firmino and Lallana in the front three. The crowd, who Klopp had specifically asked to make Anfield a cauldron ahead of the game, could barely muster a peep as a dull first half ended goalless.

Half-time thoughts had been of whether they could break down the wall in the second period, or if they may have to settle for an unwelcome goalless draw.

It was then with some surprise that Swansea came out in the second half on the attack, and soon forced a corner from a Lovren header. The ball in was headed into the path of Spanish striker Fernando Llorente, who prodded in to give his team an unlikely lead.

Clement had clearly had an early effect on his new team, and his two new players, Tom Carroll and Martin Olsson, had been brought in just days earlier from Tottenham and Norwich respectively, and both were excelling on debut.

It was they who linked up minutes later down the left with Olsson teeing the ball up for Carroll to cross. The perfectly arced delivery found the head of Llorente who bulleted an effort past Mignolet to make it 2-0 to the visitors.

Anfield was in shock. Klopp's men had gone from struggling to break down a resolute side to needing to score three times while trying not to leak anything else at the back.

Just as the mood was reaching desperation point, the deficit was halved as a Milner cross reached Firmino, who headed in to make it 2-1. Noise levels rose and it appeared that the home team had finally woken up.

Klopp turned to Daniel Sturridge to try and force the issue further, but it was Firmino who stepped up again with 20 minutes left as a ball in from Wijnaldum was chested down by the Brazilian and volleyed into the corner to equalise. It was a tremendous goal and felt like a complete pendulum swing. Swansea were on the ropes and Liverpool had almost a quarter of the game left to find the killer third.

Klopp had been preparing to bring Divock Origi on before the goal, and decided to do so anyway in an effort to kill the Welsh side off once and for all. However, it meant moving Firmino back into midfield to accommodate him, and this seemed to have the opposite of the intended effect.

Liverpool created a couple of chances immediately after Firmino's equaliser, but all of a sudden Swansea were back on the attack again. Leroy Fer wasn't being challenged, and neither was Carroll when he tried to dribble into the area. The ball did come loose and, in a panic, Klavan tried to scoop the ball away, but it then rolled perfectly into the path of the onrushing Gylfi Sigurdsson, who had lost Clyne at the far post. The Icelandic midfielder planted the ball into the corner of the net to restore Swansea's lead.

Exasperation all around. There were still 15 minutes plus stoppage time left but the atmosphere in the ground was gone. The shock of falling behind again consumed the fans and the players. Some chances were created before the final whistle, but there was little in the way of conviction or belief.

The final whistle went and, in the eyes of some fans, it may as well have been the whistle to end the season. So few points were being dropped in the title race that games like this were almost seen as dead rubbers. To lose, at home, to arguably the worst team in the league was like giving a bonus three points to the rest of the top six. With Chelsea playing Hull at home the following day, it was a near certainty that the gap between Liverpool and the summit would be ten points.

Even with the shock of the manner of the losses to Burnley and Bournemouth, this one felt like the biggest punch to the gut. Completely unexpected, and at a crucial time of the season. The next league game would be Chelsea at home, but the significance of it seemed lessened after defeat here.

Twitter was full of Liverpool fans at various stages of despair, with the overwhelmingly standout word being used over and over again by the masses being 'heartbroken'.

It was Liverpool's first home defeat in over a year, having gone unbeaten at Anfield for 17 games after the previous January's 1-0 loss to Stoke in the League Cup. That run was no consolation to Klopp though, who was despondent with the display and result.

He said, 'First half, obviously you could hear in the stadium it was not the most entertaining game. It was the job to do today. If you want to have a real spectacle on the pitch, you need two sides for it. In the first half, only we played, they defended. It's not that you can create in each second a chance, but we had these four or five really good moments when we did really well. That's what you have to do in a game like this, to change the situation in a positive way, [which] means you have a lead, 1-0 up, 2-0 up, whatever. That changes the game, of course.

'In this case, we couldn't score and came out of half-time and then obviously you need to be spot on immediately and in the first minutes one of the decisive [moments] was that they even got the corner. It was a throw-in and we were too late, then not concentrated in the situation, flick-on and corner. We lost the first challenge after the corner and, until now, I couldn't see how Llorente could be completely alone in the six-yard box and score the goal.

'Then they had their second chance in the game, we couldn't avoid the cross, ball in the air – brilliant cross, brilliant header. That, I can easily accept. If something happens like this, I don't speak about the mistakes around the header. But we should have avoided the pass and then the cross. That should be possible. The reaction was then very good; 2-1, wonderful goal, 2-2, wonderful goal, big chances, chance after chance. Then we had the punch that we missed a little bit in the first half, not only when we scored the goals, also when we created the chances.

'Then the most disappointing moment, the third goal, nearly everything was wrong around this goal. I think it started with a long ball – that was not a real surprise, they played a few of these. The reaction on the long ball was not good. We strode back, we were there and we scored, then we obviously couldn't switch in this moment to a defensive mood. That was the biggest mistake in this situation. We were passive. We win the ball and we could again create the next chance, but they took the opportunity and at the end Swansea players were in our box. That makes, of course, no sense.

'I don't look for where is lucky and unlucky; it was obvious we had not that much luck today, maybe they had a little bit more, especially in defending. [There were] two or three situations where it was already done nearly and we could have scored again. We showed again that when we are really on track then we are a strong side and can create chances and score goals. That's natural, if you want, and will happen. But the defending around all three goals was not good enough, 100 per cent. That's a very important part of the game. It's very disappointing today.'

When asked how damaging the loss could be to his squad and their aims for the season, he said, 'I don't know how much exactly. In Germany, that [damaging] is a pretty harsh word. If it has influence, then it has to be like this. It's a few weeks ago we [last] lost in the Premier League and it has to feel really bad – and that's what it does.

'I don't need this feeling but now we have to, like always we have to use it – we have to show a reaction. It was not like we are in this situation and think everything is going well, we are really fighting. Two-nil down is not nice, but scoring the equaliser was fantastic so then it was clear who was on the run – but then it was really hard when we conceded the third one. It is our mistake – nobody else made a mistake, only us. Now we have to show a reaction.'

The bones were picked out of the performance, and Liverpool's overall abilities and expectations for the future on various websites, podcasts and football television shows. The general consensus was that anything other than a win over Chelsea in their next league game and they would be solely focused on Champions League qualification for the remaining 15 matches of the season.

The day before the Swansea encounter there had been some positive news out of the club. Steven Gerrard was returning.

The former captain was appointed as an academy coach, passing on his years of wisdom to the Reds's stars of tomorrow. While it was initially an overview role, by the end of the season it was confirmed that Gerrard would be managing the club's under-18 side from the 2017/18 campaign.

Klopp was pleased with the appointment. 'He said he wants to be a manager in the future. That's cool,' the German explained.

'It was important to know what Steven wants. Being a manager is a job you have to learn and he is ready to make steps.

'Combining his playing experience with all the things he has to learn, he has a bright future. Everyone in this room knows better than I do he is a wonderful guy and it's wonderful news for football.'

There was still the matter of two domestic cups to challenge for and that would be the focus of the next couple of games, starting with Southampton in the second leg of the League Cup semi-final. The determination to not let this blip turn into a crisis was evident in Klopp's pre-match notes, which read, 'We stay together, we stay positive, we come out and we punch back hard.'

The fans were equally fired up, lining the streets outside the ground to boo the arriving visitors from the south coast and to cheer their heroes as the home coach pulled in, akin to some of the big European nights from the season before. It was outright defiance from all concerned not to allow the negative feelings from Saturday ruin the quest for another final under Klopp.

The good vibes had not just been brought about by the return of Gerrard and the fighting talk of Klopp, but by the news that had broken earlier in the day that Philippe Coutinho had signed a new five-year contract. The 'little magician' had arguably been the team's best player since Klopp arrived and it was a positive signal of intent from him and the club that a deal had been done so quickly.

The manager named an attacking line-up, knowing that there was a good chance three or more goals could be needed as the away goal rule would come into effect after any potential extra time. Wijnaldum was dropped to the bench for Sturridge, meaning Lallana would go back into the midfield three and Firmino would play on the right of the front line.

There was also a necessary change at right-back as Clyne was left out after suffering further from his abdominal injury, and Alexander-Arnold came back in.

As was to be expected, Southampton sat deep and compact, seeing that this method had given Liverpool real problems against Sunderland and Swansea.

The first half was largely a similar story to the Swansea game. A slow tempo, very little in the way of creativity and barely a sweat broken into by the opposition, who came close to scoring themselves on more than one occasion.

There was a 20-minute period in the second half where Liverpool exerted extended pressure on the Southampton defence, which had been weakened by the absence of the injured Virgil van Dijk. By far the best chance of the game for the hosts came in that period as a ball into the box was headed back across goal to Sturridge, in the six-yard box right in front of goal. Somehow, he volleyed over when it was easier to score.

Klopp turned to his subs as he brought Origi and Wijnaldum on for Can and Coutinho, and the late pressure being put on Southampton should have forced a penalty as a header from a corner saw Shane Long lean his arm into the ball to block it. Then there was another penalty shout as Origi went down under a challenge from Jack Stephens. It wasn't clear how much contact there was with the player, but referee Martin Atkinson gave a corner and nothing more.

Moments later, the tie was done.

Milner swung a poor corner in that was cleared and Southampton broke. Liverpool had committed men forward in search of the goal they needed, and Josh Sims raced away on the counter to set up Long, who made no mistake as he fired past Karius. Liverpool were out.

Having lost the final in such heartbreaking fashion in his first season, Klopp wanted this League Cup, and it had yet again been taken away from him. He tried to mask his disappointment after the game, claiming that both sides had played well and that it was just unfortunate that they couldn't find the goal they needed, but there was a clear sense of growing anger and frustration in his voice.

He revealed, 'I'm disappointed, there's big disappointment. First of all, big congratulations to Southampton – they won both legs so deserve to go to the final, but I think especially in the game tonight we could have won [the tie], that's why I am disappointed.

'The plan of Southampton was counter-attacking, which they did really well. In the first half, one or two counter-attacks could have been defended better and we should not be in one-on-one situations with Redmond, but all the rest was good play of Southampton.

'We are out and we have to accept it. For me as a coach, it is very important to know about the performance and I will not ignore this, but in this moment I am of course disappointed because we would have deserved to win the game tonight. If this would have been enough, I have no idea. We have to congratulate Southampton and we wish them all the best.'

Klopp was also asked about his side's ability to break teams down, with more and more appearing to realise that playing with a low block bore more fruit against the Reds than any other tactic.

'If we would doubt the way we are after these little, little problems we've had now, it would really be a strange thing,' he replied. 'We are absolutely in the situation – we don't have the points we want, that's not the problem, that's how it is. We know what we want to do, we know what we have to do and we know about the football we want to play, so that's all good.'

Just 62 hours later things got even worse. Liverpool hosted Wolverhampton Wanderers. Paul Lambert's side were 18th in the Championship and generally having a poor season.

Klopp knew Lambert from his time at Dortmund, with the former Scottish midfielder still revered at the German club after being a part of the 1997 Champions League winning side. He was also on the same coaching course when the two were earning their badges in Germany.

It turned out to be another torrid game of frustration and mistakes for Liverpool as Lambert got one over on his old friend with a 2-1 win. Two first half goals from Wolves were enough, with Liverpool only registering a late consolation through Divock Origi.

The Reds fans headed for the exits, keen to turn their back on a week where they had lost three home games after having gone a year undefeated at Anfield. Not only that, but all three games were lost to weaker opposition who had played the same way; turning up to defend and hit Liverpool on the break. It was a simple tactic, but it had worked, three times.

Klopp had claimed that his side had played well against Southampton and had been unlucky in that particular defeat, but there was no sugar-coating this one. It had been a drab performance from a team drained of confidence.

The manager said, 'Very [disappointing], again. Cup games like this are always difficult [and] in our situation, after losing two games, not full of confidence, not flying through the league. We made a lot of changes, of course, most of them because we couldn't do it differently, but a few because we wanted [to].'

When asked about the effect of the bad run of form on confidence, Klopp added, 'We spoke about confidence a few months ago and I said it's a little flower. If something bounces on it, then it's away. Obviously, that happened kind of, but it's not that we play without confidence. I can see a lot of moments when we really still believe in our skills and all that stuff. So we don't have to make it too big, but it's not that difficult. It's not that I say there's no chance until Tuesday to make a real turn.

'Somebody asked me a second ago if this is the lowest point of my Liverpool time until now – I don't know. But if it is, it's the perfect point to turn because it's not possible to go lower. That's all we have to think about now. It's not that hard but it feels in this moment – and is absolutely right – bad.

'We have to use it. In this moment, it's not the right time to talk too much about being positive and optimistic. No doubt from tomorrow on we will be, but in this moment we feel really bad.'

The media were scathing in their comments about Klopp's team selection, with former England strikers and *Match of the Day* pundits Gary Lineker and Alan Shearer the most vocal in their criticism.

Lineker tweeted during the game, 'Don't get Klopp playing his reserves with no European football. Shows a lack of knowledge of the depth in English football and respect.'

Shearer said during the BBC's FA Cup coverage the day after Liverpool's loss, 'Clubs care about money and fans care about trophies – and it's very unfortunate.

'I don't get – and never have done – the resting of players. I used Liverpool as an example yesterday, [they] changed the team again.

'Liverpool aren't even in Europe. Liverpool have 16 league games left this season, in four months. They could have had an extra four games. It's just crazy. I don't understand it.

'I'm all for bringing young kids into the team, but not six, seven or eight of them. One or two, yes, so they can mix with the experienced guys and get a taste for first-team football – but not for seven or eight.'

Klopp had actually only selected four young players. Plenty of other Premier League and even Championship clubs had also made significant changes to their team over the same weekend due to a full programme of league games being scheduled for the following Tuesday and Wednesday. Southampton made ten changes from the team that had won at Anfield and were duly thrashed 5-0 at home to Arsenal.

However, the three home defeats had drastically changed the tone at Liverpool, certainly among fans who were beginning to become concerned that their season was getting away from them. After all the good feelings around the club through the first half of the season, in the space of eight days they had been eliminated from both domestic cup competitions and fallen ten points off the pace in the race for the title.

Some believers were starting to become doubters again.

26

'As long as this club keeps the nerve and what kind of power we can create, it's outstanding. Let's stay cool and have a little bit of fun when you think about Liverpool and look ahead.'

AS the home clash with Chelsea came over the horizon, things looked bleak for Liverpool. Just a couple of weeks earlier fans had been looking ahead to this fixture as one that could get them back into the title race. Now it was being billed as a must win just to stay ahead in the fight for the top four.

The Blues were running away with the Premier League title. After Liverpool had defeated them at Stamford Bridge early on in the season, Arsenal beat them 3-0 at the Emirates Stadium. This led to Antonio Conte switching to his favoured three at the back system, and from then on Chelsea were practically faultless, winning 15 of their next 16 league games.

Even an in-form Liverpool side would have found the fixture daunting, but this Reds team was shorn of confidence and coming off three home defeats in a week. If Chelsea added to that run, Klopp's side would become the first in English history to lose four home games in 11 days.

One plus for Klopp was the return of Sadio Mané. The influential attacker had agonisingly missed the crucial penalty in a shoot-out between Senegal and Cameroon in the African Cup of Nations quarter-final, and after his tears had dried, Liverpool tried to get him on a private flight back to England. Complications meant that the departure was delayed until the Monday, but he arrived in time to make the squad.

Klopp decided to leave him on the bench in the hope he could be an impact sub should the game call for it.

Chelsea's team was as expected. Conte had enjoyed the luxury of being able to field near enough the same 11 players in every game during the season, though the Italian did make one slight alteration, bringing Willian in for Pedro.

Klopp named close to his full-strength team, giving Matip his first league start of 2017, while Lallana remained a part of the front three with Coutinho and Firmino.

Nerves were jangling ahead of the clash, but they didn't show in the opening minutes as the Reds took the game to the league leaders. Chelsea had built their season on being incredibly strong and organised, and it was showing here as, although Liverpool were dominating the ball and moving it around at a good pace, they were unable to create much in the way of chances, barring one good strike from distance from Wijnaldum that Thibaut Courtois pushed wide.

Klopp will have been pleased with his team's start though. They were showing no fear and playing a patient but dominant game. It then came as somewhat of a shock when the visitors took the lead.

Eden Hazard won a free kick by suckering Lallana into a challenge 30 yards from goal. As Simon Mignolet was organising his wall, David Luiz ran up and smashed the ball hard and low and it found the net via the inside of the post. Mignolet protested but referee Mark Clattenberg had blown his whistle and Luiz took full advantage.

Liverpool were deflated, and didn't manage to provide a reply before the end of the first half.

An issue Klopp's men had been having in recent games was going behind and then being unable to break through an opposition that had something to protect, and this Chelsea team had been comfortably the best in the country at holding on to leads. The key for the Reds was to not become desperate, and they remained calm and patient in the second half. Eventually it led to a clear-cut chance as a neat move and a kind deflection presented the ball to Firmino inside the box, but he snatched at it and side-footed well over the bar. It felt like a big chance gone, but another was on its way.

Henderson received the ball on the edge of the box and whipped it to the left. Coutinho headed the ball back across the area and Wijnaldum got on the end of it to head the ball low and out of the reach of Courtois. Anfield erupted and Liverpool were level.

With 15 minutes to go, Klopp brought Mané on to try and force a winner against a tiring Chelsea defence. The crowd cheered with appreciation and relief that the Senegalese was back in red, but their relief was soon tested as mere seconds later, Chelsea had a penalty.

Diego Costa had run through on a counter-attack and gone down under a challenge from Matip. The Spain international stepped up himself as the Kop held its breath. They soon exhaled with more relief as Mignolet tipped the penalty wide.

After the save, Klopp was seen to turn to fourth official Neil Swarbrick and scream aggressively in his face. Swarbrick did not react though, even raising a smile, and Klopp did not receive any punishment from Clattenberg.

After the game, a sheepish Klopp revealed that what he actually said was, 'Nobody can beat us!' and apologised to Swarbrick for the outburst, who apparently just responded by saying he liked Klopp's passion, but the German added, 'I can't give a guarantee that it won't happen again. I could say now that it won't, but that would be a lie. That's why there are fines for it. If we go over the top, then give us a fine. It's right that we should pay the penalty.

'Managers are not by nature the kind of people who want to have a go at the referee. Do you think Arsène Wenger is a person who, when he sees the fourth official, wants to punch him? That's not how he is and everybody knows it. It happens because of the circumstances, not because of the personality.

'Sometimes you can't control yourself and you say things like, "Nobody can beat us." I have never heard a more silly sentence, given that we'd lost the three previous matches.

'And as for how I looked when saying it ... I was lucky in the way the fourth official reacted and I hope he didn't get into trouble because of it. His was the reaction of a human being.'

Both teams tried to win the game in the late stages, with Pedro whizzing a shot past the post before Firmino could only head a good chance straight at Courtois in stoppage time.

Klopp had to settle for a draw, but it was only the second time a team had prevented Chelsea from winning a league game in their last 17.

While it meant that the gap between the two remained at ten points, Arsenal had been beaten at home to Watford while Tottenham could only draw at Sunderland, so it was a helpful point in the race for the Champions League.

Klopp was satisfied with his team's performance, and in particular because he could see that they were carrying out his instructions. He said, 'I am happy about the performance. I think it was obvious we played against an outstanding strong, outstanding experienced side. I thought we did well; from the first second we were in the game and were aggressive. It felt a little bit to me tonight like [in the] red shirt, we played with readiness, passion, will, greed against experience and coolness, and that's quite difficult.

'I've said it again a few times – I really prefer a draw like this with a good performance than to have three points and no idea why we got them.

'I am really fine with the performance and I am happy we could give a little sign we are still part of the league and we're still playing football – and sometimes, really good.'

Klopp also seemed to be upbeat about what this meant for the remainder of the season, and urged people to be cool about where things were headed.

He continued, 'Unbelievably good atmosphere, I have to say, but this club – we all have to learn. We need to learn to keep our nerve. If you put us in a time machine and brought us 15 matches before the end in fourth position ... "Come on, let's play 15 games with all you have, with everything, full squad, go for it," who would say, "Oh no, please"?

'I'm pretty sure if we'd won tonight a few guys would have said, "Yes, but we lost at Burnley." I don't understand this, but when we were really good in the season then we conceded too many goals, then we should've already bought new defenders, all that stuff.

'Stay cool, that's a season, a football season, we've worked really hard. As long as this club keeps the nerve and [then with] what kind of power we can create, it's outstanding.

'Let's stay cool and have a little bit of fun when you think about Liverpool and look ahead and, yes, nothing has been decided until now, but we have a chance. So, go for it and then if not, then it's 14 games, 42 points – go for it. There's a lot to get for us and we will see where it ends.'

One person who did not take kindly to Klopp's behaviour on the touchline was José Mourinho. The former Chelsea boss raised it in his post-match comments following Manchester United's 0-0 draw with Hull City, insinuating that Klopp was getting preferential treatment whereas he would be punished for such an act.

'I don't want to speak much because I pay lots of fines,' Mourinho told Sky Sports. 'I pay more than others, much more than others. For example, yesterday one manager was told by an official, "I love your emotion."

'Today I was told to sit down or I have to go to the stands. On the pitch was the same. I don't want to speak much because I don't want to pay fines.'

It was not the first time that the Portuguese had aimed a jibe at Klopp unprovoked.

In response, Klopp stated that he may well have been lucky, but seemed surprised that the United manager had chosen to comment.

'Maybe I was lucky that fourth official said something like that, I never heard something like this before, it was the first time,' he responded.

'There are different ways to handle a situation, it is quite an emotional game and switching off emotions is not that simple.

'Myself, José, Arsène, we struggle in moments like this. We are all different, sometimes we get a fine, sometimes not. It's not what we want to do, nor is it a tactic. It was worse for me when I was younger! I have already improved.

'I have no idea why he [Mourinho] spoke about me, you will have to ask him.'

For some reason the Chelsea game had been scheduled for 31 January, which also happened to be transfer deadline day. Several clubs were having to juggle playing games with trying to seal last minute deals for players. That was one distraction that hadn't affected Klopp though as he had no incoming business to take care of.

The only deal involving the club that went through saw Mamadou Sakho join Crystal Palace on loan. The Frenchman hadn't played all season after his summer falling-out with Klopp, and after reportedly refusing to go out on loan the previous August, had decided it was time to play first-team football again and headed to south London.

The lack of new faces in the January transfer window was a bit of a sore spot for fans, who believed that the recent poor run was indicative of a squad that was too thin and too lacking in quality.

Many had assumed that the club had a plan in place for when Mané went off to Africa, but no signing was forthcoming. Reports suggested that questions had been asked about the likes of Julian Brandt from Bayer Leverkusen and Christian Pulisic from Dortmund, but that neither club had been willing to listen before the end of the season. Those same reports said that Klopp had been interested in trying to bring in Julian Draxler from Wolfsburg, but the German international opted to head to Paris Saint-Germain instead.

As the window went on and as Liverpool continued to play poorly, lose games and exit competitions, the ire from fans and pundits grew and grew. Some were questioning Klopp and whether he was being too frugal with the club's money, or trying to be too clever for his own good, while others looked to the owners, claiming that FSG were not giving Klopp money to spend.

Klopp maintained that he had the full backing of his employers, and that he was not interested in short-term fixes or panic buying for the sake of it. He wanted the right players and was prepared to wait for them.

However, what happened in the next game at Hull brought the questions right back at him.

The Tigers had been comfortably dispatched 5-1 at Anfield earlier in the season, and had since changed their manager, bringing in former Olympiakos and Sporting Lisbon coach Marco Silva. The Portuguese had gotten Hull organised, and just days earlier held Manchester United to a goalless draw at Old Trafford.

Liverpool knew this would be a harder test than the reverse fixture, but with the creative foursome of Lallana, Mané, Coutinho and Firmino starting together for the first time since November's thrashing of Watford, hopes were high that the Reds could finally record their first league win of the year.

However, that didn't happen. Klopp's men were lacklustre once again, and predictably struggled to break down a resolute Hull team. They were dominating the ball but doing nothing with it. Over the course of the game they put 45 crosses into the box, and had managed just two attempts on goal from them.

As if the game wasn't running to the 2017 script enough, they fell behind from a set piece just before half-time. A corner was headed down into Mignolet's hands, but the Belgian goalkeeper dropped it under pressure from Abel Hernández and Alfred N'Diaye prodded home.

Reports after the game said that the half-time break saw Klopp react furiously with his team, giving them a dressing down for failing to execute the agreed gameplan. It led to a slightly improved performance in the second half, but not in terms of being able to find a way past the hosts.

Sturridge, Moreno and Origi were sent on in search of the equaliser, but it was no good, and just to put the cherry on the cake, Hull broke on the counter at the death and doubled their lead. To make matters worse, it was an Everton player who scored it. Oumar Niasse, on loan from the Toffees, slotted past Mignolet to seal the game.

After providing hope that their slump was over against Chelsea, Liverpool had put in what many called their worst performance of the season at the KCOM Stadium, and those who had been denying it previously were now admitting that this was becoming a crisis.

Any doubts that lingered about the severity of the loss will have disappeared after Klopp's press conference, where for the first time in the entire period he looked a broken man.

'I have done four or five TV interviews, three or four radio interviews, and usually after half an hour you feel better because you have no time to think about a lot of things after the game, and then you immediately start answering questions. But this time, it doesn't feel better,' he said.

'We have to take all of the criticism. Not even a week ago in the press conference, I spoke about expectations at Liverpool and said, "Come on, it's allowed to have a positive look on the situation, we are still fourth in the league," and everything like this – but after a game like this, it's not allowed to say something like this.

'We expect more from ourselves and we have to show more than we did today. It is my responsibility to make it possible for the players to show more than we showed today. A few things, little, little explanations, you could see – a lack of rhythm in a few players and all that stuff.'

Hard questions were being asked, including whether this defeat had been a fatal blow to Klopp's targets for the season.

'That's not my biggest problem. I want to play much better football with my team. It's not about where you want to be, you have to show what you should reach in a season. We showed it a few times, but obviously it [was] long ago we showed it consistently. This is, first of all, what we have to change, immediately. We need to show much more consistency than we do now on the positive side.

'The Champions League is an outstandingly big, big, big target. It's fantastic and so many teams want to play there. To qualify for the Champions League in England is outstandingly difficult because of so many challenges – but after the performance of today, we don't have to talk about this. We have to show now, really, that we are really ready to go for everything. I can say it, but it will not change a lot – we have to show it together.'

It was a body blow, and put Liverpool 13 points behind Chelsea. Any faint hopes of the title were over. After Manchester City beat Swansea the following day, the Reds dropped to fifth, and were just one point ahead of Manchester United.

As expected, the fallout wasn't pretty. Liverpool had gone from a title challenge to questions being asked about whether top four was even likely in a matter of weeks. Articles were being written left, right and centre about their collapse in form, with most fingers pointing to the idea that the players simply couldn't sustain the high-energy, high pressing game that Klopp had implemented.

For the first time in his Liverpool career, Klopp was being seriously questioned. There was never really any notion that his job might be under threat, but former players were starting to stick the knife in. Dietmar Hamann suggested that it was 'madness' to give him a long-term contract the previous summer, while Jamie Carragher said that it was no longer difficult to beat Liverpool, and that Klopp's side had become 'predictable'.

It felt eerily similar to Klopp's final season at Dortmund, where his side suffered numerous defeats despite dominating possession, and conceding soft goals to teams they should have been beating. The concern was that this run of form had come at Liverpool far earlier in the process.

The other side of the argument though pointed out that while that season had largely been a disaster for Klopp, he was able to turn it around in the second half of it after a winter break where he was able to get his team back to basics on the training field. He would not enjoy such a luxury at Liverpool, but would at least be getting far more time between games from February onwards.

His team had been forced to play 12 times in a 40-day period after Christmas, but would only have four games over the next 40. This would give Klopp and his coaching staff time to try and rectify the errors that were creeping evermore into the team's play and to push on in the final 14 games of the season to at least secure the season's original aim of Champions League qualification.

Klopp made just one change from the side that lost at Hull when he welcomed Mauricio Pochettino and Tottenham to Anfield.

On paper it was the last game Liverpool wanted in their current form. Spurs had the best defence in the league, and the Reds had been struggling to break down some of the worst. Pochettino also had his best attackers available, with Christian Eriksen, Son Heung-min, Dele Alli and Harry Kane collectively firing Tottenham to second place.

The north London side were also in form heading into the clash at Anfield, having been the only team to beat Chelsea since September and comfortably dispatching Middlesbrough the week before.

More than ever, Klopp needed a big performance from his team. He needed to see that they were capable of being the Liverpool he knew they could be, and he wasn't left disappointed.

From the first whistle his team were at Tottenham's throats; Firmino pressing from the front, Lallana backing him up, Mané and Coutinho keeping the full-backs under pressure, and Matip and Lucas mopping up anything that went anywhere near Kane.

The one change Klopp had made was to bring Wijnaldum back in for Can, and it proved to be a very good decision. The Dutch midfielder put in his best performance since arriving in the summer, and was almost single-handedly dominating what was a very strong Tottenham midfield duo of Victor Wanyama and Mousa Dembélé.

His influence bore fruit on 16 minutes as some Reds pressing saw the ball come to him on the halfway line, and seeing the run of Mané, he put the Senegalese attacker in on goal. Mané outpaced the chasing defenders and lifted the ball past Hugo Lloris to open the scoring. Klopp punched the air in delight, as did the rest of Anfield.

They didn't stop there though. Just two minutes later Mané won the ball high up from Toby Alderweireld. He squared it for Lallana, whose shot was saved by Lloris. The Frenchman also stopped Firmino with the follow-up, but Mané was there again to slam into the roof of the net and make it 2-0.

This was Klopp's Liverpool; back to their best in an instant and Mané was running the show. His pace in behind had been sorely missed during the African Cup of Nations, but it was the catalyst in Liverpool returning to their devastating selves.

He had made headlines a couple of seasons earlier with a hat-trick for Southampton against Aston Villa that took just under three minutes to complete, smashing the record previously held for the fastest Premier League treble by former Liverpool hotshot Robbie Fowler. He wasn't in danger of breaking it again in this game, but came very close to what would have been a six-minute hat-trick as he ran through after a mishit backpass, only for his shot to hit the inside of Lloris's leg and just go wide.

The key thing for Klopp in the second half was to manage the game. There was noticeably less all-action pressing and racing forward, but it appeared to be deliberate as Liverpool did indeed play out the game. Spurs barely threatened at all, and Coutinho nearly made it three late on with an effort that was dragged wide.

A comfortable 2-0 win against top six rivals was just what Klopp and his team needed as they recorded their first league win of 2017.

Such was the high level of performance, it was back to the familiar sound of the Reds being praised by the opposition post-game.

Spurs midfielder Eriksen said, 'They pressed high, we knew that but we didn't come out properly and that gave them gaps that they managed to find a way through.

'We know it's tough at Anfield but we could have done much better. They played like we normally play but today, there was really only one team on the pitch.'

Klopp was effusive in his praise of his players. The relief was clear in his voice that the team had rediscovered their verve and proven the doubters wrong who had questioned their ability to return to that level. Asked how happy he was with the result and performance, he answered, 'Very – with both. It can be different, you can win a game and you are not happy with the performance. Tonight I'm really happy with the performance, with a few specific things of the performance. First half, the offensive part of the game was really strong, really direct, really clear, really together. The second goal showed [it]. I don't know how many players tried to finish, at the end Sadio could finish.

'Then in the second half, in a situation like our situation – of course, we knew that we had to show a reaction – you cannot expect the highest confidence. It's more you have to fight yourself [into] the game. It was very important that today we did both – we fought and we played.

'Then, the second half was another game and a different game. Tottenham changed formation a little bit already in the first half. [We had] to adapt to this a little, it's difficult with three offensive players in the centre. But we really dealt well with it and were really concentrated, improved defensively in this game and learned from the game. That was really good and I think it was absolutely well deserved. The atmosphere, fantastic, you could really feel that everybody was waiting for a game like this again. So, for tonight everything is good.'

When asked where such a good display came from, he added, 'Maybe only the older people in the room can remember when we played really well in other games in the first part of the season. I know when we struggle and I know the reasons – it's about rhythm, it's about shape. If it's not about attitude, which I'm sure about, then it is rhythm, shape and a little bit of luck. So, being injured in the wrong moment is really difficult to deal with. We had a few of these things. Of course we missed Sadio in January – each team in the world would have missed him. So that's all part of the truth, but it's not that we played 20 games really bad. We played a few.

'Now we are back in this race and we have to use this situation. Even [though] we didn't perform fantastically in January, we are still in a really good position in the league. I don't want to find excuses for the not-so-good games or whatever. I know that it will come up before the Leicester game and everybody will ask, "What will you do now against a counter-attacking team … deep defending?" all that stuff. It's not that we have no idea about it, but we need the boys in the best shape and then you need to make the right decisions on the pitch.

'For this moment, we are there and we now have 14/15 days [until the next game]. There will be two or three days' rest for the boys and then it is pre-season [training] for the rest of the season. We have to use this. Whatever I could say tonight, in a very good mood obviously, would not help. We have to use the team and show them again that we are there.

'I thought tonight it was really nice to watch how the whole of LFC reacted – not only the team, but the crowd. They could have been much more critical – I am not long enough here to understand how the crowd reacts here, but the reaction tonight … they were waiting a little bit for us, "Come on, show something." Then we showed something and it was fantastic.'

Inevitably, the question of whether this meant his team were looking to catch Chelsea again came up. 'What would you think about me if I would say now that I think we can [catch] them? Really ambitious or crazy? Maybe you can imagine that I'm not too interested in this in the moment because the only possibility to win something is to win football games and we started 2017 – if you want – tonight and we should not go nuts immediately and talk about all the rest. Let's take it step by step. Chelsea don't look too much like they could struggle … If they do then [there] will be somebody. I'm not sure if we [will be] there but we'll try everything to get as many points as we can get from the season and then we count and see what it was worth.'

The following day Chelsea did drop two points in a 1-1 draw at Burnley. The Blues remained eight points clear at the top of the league with 13 games to play, and 11 clear of Liverpool. However, second to sixth was gearing up to be a fascinating tussle where three out of the five teams would qualify for the Champions League. Manchester City were second on 52 points, but Manchester United were sitting sixth on 48. In just a couple of weeks the entire order could swap round, and so it was imperative that Liverpool followed up the Spurs win in their remaining fixtures.

27

'Usually, you win games and you lose against the big teams because at the beginning, when they are at a higher level, they are smarter and more experienced and you lose the games. We've chosen another way but it's still part of the deal and we know that we have to keep on going – and we will.'

KLOPP had mentioned in his post-Tottenham press conference that he would be using the 16-day break between that game and the next one at Leicester to prepare his squad for the remainder of the campaign.

The previous season during an international break in the March, he took the players who didn't travel with their respective countries to Tenerife for a warm-weather training camp. It worked wonders as his team finished the season strongly so he did a similar thing here, only with his whole squad.

The club booked four nights at the five-star Hotel Principe Felipe in La Manga, Spain. It was a resort that Klopp knew well as he had taken his Dortmund teams there in previous years.

Klopp indicated that this would essentially be a mini pre-season, and that with the gap between games, he could prepare the squad to take to the field at Leicester almost as if it were the first game of the campaign.

He gave the squad three days off after the Tottenham win so that they were fresh and prepared for hard work in the warm climate of the south coast of Spain.

All first-teamers who were fit were taken, as were selected youngsters including Trent Alexander-Arnold, Ben Woodburn, Harry Wilson and Conor Masterson.

The players and staff cycled to and from their double training sessions. The weather wasn't typical of southern Spain, but it was better than back in England and ideal for training at optimum intensity.

As well as training, Klopp organised small-sided games, and the squad were divided up into four teams – red, yellow, white and black – for a six-a-side tournament on the Thursday afternoon.

Fittingly, the red team won, consisting of Roberto Firmino, James Milner, Joe Gomez, Gini Wijnaldum, Connor Randall and Masterson.

As a punishment, the team that finished last was made to jump into a freezing cold outdoor swimming pool. The black team was made up of Sadio Mané, Adam Lallana, Ragnar Klavan, Nathaniel Clyne and Kevin Stewart, and jumped into the icy water that no one else had dared to all week.

One player who didn't have to face the same fate was Daniel Sturridge, but that was because he was already suffering from illness. As his virus was contagious, he was sent home from the trip to recover in England.

Another of Klopp's attempts at building team bonding scenarios was to make his players share rooms. They usually had a room each for away trips, but for their stay in La Manga the manager decided to pair them up, and at random as well. He conducted an FA Cup style draw to determine who would room with who. Some of the pairings included Jordan Henderson and Sheyi Ojo, Milner with Mané, Firmino with Loris Karius and Lallana with Alex Manninger.

Klopp told the *Liverpool Echo* during the stay, 'Simon Mignolet is with Conor Masterson, I'm not sure that Simon even knew Conor before this trip. But after four days here he really will.

'The players are learning more about each other. Everything has been perfectly organised.

'We've had a few meetings and we'll have a few more of them. I'm enjoying it and I think the players are too.'

On the first night of the trip, Klopp and his staff were in the hotel bar watching Bayern Munich decimate Arsenal 5-1 in their Champions League round of 16 first leg. While he was happy that he could take his squad away for a mini-break from the stresses of domestic football, he clearly would rather have been testing his wits and his squad against Europe's best instead.

In a separate interview with the *Echo*, he said, 'Things that I don't have, I don't miss. But of course I enjoyed being in that competition [the Champions League] a lot and that's where we want to be.

'To achieve that we need to qualify. We didn't qualify this season. We are working to go there as soon as possible.

'We saw this week again what a strong competition the Europa League is too. Strong teams, intense games. We enjoyed it last season, well we did until the last matchday! We had some wonderful games in that competition.

'But of course the Champions League is *the* competition. We want to be part of it. To get there we have to win a few games.'

The Reds had not been in Europe's premier competition since the 2014/15 season, when they had softly bowed out in the group stage. They also missed out on qualification under Klopp when they lost the Europa League Final, but it was clear from Klopp's words that he felt his team were ready to be back there. In order to do that, they would need to ensure a top-four finish.

The squad returned to Merseyside on the Sunday night, with eight days until their next game, which would allow them a full week at Melwood to prepare.

Melwood had been Liverpool's training base since the 1950s, housing the most successful teams in the club's history along the way. Bill Shankly revolutionised it when he arrived in 1959 and Gerard Houllier had overseen a modernisation just after the millennium, but by now it was too small and dated for a club of Liverpool's stature.

Klopp also didn't like that it was only home to the first team, while the youth teams trained at the academy complex five miles away in Kirkby. He often brought youth players to Melwood to train with the first team, but would rather have been able to watch all of the youngsters at close quarters without having to go between the two sites.

Rumours had been swirling about Klopp's desire to merge. The previous July when he had signed his new six-year contract, the German had said, 'We think about building a new academy or bringing the academy and Melwood together. Things like this – it's much longer term than my contract.

'It's important we do the right things so this wonderful club can be successful both in these six years but later on too. We are very responsible for the club.'

News was confirmed just after the squad came back from Spain that the club would be paying £50m to turn the Kirkby site into an all-encompassing world-class club training facility. The work would not be completed until the summer of 2019, but it was yet another example of the forward planning from Klopp, and the extreme faith in his ideas that the owners had.

The elongated break was over and Liverpool had to prepare to visit the home of the stuttering champions, Leicester. The Foxes had stunned the world with their unlikeliest of Premier League title wins the season before, but had struggled so badly to repeat the trick that they went into this game in the relegation zone.

They had been largely schooled by Sevilla in the first leg of their Champions League last-16 tie a few days earlier, but had scored an away goal and ended the game strongly. In spite of that, a day later the club shocked the world for the second time in a year when they sacked the manager who had won them the only league title of their 133-year history, Claudio Ranieri. The popular Italian paid the price for poor form, but received almost universal support from the football world.

The obvious concern for Liverpool was that Leicester would go into the game with so-called 'new manager bounce', with caretaker boss Craig Shakespeare on the sidelines opposite Klopp.

The Liverpool manager was inevitably asked about Ranieri's sacking at his pre-match press conference, to which he responded, 'There have been a few strange decisions in 2016/17. Brexit, Trump and Ranieri. You have to ask Leicester why they have done it.'

Klopp had also warned in the build-up, even before Ranieri's sacking, that Leicester could well find their form again soon, and that Liverpool might be the first team to face the 'new' Leicester.

A big blow was dealt to Klopp before the game after it was confirmed that Jordan Henderson had picked up a foot injury in training. He would not play again for the rest of the season. Dejan Lovren and Daniel Sturridge had also failed to recover in time, and so Klopp was once again down to the bare bones, with the likes of Kevin Stewart, Trent Alexander-Arnold and Ben Woodburn named on the bench. Lucas continued at centre-back with Joel Matip, while Emre Can came in to replace Henderson.

In spite of Klopp's warning, many were uncertain which Leicester would turn up. As it turned out, they very much bounced.

Dominance from the league champions saw them go 3-0 up by the hour mark. Jamie Vardy in particular had again been a thorn in Liverpool's side with two goals, and despite a nicely worked Coutinho consolation, it was another drab performance and defeat.

Many thought a corner had been turned against Tottenham, but all it had really done was shine a further light on Liverpool's uncanny ability to play well against rivals and not be able to even play acceptably against weaker teams.

The defeat left the Reds outside the top four and Klopp, as was the case after defeat at Hull, was at a loss to explain what had happened.

'It was not good enough in the beginning, not good enough in the middle and not good enough in the end,' he told the media after the game.

'For us, it is very important to say we cannot blame anybody else for this performance – it's only our responsibility. That doesn't make it better, but we don't want to look for excuses. The job we have to do is to react again on it and then react, react and react. What happened tonight has happened too often this season already. Everybody who has followed us over the whole year knows how good we can be, so that makes it even worse to accept a performance like this tonight.'

Klopp was asked about the inconsistency of his team since the turn of the year, and replied, 'Consistency is to do what you have to do always. We've brought ourselves into a situation where everyone can doubt our attitude. That's really our fault, our mistake and nobody else's. I cannot change the result now but the only thing we can do again is to work on it because you have no other solution.

'You have to work on it and show again, show again and show again. The most important thing is that everybody who is with us, likes us and wants us winning needs to see – and has a right to see – that we only play football for one reason and that's for winning. Even I couldn't see this tonight and I knew we were here because we wanted to win. So, that's a problem. There's not a lot more to say, but a lot to work on.'

After the positivity of the win over Tottenham, the defeat at Leicester did not sit well with the fans. The forums and social media were all of a sudden filled with people questioning Klopp, with accusations ranging from him being too stubborn, not tactically astute enough, not having a 'plan B' and generally being incapable of setting his team up to beat the lesser teams of the league. The doubters were getting louder.

It would be just five days until Klopp would get a chance to make amends, though it came in the form of a top-six encounter with Arsenal at Anfield. The Gunners had been licking their wounds after getting a sound 5-1 thrashing at the hands of Bayern Munich in the Champions League a couple of weeks prior. Since that game

Arsène Wenger's men had only played once, a fairly laboured 2-0 win over non-league Sutton United in the FA Cup, and they had not had another game in 12 days thanks to Southampton's participation in the League Cup Final.

Just as Liverpool had looked rusty at Leicester, Arsenal did here as the Reds came out of the traps fastest, and it took just nine minutes for them to take the lead. A long ball from Mignolet was flicked by Coutinho to Lallana, who released Mané down the right. The Senegalese fired the ball across the box to Firmino, who took one touch to control and another to lift the ball over Petr Čech and into the roof of the net. It was just the spark that the crowd needed, and just the blow that Wenger didn't.

The Gunners boss was under scrutiny like never before. The dam of patience from the Arsenal fans had well and truly burst. There was a sense that Wenger and his team were becoming stale, unable to do any better than a limp title push and elimination from the last 16 of the Champions League. The insipid second-half performance in Munich had been the final straw for many, and a large number of fans were adamant that it was time for Wenger to end his two-decade tenure at the Emirates. As it turned out they went on to win the FA Cup and Wenger signed a two-year extension to his contract, but that prospect won't have calmed Gunners fans during this encounter.

Something that added fuel to the fire was the fact that Wenger had started Alexis Sánchez on the bench. The Chilean was Arsenal's talisman, but he was dropped in favour of Olivier Giroud. Wenger insisted after the game that it was tactical, but stories emerged the following day that Sánchez had been involved in a training ground bust-up over frustrations with the lack of fight from his team-mates in recent games.

Liverpool took full advantage of the civil unrest in the away camp, and made it 2-0 with the greatest of ease on 40 minutes. A move down the left saw Wijnaldum tap the ball inside to Firmino, who remained calm and found Mané in acres of space on the far side. Mané composed himself and smashed the ball into the net to double the lead.

Almost inevitably, Wenger turned to Sánchez at half-time to rescue the game for his team. The former Barcelona man made a difference, forcing the hosts further back and soon finding a way through as he played in Danny Welbeck, who lifted the ball over Mignolet to make it 2-1.

All of a sudden things started to get slightly nervy for Klopp. Both teams were looking for the next vital goal, with Matip failing to connect properly from a Coutinho ball, while Sánchez continued to be a menace at the other end.

Origi came on and nearly made an instant impact as his header from a free kick crashed against the post. However, he would make an impact before the end of the game. Sanchez had a great chance in stoppage time to equalise, but Matip blocked it. The ball came to Lallana who headed upfield. He was surrounded by Arsenal defenders, but turned and somehow played a ball through three players out to Origi on the right, who ran down the touchline, before an early ball in found the marauding run of Wijnaldum and the Dutchman made no mistake in placing the ball with a forceful first-time shot past Čech and into the corner for 3-1.

It was just the response that Klopp needed from his players after the poor showing at Leicester, even if it did just add to the argument that his team could only raise their game against top-six rivals.

Klopp didn't mind though as he warmly spoke of his players' efforts after the game, 'First of all, we were absolutely spot-on from the first second in the game. We played a wonderful first half. It was clear it would be a very intense game, you could see it already with the line-up of Arsenal; okay, Mesut Özil was not in, Sánchez was not in, but pretty much the rest.

'It was clear a response would come from Arsenal and especially when Alexis Sánchez is then on the pitch. On one side, he is a world-class player, no doubt about this. On the other side, he is completely different to Welbeck for example; not better or worse, only different. It took five minutes, but they felt actually like 50, to adapt to the situation.

'We had a really hard week. Directly after the [Leicester] game, I found a few words and it was not asking for friendships. It was pretty clear. Next day, we made the analysis, which was nothing to enjoy for me when I did it and not for the boys when they saw it. But there was a point in the week when we actually had to finish the Leicester game.

'It was absolutely exceptional; we have played and lost games, and not played well in all the games, but in this game [there were] so many bad individual performances and it's really difficult to win a football game. It was frustrating. We are kind of the rollercoaster of the league – a lot of ups and, meanwhile, too many downs.

'But only if you are really silly then you let the bad things have more influence on you than the good things. We have to remind ourselves of the good things and we are ready to go again, if you want.

'The boys showed again what they are capable of. I've said a few times now, I don't like the fact that inconsistency is part of the deal in development. Usually, you win games and you lose against the big teams because at the beginning, when they are at a higher level, they are smarter and more experienced and you lose the games. We've chosen another way but it's still part of the deal and we know that we have to keep on going – and we will.'

The benefit from the win was not only that Liverpool gained three valuable points in the race for the Champions League places, but that rivals Arsenal had not, and were looking likely to drop more if they didn't sort their house out.

It had been a very good response to a setback from the Reds, but right around the corner was another potential hazard. Burnley at home.

The game was supposed to take place in the second weekend of the season, but due to ongoing work at Anfield with the Main Stand, it had to be played at Turf Moor, and Liverpool slumped to a 2-0 defeat at the newly promoted side.

Sean Dyche's men had not just saved their form for Liverpool though. They had been beating all kinds of teams at home since then, and were safely ensconced in mid-table in the Premier League, which was remarkable for a club of their size. They had done it through discipline, organisation and a willingness to win ugly. They were practically everything that usually tripped Liverpool up, and so when they came to Anfield, many anticipated another hiccup.

A blow for Klopp before the game was that Firmino had been ruled out after he picked up a knock against Arsenal, and so Origi started in his place.

The secret to Burnley's success in August had been a fast start, going 1-0 up in the opening couple of minutes, and then sitting back and soaking up pressure. Liverpool enjoyed 81 per cent possession that day, and yet still lost relatively comfortably.

Yet again, the Clarets started quickly and enjoyed much of the early going at Anfield and in the seventh minute they took the lead. An early cross from Matt Lowton somehow got through to Ashley Barnes, who guided the ball past Mignolet.

There was an audible groan around the ground as the same old feelings of impending doom loomed.

However, despite labouring somewhat throughout the half, in first-half stoppage time a ball in from Origi on the left bounced kindly for Wijnaldum, who took a moment to wait for the perfect opportunity before calmly slotting the ball into the net to equalise. Relief was all around at half-time as the Reds went in level, with 45 minutes to go for a crucial winner.

It was a slightly different story in the second half, with the visitors sitting back more and Liverpool performing the basics a little better than they had been. It was still far from a vintage performance though, not least from Coutinho, who to some surprise was subbed off on the hour mark to be replaced by Ben Woodburn.

Just moments later, Origi laid the ball inside to Emre Can, who took aim and fired low and hard into the corner of the net from over 25 yards. It was an inch-perfect strike and sent the Kop wild as the big German slid on his knees in celebration.

There was still time for one more heart-stopping moment as a long throw ended up bouncing to Lowton at the far post, but the full-back could only hook the ball over the bar.

Liverpool held on for the 2-1 win and for possibly the first time in the whole season they had won a game without playing particularly well, which if anything made Klopp even happier.

He said, 'Obviously we all have to get used to it a little bit because it's the first "ugly" game we've won. Usually when we were not at our best we've lost and in a few parts of the game we weren't at our best actually. If you're not at your best it's a close game and that's how it was.

'We knew we had to do better, of course. It was about formation, it was about orientation, that's what we spoke about at half-time. When we played the long balls, we felt not that comfortable today. The plan from the beginning was to mix it up, playing build-up and long ball in a formation for the second balls. Like I said, Burnley was for sure in this part of the game better.

'We defended passionately, that's how it should be [and] our organisation was better. There were a few counter-attacking moments, when we played football in a few moments obviously it felt better, and in the end we won the game and it felt well deserved.'

He also had some specific words of praise for Can, 'Emre is a boy with an outstanding attitude. He's had a few problems with his calf in the last few months, which we couldn't sort quickly enough – not because of our medical department but because sometimes he had it, sometimes not. A lot of specialists have been around to try and find out, but the situation was like this, that we could not say, "Go on holiday for four weeks and maybe it's better then" – that's not the situation. So it looks like we've found the solution now and he doesn't have these problems any more.'

The Reds had won ugly, and gained three points on a weekend where all of their near rivals had been playing in the FA Cup, and so the table was starting to look healthier, five and six points ahead of Arsenal and Manchester United in fifth and sixth, though they did both have games in hand.

There were ten games to go and the race for the Champions League spots was hotting up. Next up for Liverpool was a trip to the Etihad Stadium to face Pep Guardiola's Manchester City.

Guardiola's side were coming off a somewhat ignominious Champions League elimination at the hands of Monaco just days earlier, and would either be lacking confidence or thirsty to get revenge on someone.

A piece of good news for Klopp was the return of Roberto Firmino to fitness and the starting line-up, though he hadn't been able to train for most of the week. There was still no sign of Henderson, Sturridge or Lovren, though the Croat had come through an under-23 game unscathed a few days earlier. He sat on the bench as Klavan continued in his place.

Arsenal had lost again the previous day, 3-1 at West Brom, but Tottenham and Manchester United had both won, and so the pressure was on for City and Liverpool.

The hosts started strongly, trying to utilise the wicked pace of Raheem Sterling and Leroy Sané out wide, particularly the rapid Sterling against the less rapid Milner. The former Liverpool player kept getting caught offside though and breaking down attacks.

Chances were coming at both ends as rain poured down from the Manchester sky. Coutinho received the ball on the left and cut inside, only to fire over the bar. Then the chance of the half came at the other end as a ball across the box from David Silva somehow wasn't turned in by either Sterling or Fernandinho. Replays showed that Sterling was clattered by Milner and the hosts were unfortunate not to get a penalty, but as Wijnaldum had also been brought down in the box by Yaya Touré earlier, it seemed fair that neither were given.

The pace if anything got quicker in the second half. Mané was denied by a last-ditch block by John Stones, but the Reds soon had a better opening. A ball over the top from Emre Can found Firmino in all sorts of space in the City box. The Brazilian went to control the ball with his chest, but was bowled over by a recovering Gaël Clichy, and the referee pointed straight to the spot.

Up stepped Milner, who had been getting booed all game by the City fans after he left them to join Liverpool almost two years prior.

Klopp couldn't watch as Milner sent Caballero the wrong way to notch his seventh penalty of the season. He celebrated, his players celebrated, but there was a long way to go.

The pressure from City was ramped up as the half went on. Guardiola made a tactical change, removing the cumbersome Touré and introducing Bacary Sagna, moving Fernandinho into the middle and pushing Kevin De Bruyne out wide. It worked on 69 minutes as a ball out to De Bruyne on the right found the Belgian in plenty of space, and his inch-perfect ball into the box was finished by Sergio Agüero.

It had been coming, but with over 20 minutes to go it still felt like the game was there to be won by either team. City came very close to a quick second as Agüero and Sané linked up in the box. The Argentine slipped before he could shoot, and De Bruyne could only rattle his effort off the post.

Then it was Liverpool's turn to somehow not score. A wonderful move ended with Wijnaldum chipping the ball into Firmino, who guided the ball into the path of Lallana and he just had Caballero to beat from point-blank range, but somehow missed the ball and the chance was gone.

There was still time for City to have another agonising opportunity come and go as a ball across the box arrived for what appeared to be a simple tap in for Agüero but he managed to volley over the bar from close range.

It had been an exhausting game to watch, akin to a Rocky movie as two heavyweights traded blows, with one clearly on top for a while, until the other fought back with gusto. The game ended with noses proverbially bloodied, but neither able to land the knockout blow. A respectable and very well-earned point to both.

It was a great advert for the Premier League, but also for the impact of outside sources. Both Klopp and Guardiola had come in for criticism from some quarters for their approaches, but both had served up a fantastically exciting and high-quality encounter, not always in terms of defensive play, but in terms of tactically going for the win for the whole 90 minutes. There was no sitting back, no consolidating, just pure unadulterated intent to beat the other team down.

Guardiola said after the game that it had been one of the best of his career. 'I am so proud,' he told the BBC. 'This is one of the most special days of my life.

'Liverpool had all week to prepare and they always fight until the last moment. That is why I am so happy.'

Asked whether he felt his team should have gone on to win the game, Klopp said, 'I feel better [now]. I thought the whole time that everybody around me was so excited, but not in the dressing room actually – they felt a little bit like I did. The wonderful piece of football we did that Adam couldn't finish, unfortunately, that's what brought this situation. But, of course, I know Sergio Agüero could have scored once or twice.

'It's not that I'm not satisfied; it's more that actually I expect things like this from us. That's it. I cannot run around after a draw against Man City. But, of course it's a success. It's good if you get a point here in a game like this. If you can perform like this, that's positive too. I'm fine.'

When asked about Lallana's miss he added, 'Obviously he's one of the best – if not the best – player, technical-wise, I have ever worked with. If he couldn't [score] in this moment, I thought it was because he worked so hard before.

'Immediately after the game, Adam said "sorry" to me and I thought "why?" – but now I know why he thought he had to say sorry. But he didn't have to because his performance was outstanding again.'

There had been tremendous performances all over the park from Liverpool. Matip was solid, Clyne was much improved on recent showings, Can put in possibly his best game of the season, Wijnaldum and Lallana had been imperious in midfield and Mané and Firmino had both done their bit in attack.

Klopp was asked about the race for the Champions League, with five teams fighting for three places, and whether he was confident that his Liverpool would be among Europe's elite next season.

'We are still in a battle, that's how it is. It's a really important sign that we can already do this. We have to improve – in a game like today, we have to improve and in all of the other games, we have to improve. I know a lot of reasons why we couldn't and, as I said, it's a long-term project and if I wake up every morning and think, "Oh my god, we lost the points there and there," it wouldn't make it better so I don't do it.

'The next game is against Everton, they have come from behind [in the table] and it is quite impressive, so it is not only a derby, it's another very important game.

'The problem is, if you do something like this [draw at Man City] usually it is really positive, but in our case it is not only because it means we could have done better in the other games. In a few of them, yes, but not in all of them because of different reasons.

'There is one outstanding side this year – an outstanding and consistent side – and they will be champions probably [Chelsea]. That is then well deserved and all the rest fight with all they have for the Champions League. We are one of these sides and that's good. If you do it, it's a success and if we don't do it, we will be disappointed, but we would not stop working and would not stop believing in this project. We are really convinced about the circumstances we have and we want to use it.'

28

*'I said it pretty early in the season: bad things
are my responsibility and good things are the
responsibility of the players. I thought that's a
fair deal because I have the shoulders to get it,
the age to get it, the experience to get it.'*

BEFORE the Manchester City game, Klopp had been interviewed by Sky Sports. He gave an update on how he was feeling about life at Liverpool, and in spite of the recent setbacks, he seemed very positive.

'It's a fantastic club, it's actually better than I could imagine before I came here,' he said.

'I spoke to Antonio Conte a few weeks ago before the game [against Chelsea] and he said, "How is it?" I said, "Everything perfect apart from the points!" We could have a few more but I really enjoy it here.'

He also spoke of his fondness for his new surroundings outside of work, 'I didn't think too much about the city of Liverpool before, I knew the club obviously but I didn't think about the city.

'That's much better than I thought. All cities in the world have an image, I'm not sure if Liverpool's is the best in the world. But [if you] were never here, please come here and visit this city, it's really nice! Especially the surroundings – we live close to the sea.'

He continued, 'Is it important how long [since] you won something? Or how much you want something? There are a lot of fans who were not alive when we won the last title, my job is to make it more likely.

'I said it before, we cannot have this fantastic history of this fantastic club in our backpack and carry it around, it makes no sense.

There's pressure, yes, and sometimes we are maybe still not patient enough. In January/February you could feel everybody thought, "It slips – again – through our fingers." But it wasn't again, it was the first time for us, and that's different.

'I feel the maximum support of all the people around, especially of the fans. Supporters still think I'm the right person in the right place, so we feel this trust and faith, and we have to use it.

'Around us is a lot of quality and we need to respect this. Because we want it more or [for longer], doesn't make it more likely. We have to do it better, and that's what we're working on.'

It was time for another international break, with the Merseyside derby at Anfield waiting on the other side.

The vast majority of Klopp's squad had gone, but the ones he was left with went with him to another mid-season training camp in a warmer climate. After the trip to La Manga just a month earlier, the remaining Reds were off to Tenerife for a few days, where they had been 12 months before.

Jordan Henderson was joined by the likes of Alberto Moreno, Loris Karius, Joel Matip, Dejan Lovren, James Milner and Lucas Leiva, as well as a selection of youngsters. Klopp would have them training hard, but also allowed wives and girlfriends to join them, and would then give everyone the weekend off once they returned.

Klopp told the club website, 'The players are here because we have to train. It's a wonderful opportunity that the club gave us, that we can bring all the families with us here, that we have this time and can combine different things.

'We have new players since we were here last year, so we see the kids, we see the wives too. It's really nice. When we flew here yesterday the mood and atmosphere on the plane was outstanding – I think we had 30 or 40 kids on the plane!'

When asked about the idea to bring the players' families along he added, 'We believe in things like this, we believe in atmosphere and that's what we try to create. Having families here helps the players. [Also] Mrs Klavan is here with her two boys, while Raggy is with his national team, and that's really nice.

'It's not easy to have a completely normal private life as the family of a professional football player but it's important that the girls know each other and we try to do things like this as often as possible so they all feel comfortable.

'If you [the players] feel comfortable, it's more likely that you can perform.'

The players may have come back refreshed from Tenerife, but not everyone came back from the international break in prime condition.

Adam Lallana picked up an injury in England's World Cup qualifier with Lithuania and was ruled out for the next four weeks. It was a big blow to lose such a vital player for a crucial and busy period of the season, but was not the first time Klopp had needed to shuffle his pack at the worst possible moment.

There was also the issue that Philippe Coutinho and Roberto Firmino had to be flown back on a private plane from South America to get them back to England in time for the derby. They did make it back in time but it was anyone's guess as to how fit they would be for such a blood and thunder game.

Going into the derby, Everton had a serious injury issue of their own, with right-back Seamus Coleman ruled out for several months after breaking his leg in the Republic of Ireland's clash with Wales. Ramiro Funes Mori was also out for the season, while newly acquired midfielder Morgan Schneiderlin would not be fit in time.

Despite those setbacks, the blue half of Merseyside went into the encounter confident of halting a run that had seen them fail to win a single game against Liverpool since Roy Hodgson's tenure in 2010, and had not won at Anfield since 1999. However, they had been on a run that saw them lose just once in the 12 league games that had gone since the Reds beat them at Goodison Park in December. It meant they started the game just six points behind Liverpool in the table.

Klopp was determined to halt their rise and cement his side in the top four. He was able to start the two Brazilians, but it was the selection of another Brazilian that raised eyebrows.

Lucas was named in midfield, which had been his position for most of his career, but he had not played there for over a year, having been utilised at centre-back throughout the 2016/17 campaign.

Social media practically exploded with Reds fans unhappy that Lucas was getting the nod over a more attacking option to replace Lallana, such as Divock Origi or even young Ben Woodburn.

Before the game there was a minute's applause to honour the memory of club legend Ronnie Moran, who had passed away a week earlier. Moran had spent 49 years at the club as a player, coach and assistant manager, and had been a key member of the legendary 'boot room'. The respect from both sides of the city was a nice moment, and Klopp had said pre-match that he wanted his players to put in a performance worthy of Moran's high expectations.

'Bugsy', as he was affectionately known, would have been smiling down on Anfield in the eighth minute as Mané dribbled through Everton's midfield, played a one-two with Firmino, before running diagonally to the edge of the penalty area and dragging a shot with his left foot towards the far post. Joel Robles was caught flat-footed in the Everton goal as the ball rolled into the corner to give the hosts an early lead. The man who had broken Everton hearts in the late stages of the game at Goodison was at it again.

The visitors had been comprehensively beaten 4-0 in the same fixture the previous year, on a night where they managed just three shots to Liverpool's 37. They would not roll over as easily this time and tried to fight back, with results.

An earlier corner had been whipped on to the head of Phil Jagielka, nearly resulting in a goal. So just before the half-hour mark, they tried it again. Jagielka won it again, and the ball rebounded into the path of Matthew Pennington, who couldn't miss. It was 1-1, and yet another goal conceded from a set piece.

It was a blow for the Reds, but the fans sang in defiance, which could have played a part in the almost instant reply. Coutinho, whose diversionary run off the ball had created space for the first goal, picked up the ball and ran at Idrissa Gueye, taking it past the Senegalese midfielder, before squaring up Pennington. A trademark drop of the shoulder, cut inside and shot into the far corner gave his side the lead again.

The former Inter attacker had struggled to regain his early season form after recovering from a foot injury picked up before Christmas, but it seemed that the trip across the world did him well as he appeared to be back to his best on derby day.

One subplot to the game had been the ferocity of some of the tackles. It is sometimes known as the 'friendly derby', but has also seen far more red cards than any other fixture in Premier League history, and that total should have been added to in the second half as Ross Barkley – as he had done in the reverse fixture – went in studs up on a Liverpool player, in this case Dejan Lovren. The Liverpool-born midfielder again got away with a yellow.

However, disaster was to strike from a more innocuous challenge. Mané and Leighton Baines battled near the touchline, and the England left-back put his foot through the ball to clear it upfield, but Mané caught his leg under Baines's trailing leg on the follow-through. His knee bent in a funny direction and he was down. After some treatment he tried to play on, but immediately fell to the floor again.

After the game it was reported that he left the stadium unaided, but scans later showed that he had suffered meniscus damage and required an operation that would end his season.

Mané had been a sensation in his first year at the club, scoring 13 goals and getting five assists in 27 league games. His team had struggled badly without him when he had been at the African Cup of Nations, but they would have to make do without him again for the crucial league run-in.

His replacement was Divock Origi, who ensured that Reds fans didn't have too long to panic about Mané's situation. Coutinho went on another mazy run and slid the ball behind Origi, who allowed it to run across and on to his right foot, before blasting past Robles and making it 3-1.

After a brief surge from Everton, Klopp's men ended up seeing the game out comfortably, even allowing Trent Alexander-Arnold time to come on and have a speculative effort on goal that nearly made it four. It was one more shot than Romelu Lukaku had managed at the other end. Everton's star striker had been nullified entirely by Lovren, who won headers against him all game.

Another success story had been Lucas, who was an assured and calming presence in the middle, winning headers, tackles and making vital interceptions. Some sheepish Reds fans conceded after the game that not only had Lucas played well, but he may have been man of the match.

Klopp was delighted with the performance, 'I thought it was deserved. Like always, you have to learn a little bit from the game.

'We knew about the intensity we needed to be ready for, and I thought we were. After the first few minutes we controlled the game, we found the spaces between their lines, we brought Phil into really good positions.

'I said to the boys before the game that it needs to be a mixture of being really smart and emotional – not only emotional. I thought they did really well, controlled it and scored fantastic goals. I'm not sure anybody has the assist for Sadio's goal or Phil's goal, they did it pretty much by themselves. It was really nice and important, especially after the equaliser, after a set piece.'

There were also interesting comments regarding how his team had kept themselves relatively composed during a game that had the potential to boil over at points. 'I thought in all three derbies we've played until now, we were exactly like this. I know a few people – especially from other clubs – think I am crazy because I look like I look, I'm sorry for this but I am really emotional. As I have said a few times, my teams are always top of the fair play table because I think aggressiveness is to hurt yourself.

'I thought we did really well, again with the importance of the game, not to show anybody that we would do everything for this derby – we had to play football and use the football to do it. We want to be hard, yes, but against ourselves and we want all the players to leave the pitch without injuries. You cannot avoid injuries in football, as we all know, but a few of them you can.'

Just a few days later they would be back at Anfield hosting Bournemouth, and Klopp was eager to get a rallying cry in ahead of another vital game in the race for the top four. 'The next game, Wednesday, we will be ready. It's another home game and a night game, and I can say immediately to everybody who will be here: please start warming up already. We need each voice and we need everybody to create another outstanding performance.'

It was a big win for Liverpool, not only bursting the bubble of their rivals and opening up a nine-point gap, but it came on a weekend where others around them dropped points. Manchester United were held to a draw by West Brom at Old Trafford, and the following day saw Manchester City and Arsenal cancel each other out in a 2-2 at the Etihad Stadium. There was also the fact that leaders Chelsea had been surprisingly beaten 2-1 at home to Crystal Palace. Thoughts of catching Antonio Conte's side weren't overly realistic but it pleased Liverpool fans nonetheless, especially as at the heart of Palace's resolute defence at Stamford Bridge was Reds loanee Mamadou Sakho.

The game with Bournemouth was a chance for payback. The reverse game on the south coast had been seen by many as the catalyst for the collapse of Liverpool's title challenge, given the dramatic way they managed to lose despite having a 3-1 lead with a quarter of the game remaining.

On this night they would be left frustrated again. After falling behind early on, Liverpool turned it around to 2-1 thanks to Coutinho and Origi, only for Bournemouth to equalise late on.

The wave of elation after the Everton win was replaced by a 'not again' feeling, exacerbated after it emerged that Tottenham and Arsenal had both won. Manchester City lost at Chelsea, while Manchester United had been held to another draw by Everton the previous night. With five minutes to go in both games, Liverpool had been level on points with Tottenham, but after Spurs turned their game at Swansea around from 1-0 down to 3-1 up, and the Reds conceding the late equaliser, by the end of the night there was a five point gap.

Klopp was visibly irked by the result, but tried to remain philosophical, 'When you start like this, it makes the game not easier, it makes it more difficult, and you could feel the atmosphere in the stadium was then kind of nervous. The noise was not very optimistic, I would say, with each backpass we played. But in a situation like this you need to stay patient, you need to stay calm and play football.

'There were still a few situations when it looked a little bit stiff and this stuff, but then we scored the goal and that was fantastic, a fantastic moment. We could go in at half-time and start the game new in the second half, which we did.

'We played much better second half, we used the wings better, we played simpler in many situations, we played clearer from behind – in the run of the full-backs, for example. So how we created the second goal was a nice pass from Ragnar to Millie; Millie plays it pretty simple to Phil; Phil very nice to Gini in the box; Gini makes this wonderful move, cross, goal.

'We could have scored the third probably – we had the chances, we had the counter-attacks. But then we had to change Phil because he felt sick at half-time. He vomited. He said he feels better now – that's good – but it was clear when he gave the sign then we had to change. It's no joy when you have to take off the best player in this moment on the pitch, because he played really well.

'The decision was then to organise a little bit differently, three at the back plus the two in front with Lucas and Emre to still give the full-backs the opportunity to use the space on the wings. Against a 4-4-2 system that makes absolute sense. We had the moments and we scored a wonderful goal, and usually you could close the game in one moment. We didn't, we left it open. And then a second ball after a set piece and that made me nearly vomit, actually.

'That's, of course, not nice. But we have to take it. It's my responsibility, all of this. I have to be clearer in these situations, obviously. But I will find a solution for this.'

Klopp was also asked why he insists that he shoulder the responsibility when setbacks such as this one occur, and replied, 'That's life. When my son is doing something that's not right, probably I have a big part of the responsibility. I should have explained better. The boys are obviously not my sons but the situation is not too different – it's my responsibility. I will tell them that they have a part of it, how you can imagine, but there is nothing else to say about it.

'I said it pretty early in the season: bad things are my responsibility and good things are the responsibility of the players. I thought that's a fair deal because I have the shoulders to get it, the age to get it, the experience to get it. But we have to work on it. It's not that I felt immediately it's my responsibility. I thought: what is this? That's really hard to [take] but it's my responsibility.'

The draw with Bournemouth had felt particularly bad because of the games on the horizon. With an increasingly depleted squad, Klopp would next have to take his team on two of the hardest away trips of the season, Stoke and West Brom.

With just three days between Bournemouth and Stoke there was very little time for recovery for any of the players and so many expected a couple of surprises when the team was announced at the Bet365 Stadium. There were more than a couple.

Klopp opted to start with three at the back this time, with Matip, Lovren and Klavan, but decided to move Clyne to the left side and Milner into midfield, starting Alexander-Arnold at right wing-back. He wasn't the only teenager starting though, as Ben Woodburn also came in from the start. Coutinho had not recovered fully from his illness, but there was also an issue with Firmino, who told Klopp that his tank was empty after playing so much football since returning from injury against Manchester City, including his international break trip to South America.

Liverpool's starting line-up was without Jordan Henderson, Lallana, Mané, Coutinho and Firmino, five of the usual starting front six, and so it was little surprise that Stoke dominated the first half. The likes of Xherdan Shaqiri and Marko Arnautović were marauding down the wings and getting balls into the box, as well as getting shots on goal themselves. Shaqiri had a goal disallowed for offside while Arnautović hit the side-netting after Lovren sliced a clearance into the air.

Just before half-time, a rare venture forward from the visitors saw the ball arrive at Woodburn just inside the penalty area. He turned Erik Pieters, only to be clattered to the floor. The referee waved penalty appeals away and played on. Moments later, Stoke were ahead.

Shaqiri took advantage of Clyne being out of position, sped past the covering Klavan, crossed the ball past Matip and on to the head of Jonathan Walters, who scored his seventh goal against Liverpool of his career.

Woodburn and Alexander-Arnold had struggled with the increased physicality of the game, but had far from disgraced themselves. Even so, they both made way at half-time as Klopp felt it was necessary to introduce Coutinho and Firmino. The team had really laboured with the new system, and reverted to a more familiar setup with Clyne back on the right and Milner on the left.

The change made all the difference. Liverpool were vastly improved in the second half, with both Brazilians forcing Lee Grant into saves. A Coutinho corner was then headed against the bar by Lovren. A goal was coming.

Sturridge was introduced for Origi, and he was part of the move that saw Emre Can clip a ball into the box. It fell kindly for Coutinho on the edge of the area and he drilled low into the corner of the goal. Milner collected the ball and the players headed straight back to the halfway line, sure that their momentum would lead to further joy.

Two minutes later, Wijnaldum clipped a long pass over the top for Firmino. The ball held up so he had to slow down slightly, but decided to just hit a shot from range rather than try and shake off defenders. The ball flew over Grant's head and into the net to give Liverpool the lead. The fans went wild and so did Firmino, whipping his shirt off and throwing it into the air. It was the seventh time since arriving in England that Firmino had been booked for removing his shirt in celebration, but no one seemed to mind.

There followed a very nervous moment when a Stoke ball in from the left found Saido Berahino, but Mignolet pulled off a remarkable save from point-blank range. He had also made an earlier save at 1-0 from former Red, Charlie Adam when it looked for all the world that the Scot would score. Mignolet had come in for a lot of criticism at times during his Liverpool career, but he was having an afternoon to remember.

It was a hard-earned three points, and the perfect way to recover from the Bournemouth draw. Klopp thought so too.

'It was very, very important for us. For different reasons, it was really difficult. Stoke is a difficult place to play, to come here it's really difficult to take the points. In our situation, we knew before it is much more difficult but we still thought it was possible.

'The first half was actually not as good as we thought it could be. They were two completely different halves, obviously. We had to change the system; we couldn't train it really. I don't like it too much but the situation forced it.

'We didn't defend like we usually do – we couldn't play high pressure, so we had to stay a little bit deeper, but they didn't create a lot of chances. They scored a goal. This situation was not a question of system, it was only losing two challenges – the first and the second ... goal.

'Then, half-time, it was a difficult decision to make because it was not clear that Roberto and Phil would be ready for 45 minutes. Roberto, after the last game, a guy who usually never says anything about how he feels, said, "I'm really done."

'Phil lost three kilos in the last three days. For most of us that would be good news! But for Phil and a professional football player, it is not as good. He came to the hotel this morning and said, "I'm fine." But we knew he would have a low energy level, full enough for 30 minutes.

'We scored two fantastic goals and played football in the second half. In the first half we didn't play football; it was not because of Trent or Ben, they were not even involved because we [played] always long balls, we tried to find Divock.'

Klopp had words of encouragement for the two youngsters after their 45-minute outing. When asked if he was reluctant to take them off so early he said, 'Usually I would be but we have such a close relationship. All the players went in the dressing room and didn't celebrate and the boys [Woodburn and Alexander-Arnold], they didn't look like it's the best day of their lives. It started like this but didn't end like this, that's life. They don't have to react like adults and they can be disappointed, we will help them more than we help anyone else, but everything is fine – it's not about them, it was not them.

'They have outstanding talents, they are fantastic boys, our boys, so everything will be good. It didn't feel like I want to do it more, or every week, but that's the job.'

Finally, he emphasised just how big he thought the win was in the circumstances, 'Massive, it's absolutely massive. That's how it feels. We have won a few games this year, but this was really special. Today you could feel it immediately in the dressing room ... immediately everybody was like, "That's very important!" Of course, we have to prove it next week and then the next week and then the next week, that's how it is, but it feels outstandingly good in this moment.'

One team who didn't feel outstandingly good was Klopp's former club Mainz. The Bundesliga side had been struggling in the league and found themselves just one point above the relegation zone after a run of five defeats. A group of Mainz fans travelled to Liverpool to meet Klopp and asked him to provide a motivational video message to the club and fans. He reluctantly agreed.

Klopp said in the video, 'Why I was up for talking about the situation? It's just dead important to me.

'When I got asked about my biggest success in my career, everyone expected me to reply the domestic double at Dortmund. And yes, that was extraordinary and fantastic. But looking at our starting position in Mainz in 2001, then it was definitely 23 May 2004, when we won promotion. I will never forget this day.'

He added, 'The people are no longer aware of their responsibility and Mainz was the city where every single person, in the stadium or in front of the TV, was involved in the fight to achieve sporting goals. I loved that.

'We took more knocks than maybe most of the other clubs but we all came out of the situation stronger. Since I will one day return to Mainz to live there, I'd be delighted if it were a still a Bundesliga city.

'I hope that everyone knows what's at stake. We all know that football is not the most important thing in the world, but it's a wonderful way of celebrating success together and also sometimes suffer defeats.

'Nobody's shown that better than Mainz and thus I'd say get up, buy a ticket and shout your heart out. All of Mainz for one goal!'

Whether the video made any difference or not, Mainz did indeed stay up.

Being asked to comment on his former teams was becoming a common occurrence. Borussia Dortmund were due to play AS Monaco in the Champions League quarter-final first leg at Signal Iduna Park.

However, on the way to the game, a bomb went off next to the Dortmund team coach, causing damage to the vehicle and injuring defender Marc Bartra. The Spaniard had surgery on his hand and faced four weeks out, but it was a miracle that there wasn't more damage done to those on board as nails were found embedded in headrests.

UEFA decided to cancel the game, but only for 22 hours. They played the following day, with Dortmund losing 3-2. Former Liverpool player Nuri Şahin and coach Thomas Tuchel both emphasised that the team was in no condition to be playing a game of football, and Tuchel in particular made his frustration with UEFA clear.

At his pre-match press conference ahead of the West Brom game, Klopp was asked for his thoughts.

He said, 'First of all, I don't think what I say is too important, but how everyone can probably imagine, it was a really difficult moment for me because I was, I don't know how often, in the team hotel at

Dortmund with my team. I know exactly the road, exactly the place where it is. A lot of my friends were in the bus.

'At first, I was on the way home from Melwood and I got a call telling me that something happened with the bus. I tried immediately to get some information, it was strange and I was really concerned and I was scared for them. Then how it was for everybody, in the first moment it looked like a little bit of relief or not too serious, then the more information you could get, the more serious it got and that was really difficult.

'Of course, I had contact with a few people but I didn't want to bother them with my silly questions that I had, so I was waiting like all the rest of the world for more information in the media. I tried to watch everything I could watch, I tried to get the information I could get. The last thing I thought about in this moment was the game, actually.

'I watched the game yesterday and I can 100 per cent understand both sides – it was difficult, first of all, to find another date in this really tight schedule because when would you want to play the game? But of course, I think everybody would have understood if [they had said], "Okay, we don't play it, we find a solution next week."

'I saw the game and I was really proud of Borussia Dortmund, how they handled it, how they created this atmosphere. Again, the game was not too important but when they then played the game, they tried to be at their best.

'I heard the interviews after the game and I saw the faces of my former players, saw the shock in their eyes and that was really, really hard, so I forgot the game again immediately, I only thought about them. It was really difficult but a very serious thing and actually that's pretty much all I can say about it.

'It will obviously take time to deal with it in a proper way because I'm pretty sure if somebody of the people who made the decision afterwards would have been in the bus then they wouldn't have played the game. When you're not in the bus then I'm sure you cannot really imagine how it was exactly. The game is over and it's done, it was a football game.

'Now they have a few days to try to learn to live with it, that's how it is. I'm like all the other football fans in the world but the only difference between me and them is that I know all of them, so that makes it more difficult for me, but that's all.'

29

*'Obviously we care; I could see it in a few faces,
I could hear it a little bit from outside. The
boys have delivered a lot of this excitement, but
now it's really about serious football. Do what
you have to do – and we will do.'*

AFTER the tricky away tie at Stoke City, Liverpool now had
to negotiate an arguably trickier game at West Bromwich
Albion.

Trickier not just because they were playing a team in eighth place
who had caused them problems in the past, taking two draws from
the Reds the previous season, but managed by Tony Pulis, who had
never lost a home game to Liverpool in his entire career.

He had built a reputation for creating teams from the most
meagre of ingredients and keeping them in the top division by any
means necessary, but at the Hawthorns he had taken his side to the
top half of the table, and was on course to achieve West Brom's highest
Premier League points total, just two wins away from breaking 50
points for the first time.

Klopp was able to get experience back into the team, with
Coutinho and Roberto Firmino fit to start, while Lucas came back
into midfield.

It was a slow-burning start to the game with little by way of real
chances for either side. Firmino and Coutinho both dragged left-
footed efforts wide, while the hosts could only wonder what might
have been at the other end when Firmino just managed to flick the
ball away from the onrushing Nacer Chadli, who was set to tap in at
the far post. Simon Mignolet then had to deny Wales international

Hal Robson-Kanu, who managed to get through on goal, but his tame effort was easily parried.

It seemed set to go in at the break without the scoreboard being needed, but just before half-time James Milner played in what appeared to be a poor free kick, but Lucas diverted it with his head and Firmino found himself unmarked at the far post to nod in the opening goal.

It would have been a stretch to suggest it had been coming, but there were no complaints from the visitors.

The midfield trio of Lucas, Emre Can and Gini Wijnaldum contained the game well, while anything that got through them was mopped up by the defensive pair of Joel Matip and Dejan Lovren. The duo had only managed to play 13 games together in their first season as Klopp's first choice pair due to persistent injuries to both, but the Reds were yet to lose when they had done.

A wave of pressure came late on, with substitute Salomón Rondón getting past Matip and passing to Matt Phillips, but he was denied superbly by Mignolet.

In injury time the Baggies's goalkeeper Ben Foster decided to go up for a corner. It was cleared and Reds substitute Alberto Moreno snatched the ball and charged up the field. Fellow sub Daniel Sturridge was screaming for a pass, but would have been offside, so Moreno attempted a shot from all of 45 yards at the empty net. Perhaps due to the rustiness that comes with spending the season on the bench, the ball trickled wide. However, the final whistle soon went and Liverpool had clinched the points.

A smiling Klopp put his arms round Moreno, not to strangle him, as he may have done if West Brom had equalised, but to laugh with him about his miss. The relief was clear to see that a big three points had been sealed, the first time a visiting Reds manager had defeated Pulis.

'It is one of the most difficult places to come because in no game can you feel comfortable,' Klopp said. 'Somebody asked me which result would have kept me a little bit calmer in the last few minutes and I said only 4-0 after 86 minutes! Maybe then I would have felt okay, but now it's done.'

One key to the win had been Liverpool's ability to limit the number of set pieces they had to face, keeping the Baggies to just four corners, but Klopp knew that they couldn't overlook the rest of their game.

'With West Brom, it is not only set pieces, they have really good footballers on the pitch and if you're a little bit less aggressive then immediately they use their threat around set pieces to play football because you don't want to go in with real challenges. That makes it really difficult, so you need to be at your highest concentration level – but we have been.

'For us, it was very, very important because showing this concentration level until the end didn't work each week in the last few months – but today, it was really good and I am happy about this.'

Klopp was also asked about the team's record at West Brom.

'Actually, I thought we'd won here last year but that was a draw, so I'm not too good at remembering results! I had no idea [about the record], but you can imagine it's a difficult place to come. It's really three very important points at a difficult place and that's improved our base for the rest of the season so I'm happy about this. Let's carry on.'

Carry on they would, and up next was a home game with yet another side known for their organisation and physicality, Crystal Palace.

In the week leading up to the game Klopp was asked about his plans for the summer, and whether he thought players might be starting to see Liverpool as a more attractive destination than they would have done a year earlier.

'I think that Liverpool at this moment is a really interesting project for players,' the manager said.

'We cannot say 100 per cent we will play Champions League football next year, but it's a young team, it's a fantastic club, it's a good situation where we really can see the progress of the team.

'So I would say together with Tottenham, the average age of the team is such that there's still a lot to come. They are obviously a few steps ahead, but they have played longer together maybe. We feel in a good way, and if a player wants to be part of this way, then it's easier to make this decision this year than last year.

'But actually not a lot of players told me last year, "I don't want to be part of this, but let me see what happens next year and then we can talk again."

'It's more my feeling than anything I could say about what a player thinks. But the talks we've had so far are very positive. That doesn't mean it will all work out, but they are really positive, and they all see the progress. That's good.'

After the West Brom victory, Klopp said that his team played 'adult football', and they would need to do so again to overcome Crystal Palace, who under Sam Allardyce had recovered from a dreadful spell where relegation was seeming to be a real possibility to getting themselves clear of the drop after surprise wins over Chelsea and Arsenal.

On paper it seemed to be a simpler task than the previous two games, but the fact remained that Palace had won at Anfield for two seasons running, including handing Klopp his first defeat as Liverpool manager.

There was more pressure put on the Reds before the game as Manchester United picked up a 2-0 win at Burnley, meaning they were just three points off them with a game in hand, while Manchester City were just two behind, also with a game in hand.

The subplot around the game was predictably the return of Christian Benteke, and the non-return of Mamadou Sakho. The French defender had been in sensational form for the Eagles since joining on loan at the end of the January transfer window, which led to some Reds fans calling for his return to help his parent club in keeping the goals out.

The breakdown in Sakho's relationship with Klopp though meant that a reconciliation was unlikely.

Benteke inevitably did play a part though.

It was Liverpool who started on top and took the lead from a piece of brilliance as Coutinho lined up a free kick he had won himself 30 yards from goal. He bent it expertly into the corner out of reach of Wayne Hennessey. It was a sensational strike and just what Liverpool needed.

Having been beneficiaries of a goal just before half-time the week before, it was Liverpool who were on the receiving end this time as sloppy defending from Lovren allowed Yohan Cabaye in down the Liverpool left. The Frenchman had all the time in the world to square for Benteke to tap in.

The hosts upped the tempo in the second half, and Coutinho was continuing his sparkling display, making a jinking run into the penalty area. He took the ball past several Palace defenders, only to be clipped by another former Red, Martin Kelly. He stayed on his feet and took the shot, which was blocked and cleared. Had he gone down, a penalty would almost certainly have been awarded.

It was starting to feel like one of those days for Liverpool, a feeling that increased when Palace won a corner after more sloppiness from Lovren allowed Andros Townsend in on the right. Milner managed to get back to make the tackle, but the resulting corner saw Liverpool defenders stand like statues and watch as Benteke stooped to head in another.

In such circumstances, Klopp would have hoped to have been able to turn to his bench for inspiration, but due to the increasing injury list he could only turn to look at Loris Karius, Moreno and five teenagers. The average age of the subs was just 19, including 17-year-old striker Rhian Brewster, who had been earning rave reviews for his performances for the under-23 side but could hardly be relied on to save a game such as this.

Klopp had no choice but to make changes, bringing Trent Alexander-Arnold, Moreno and the returning Marko Grujić on, but it was all in vain as Palace held on to record their third consecutive win at Anfield.

It was an absolute gut punch to Liverpool's season, turning Champions League qualification from quite likely to being relatively improbable assuming the two Manchester clubs achieved their expected results in the last few games of the campaign.

Klopp was not surprised that Palace had caused his team problems, but was clearly irked by the way Liverpool had allowed them to do so.

He said, 'It was not the most exciting game but we all have to learn that these games are not exciting. If you open it with 1-0, which we did, and you can then score the second, then the opponent maybe changes style of play and in the end there are spaces which they are not used to giving away, and you can use it.

'We couldn't, because we gave them the opportunity out of nothing to score the first goal. One long ball, one cross and Benteke alone in the box – there is no excuse, nothing good to say about this moment.

'You could see immediately their confidence grew in this moment, they started playing football. It was only two minutes because of the half-time whistle. But we knew all the things we did, passing these balls between the lines, we had Roberto and especially Gini and Phil – a lot of times between the lines they could turn.

'We could have used these balls a little bit better, we wanted to involve Divock a little bit more because Divock made good ways but we didn't play in this line. If they want to win the ball, it's a foul if Div does it in a good way. It would be a threat for them also, we could see with Phil's free kick ability.

'We did it again out of nothing, we gave the corner away. This corner is now really strange. I know how often we spoke about set pieces but we cannot speak about defending set pieces – if we hit the ball at the first post then it's a bad corner. We didn't hit it, so it's a goal, that's how it is. It made the game not easy. We had to go again, we changed a little bit, the system, we brought wingers with Trent and Alberto to make the game wide. We had Marko on the pitch as another header, a threat.

'And wanted to have Roberto in the box, and Gini and Phil around for second balls. But how everybody could see, especially in added time, we lost a little bit of nerves, it was not clear any more. We gave them the opportunity to win these balls too easy. We had not a good formation for second balls.'

Klopp was asked about how much of a setback this would be to his and his team's ambitions for the end of the season.

'I'm pretty much used to nothing more in my life than to get up after a knock,' he replied. 'Nothing has happened more often to me than this, so that's no problem. I spoke to the boys after the game and told them that yes, it feels frustrating, it's disappointing, we made these mistakes – that's all true and we have to feel it today because that's how defeats are. But they make sense, defeats always make sense. You don't like it but there's a reason for them – not only what you did in the game, but also how you react after the game.

'There is one month to go; one wonderful football month with four games, so we will not give up. 100 per cent not. You could see it today, we all need to get used to it much more than we already are – in a game like this, there is not the biggest possible excitement most of the time, but nobody cares usually. Obviously we care; I could see it in a few faces, I could hear it a little bit from outside. The boys have delivered a lot of this excitement, but now it's really about serious football. Do what you have to do – and we will do. We tried to do it today, but two times they gave us an answer we didn't want.

'I've said it now five or six times, I know a lot of people around think now, "Oh my god, Champions League slips through our fingers again." Only if we let it slip. We have to try everything, we will try everything. Our job is to squeeze everything out of this season that we can squeeze. Obviously it is not easy for us, but that's no surprise.'

The question marks would keep coming about the defensive side of Klopp's team. Despite the overall improvement in performance of the team, Liverpool were set to yet again concede close to 50 goals in the league, with 42 going in from 34 games, while the two teams above them, Chelsea and Tottenham, had afforded the opposition just 29 and 22 goals by the same point, and Manchester United had let in only 25.

Klopp explained in a separate interview why it's not as simple as measuring goals going in for judging his defenders in the same way you'd judge those at other clubs.

He said, 'A centre-half for a top team is playing with a lot of space at the back. That's how Tottenham act, how City act and sometimes how Arsenal act. Manchester United are for sure a bit different.

'That is the situation, you have to involve a lot of players usually in offensive things, you cannot be offensive with two players in a counter-attack when there are already eight from the other team in their own half or box. So, yes, of course it is more difficult.

'If we go for a centre-half we need to know how he acts in big spaces, but on the other side centre-halves can feel pretty alone in certain moments if we don't react the right way after losing the ball. That is why counter-pressing is a pretty useful skill.

'I saw a lot of centre-halves, that is how it is,' he added. 'We cannot go for a centre-half of Bayern Munich for example, they have similar problems that we have.

'You have to imagine how he will react in different situations. All clubs defend in some moments high.

'It is about being football-smart and they have to make the right decision in the right moment, stepping back and all that stuff.

'For example, the second goal [against Crystal Palace] was after a set piece, but it came after we lost the ball in build-up and things like this.

'If he steps back in this moment then for a few seconds there could be help from somewhere. It was two wrong decisions in one situation. That then is really difficult. But defending high is not a problem, it is only a different job.'

The following weekend looked potentially like one where Liverpool could be put under immense pressure going into the last few games. Manchester United and Manchester City had drawn 0-0 during the week at the Etihad Stadium, which on the face of it was a good result for the Reds, but both would be playing teams in the relegation zone three days later, while Liverpool had yet another potential banana-skin away trip to Watford.

The Hornets had inflicted Klopp's heaviest defeat as Liverpool manager when they romped to a 3-0 win at Vicarage Road in December 2015, and though the team under Walter Mazzarri wasn't quite as potent as that one had been, they were still a danger and the chief tormentor on that day, Troy Deeney, would be starting.

However, there was not just one, nor two, but three kicks added to Liverpool's step ahead of the game. Unexpectedly on the Sunday, Manchester United had only drawn 1-1 at home to Swansea, Manchester City had needed to salvage a 2-2 draw at Middlesbrough, and Arsenal suffered a limp 2-0 defeat at rivals Tottenham. All of a sudden a Liverpool win at Watford would put them right back in the driving seat for Champions League qualification.

There was even further good news ahead of the game as Adam Lallana and Daniel Sturridge returned to training and to the matchday squad, both making the bench and significantly increasing its potency and average age. Otherwise it was an unchanged team from Klopp.

It was a surprisingly slow tempo to the game in the opening few minutes. Liverpool's need to secure three points led to many thinking their high-paced pressing tactic would return from the off, despite them having not fully employed it for several weeks. One possible causation for the start could have been yet another injury to a key player.

Just minutes into the game, Coutinho tried to run into the penalty area only to have Adrian Mariappa's knee crash into his thigh. No free kick was awarded, but Coutinho was left on the floor in a heap. After treatment and trying to run it off, he was forced to come off. Klopp had been hoping to bring Lallana on for the last 20 or 30 minutes, but now had to introduce him just 12 minutes in.

The England midfielder had missed over a month after picking up a knock on international duty, but seemed to have not missed a beat as he immediately showed off the deft touches and neat turns that Liverpool had been missing in his absence.

With just three minutes left of the half the first goal nearly came as a Liverpool corner was headed away to Lallana on the edge of the box and his left-footed volley rattled back off the crossbar. It would have been a spectacular way to take the lead, so the only way to follow it up was by trying something even more spectacular.

More good work from Lallana fed the ball to Clyne, who moved it on to Lucas. He chipped a hopeful ball into Emre Can, who with his back to goal decided to address the ball with an overhead kick. He connected perfectly and the ball looped into the far corner to leave Watford faces stunned and Liverpool fans delirious. At the end of the campaign is was voted as the Premier League Goal of the Season.

The pressure put on by Watford in the second half would have been significantly reduced had Lallana managed to control Can's ball into the box on the counter-attack, but he was denied by a last-ditch tackle.

An exhausted Lallana came off for Ragnar Klavan to try and shore things up for the four minutes of added time that needed to be negotiated, and it came with a true heart in mouth moment as a ball into the box somehow found Sebastian Pródl at the far post. The Austrian defender fired at goal but his shot thudded back off the bar.

Shortly afterwards, the final whistle blew and Liverpool had held on to seal a vital three points. The relief was clear to see on the players' faces as they had overcome another big hurdle and opened up a gap again between them and the Manchester clubs. They once again had their fate in their hands.

It had been a team performance but the kudos understandably went to Can, whose individual moment of brilliance won the game. Klopp was as excited and surprised by it as anyone.

'Actually, I would love to see it again – everybody is speaking about it,' he said. 'I've only seen it once, but it looked already pretty nice. I probably turned a little bit too early when I saw it would hit the back of the net.

'We need to stay focused and we need to stay concentrated. We have pressure, yes – but pressure in the end of the season, in this period, means you fight for something. It's a positive pressure, so we want to keep this – we want to keep this pressure high, we want to stay focused, we want to work hard and do everything for the points we can get. We don't expect for a second that it will be easy.

'If anybody here thinks we already have the three points against Southampton then you could not have seen Southampton this season because they are a really strong side. It will be another hard game for us, but it is like it is. Tonight, nobody can take these points away from us, so that's the best news and now we have time to work and prepare for the Southampton game.'

Emre Can had not always experienced such praise regarding his performances, but he had noticeably stepped up his game in recent weeks and Klopp was keen to state his thoughts on the 23-year-old.

'If you're not positive [about Can] after this game, this goal, then something is wrong! Yes, he is a good boy, he helps us. I know how it works. He had a problem with his calf [earlier in the season] but we had no possibility to leave him out, it was not possible for us.

'We had a lot of talks about this, and everybody saw the performances and thought, "What's wrong with him?" We thought we needed him in these moments and he said, "Okay, I'll try." Sometimes it was not as good as it could have been, but meanwhile these problems are sorted and now he can build on his performances. He's a physically strong boy and very important for us. If he can score goals like this then it makes even more sense!'

Klopp also shed light on how he felt about his team allowing Prödl to rattle the crossbar in the dying seconds.

'I said to the boys after the game, "If you want to kill me, that's a good way to try!" It's crazy, it's crazy, [it gave me] 500 million grey hairs! The situation tonight, we'd already defended it and then they had three players at the second post. What can you say? We tried everything for 97 minutes, but if you want [we made] this one mistake and it could've led to a goal – that's how football at the highest level is. We didn't play perfect tonight, but it would've been really hard to accept. But we got them [the points] and I think the boys really deserved it.'

30

'When I started here I said we had to change from doubters to believers ... so look forward to it, be positive. If somebody comes to you and says "but if ..." then send him out, say, "Come on, go away, I don't want to hear about it."'

MANCHESTER City had battered Crystal Palace. The Eagles, who had proven so difficult to break down at Anfield just two weeks earlier, were ripped apart by Liverpool's top-four rivals. A final scoreline of 5-0 not only gave City three valuable points, but had significantly boosted their goal difference to the point where they had overtaken the Reds.

It was not all bad news for Klopp though as the game immediately following his side's clash with Southampton would see the other two candidates for the top four, Arsenal and Manchester United, face each other. There would be guaranteed points dropped, so a win over the Saints would cement Liverpool's place among the Premier League elite.

Perhaps due to unexpectedly playing for over 70 minutes at Watford, Adam Lallana was once again named on the bench, but on the plus side Philippe Coutinho had recovered from his dead leg and started.

Right from the start it was clear to see that Puel had not sent his men out to attack. Unsurprisingly, as so many teams had done, and in recent times successfully, he parked the proverbial bus. Liverpool probed but lacked ideas and direction, and could only muster half-chances. The first half was one of the dullest of the campaign, with Southampton failing to register a single shot.

The second half saw much the same as Southampton nullified their opponents, hoping to catch them on the break as they had done in the closing stages of their January visit. However, midway through the second half a rare lapse in concentration saw Jack Stephens handle the ball in the area, and a penalty was awarded.

James Milner stepped up, having not failed from the spot all season, or indeed since November 2009 when he missed one playing for Aston Villa against Bolton Wanderers. Fraser Forster decided to play mind games. The 6ft 7in goalkeeper stood over Milner, trying to intimidate him, kicking the penalty spot to scuff it up. Other Southampton players got around Milner, one wandered into the goal to get a drink. Referee Bobby Madley produced a yellow card but had failed to control the visitors. Milner stepped up and fired the penalty low and hard to Forster's right, but the England stopper got down and palmed it away.

As the game ticked on Southampton continued to refuse to come out and play. Klopp turned to Lallana and Daniel Sturridge for inspiration, and almost got it when Sturridge worked an opening but his right-footed shot couldn't beat Forster.

Marko Grujić made a late appearance and arguably had Liverpool's best chance aside from the spot kick as he flicked a header towards goal but again Forster was equal to it.

The final whistle went and it was two more points dropped. The third home game in a row without a win, and only the second time they had failed to score in a league game at Anfield in 2016/17.

It was a clean sheet and Liverpool had managed to stop the Saints from having a single shot on target, but that will have been little consolation to the fans, whose concerned faces as they left the ground told the story of doubt creeping back in. Doubt that the top four was still more likely than not. Worry that a season that had promised so much would potentially deliver so little right at the death, as it had done the season before.

Klopp was disappointed, but did take some solace in the fact that a point was still gained.

'We were close, but in the end we couldn't get the three points and that's how it is. As everyone could see, it was a difficult game, Southampton played in a specific way. A lot of people might say that everybody will now play here like this, but it will not be like this and if it is, we have solutions. We had them today, but you need to score at one moment and then they're open and then we can do other things. They were very disciplined and very deep; we defended their counter-attacks much better than we did against Crystal Palace, for example.

'In the end, it's all about finishing or scoring one and we couldn't do this. It made life not easy in the game. We tried until the end, but today was one of those days. Now we have only one point more, we wanted to have three points more, but it's not the end of the world. It's not exactly what we wanted and we are really disappointed about this, as you can imagine, but we will keep on going.'

On the battle for the top four, the German was understandably defiant, 'We are still fighting and nobody has given up or something like this. I spoke immediately after the game to the boys. I cannot and don't want to take away the disappointment, but what I can say is that we have one point more than before.

'The best manager I've ever had, the most experienced and in much more difficult situations said always that at the end of the season, this point will be really valuable, and I believe in this so we will see. But now we have to analyse this game. It's pretty much already done, but we will do it one more time and speak about it and then we start the preparation for the West Ham game.'

The subject of the team's recent home form came up, and while Klopp conceded that it hadn't been good enough, he did have a theory as to why this game in particular had been more difficult for his side.

'I know nobody wants to hear it, but I will be brave enough to say: the pitch was really dry. We gave it all the water we had, then after 15 minutes it was really dry with the wind. It was difficult, you could see it, a lot of passes you thought, "Why are they playing this?" but it was difficult. In a possession game you need to have the best circumstances if possible, especially in a home game. Today we couldn't have this. It's nobody's fault, it's only a description.'

Despite the setback, there was some good news later in the day as Arsenal comfortably beat Manchester United 2-0 at the Emirates Stadium. The draw with Southampton had briefly taken Liverpool's fight for the top four out of their hands, but United's defeat gave them control once again, though now Arsenal were also a potential threat.

The Gunners were seven points behind but had two games in hand and a goal difference not all that far away. One of those games in hand coincidentally came three days later at Southampton. The south coast side didn't put up the same barriers against Arsène Wenger's men and were dispatched 2-0.

The nerves and tension were building. It was starting to look like Liverpool would have to win their two remaining games to clinch

Champions League qualification, and the first of those was a trip to West Ham.

It was Liverpool's first visit to the London Stadium, where the Hammers had endured a very unhappy first campaign in their new home. However, just a week earlier they effectively ended the title race as they battled hard to a well-earned 1-0 win over Tottenham. They had also gone five games unbeaten, keeping four clean sheets in that run. This would be far from a simple match for an inconsistent Liverpool side.

The pressure was ramped up further on the Saturday when Manchester City gained a fortunate 2-1 win over Leicester after a Riyad Mahrez penalty was controversially ruled out, and Arsenal overran Stoke 4-1 in their last away game of the season.

Liverpool travelled to the capital for the Sunday clash with Slaven Bilić's men, and things weren't made any easier when Roberto Firmino was ruled out with injury. The Brazilian had been running on empty for weeks having played almost every game of the campaign, and finally had picked up a niggle, so Klopp was forced to turn to Sturridge.

The enigmatic striker had undoubted talent, and his scoring record was second to none at the club, but he hadn't played much football since Klopp's arrival. There had also been a period where Klopp simply preferred Firmino and Divock Origi to him, but he had turned to Sturridge in big moments, such as the Europa League Final in Basel where he had scored such a wonderful, albeit ultimately meaningless, goal.

It wasn't just the fact that Sturridge was being given his first start since January that caught the eye, but the formation.

Klopp had almost exclusively played a 4-3-3 system all season, but here he went with a 4-4-2 diamond. As well as pairing Sturridge and Origi up top, Klopp decided to deploy Coutinho in a deeper position, playing centrally alongside Gini Wijnaldum, while Lallana occupied the free role behind the strikers.

It wasn't the most promising of starts as Hammers full-back Sam Byram had half the pitch to himself after running towards the Liverpool penalty area, but could only fire his effort wide.

The Reds soon settled and were dominating the ball, but despite the best efforts of Sturridge and Origi, were struggling to find a way through. Joel Matip came closest in the early stages as he got on the end of a Coutinho corner, but the Cameroonian's header came back up off the turf and hit the crossbar before being cleared.

There were few chances after that until the 35th minute when Coutinho picked the ball up in his own half. He ran centrally, looked up and fired a ball down the middle of the pitch to Sturridge, who was inexplicably all by himself and onside. He ran through, rounded Adrián with ease and slotted home. It was a perfect example of the clinical abilities that Liverpool had missed while Sturridge was out, and he had provided a crucial goal with the game finely poised.

Coutinho was pulling the strings in the middle. Comparisons had been made by his own manager to Andres Iniesta in the build-up to the game, which didn't ease the fears of fans that the little Brazilian might want to leave to become Iniesta's successor at Barcelona, but he was more than emulating the World Cup winner here, picking up the ball all over the pitch and moving it around with great vision, pace and execution.

Hearts were in Liverpool mouths just before half-time as a West Ham corner reached André Ayew at the far post, but somehow the Ghanaian could only divert his two attempts on to the post, before Simon Mignolet smothered.

It was a warning sign to Klopp that the game was not yet won, so he sent his team out in the second half to make sure they completed the job. The Reds were rampant in the second 45, and had forced Adrián into three great saves within the first 110 seconds of the half. It didn't take long for the pressure to tell, and it led to a spectacular second.

Wijnaldum hit a volley from the edge of the area that crashed against the bar. While everyone – West Ham defenders included – were still standing in amazement at the effort, Coutinho had controlled the ball, dribbled past several players and fired into the far corner. It eased the nerves and gave the travelling Kop a reason to party.

Just four minutes later a West Ham corner was cleared and sent Liverpool on the counter-attack. Home fans and players alike were furious as they felt that Wijnaldum had both handled the ball and caught Winston Reid in making the clearance, but the referee played on, as did Liverpool. It was Wijnaldum who played in Coutinho, and he waltzed past James Collins and smashed the ball in to make it 3-0. A brace and two assists was all the vindication Klopp needed in his decision to play Coutinho deeper. It had paid off handsomely, but the scoring wasn't quite over.

Sturridge beat his man on the right before pulling the ball back into the box. Lallana and Wijnaldum couldn't force the ball in, but the loose shot from the latter was diverted in by Origi for 4-0.

It was Liverpool's best performance since Christmas, and arguably their best away showing all season. They had destroyed West Ham and gained three valuable points. It meant that a win over Middlesbrough on the last day of the season would guarantee a top four finish.

Klopp was ecstatic with his players after the game, hugging anyone who'd let him.

In his post-match press conference, Klopp admitted that the game had turned on moments, but said that his side had done everything he'd asked of them.

He said, 'Looking back now, it was hard work, and there were a few moments where the game could have changed. I thought we had a real deserved win, it was a really good football game.

'The start of the second half was brilliant, we played really good football and we were more direct and used the information from the first half and from half-time. We [tried] a few different moves, a few different surprising movements and [had] better timing in passing and running. It's easy to say and much more difficult to do but the boys did really brilliant. We scored the goals, controlled the game, could have scored more often but that's completely okay that we didn't. A perfect afternoon.'

When asked what he thought of Coutinho's virtuoso performance in the midfield he added, 'I can't remember when I said this but it was always clear Phil can play this [position], there's no doubt. If he starts on the wing, he is very often in this position. He was never a winger, he's always kind of a playmaker. It's not interesting where he's coming from, it's all [about] where he needs to be at one point. He needs to be in the decisive area in the middle of the park, he needs to be in shooting situations and all that stuff. That's what he did today – obviously he felt really well in this position and that was a good game.

'Part of our lives is to handle pressure; to ignore the bad part of pressure and use the good part of pressure. That's our job. I thought we did really well. We drew in the last game, we didn't finish, we didn't score with the penalty, so maybe then people said, "Yeah, well they can't deal with pressure," but the only sign for this was using a penalty or not.

'These players did so good this season that we are in the situation we are, 73 points – and nobody gives you 73 points as a present. Take it and use it, we had to work for it. The boys did it and today we saw a really convincing performance and no doubt about anything. But the first sentence the players said in the dressing room was, "One more time, one more game", and we will stay focused, 100 per cent.

We know about the situation, we know about the difficulty of the next game and nobody will go into this game and underestimate Middlesbrough even one per cent.'

As had happened the previous weekend, Manchester United provided more good news for the Reds as they fell to a 2-1 defeat at Tottenham, meaning that they could no longer catch Liverpool or anyone else in the top four, though José Mourinho's side would go on to beat Ajax in the Europa League Final a few weeks later to seal Champions League qualification anyway.

It was not as positive in the midweek as Manchester City and Arsenal both played their final games in hand, and predictably and professionally won them with relative ease, the Gunners beating Sunderland 2-0 and City triumphing 3-1 over West Brom. This meant that Liverpool would indeed have to beat Middlesbrough to be sure a top-four finish, or else be reliant on Arsenal not winning. The possible onion in the ointment was that they would be playing Everton, who would be in no mood to do their rivals a favour. There was also an outside chance of third place if City slipped up at Watford.

The week building up to the game was largely full of confidence among Liverpool fans. At home to Middlesbrough was probably the fixture most would have hand-picked if they had to guarantee victory in an end-of-season affair. Boro were already down after an unremarkable return to the top flight, relegated with just 28 points from their 37 games ahead of the final day.

They had struggled to score goals, with big signing Álvaro Negredo the only player to find the net with anything approaching regularity. They were the lowest scorers in the division, but also boasted a good defence for a team that had been comfortably relegated. By the end of the season, they had conceded 14 fewer goals than Bournemouth, who finished ten places higher in ninth, and had the best defensive record in the bottom half of the table.

The main phrase being used in the lead up to the game was that it would be like a cup final, but Klopp was keen to go against that way of thinking. He told the club website, 'I don't think we need different kinds of descriptions for this game, so it's a "cup final" or a "World Cup final" or that it's the most important game of however many years and everything.

'It is a football game. If we really – and I know we do – expect from ourselves that in each game we win the game, what is the difference?

'We always have this kind of pressure; that we want to win the game, that we have to do the right things, we have to defend well, we have to be good organisationally, we have to create chances and we have to score goals.

'So that is not a big difference and I don't think that anybody needs this special motivation or whatever. In the end, we have to play football and I am really happy I have a team able to do this.'

When asked if he had a special message for the fans and their job ahead of the crucial game, he said, 'Nothing special, actually.

'When I started here I said we had to change from doubters to believers and I think now we have a few days before the game, so look forward to it, be positive.

'If somebody comes to you and says "but if …" – and that's not the most used words in and around Liverpool – but if, then send him out, say, "Come on, go away, I don't want to hear about it."

'There's no reason for it. This team has shown so much this season and we will be ready for this game, and we should really be positive and try to enjoy the game. Maybe it's nervy for the supporters around, but it's the job to do, unfortunately.

'I'm really looking forward to it and I could use this moment then to say "thank you" for the outstanding atmospheres this season. I don't want to say "you can't do better", but it was already pretty good this season and we've enjoyed it a lot. Let's go one more time and get the full package.'

As it had the previous season, the success of the campaign and qualification for the Champions League would come down to the very final game. Liverpool had come up short in Basel against Sevilla 12 months earlier. There could be no repeat of that hiccup if belief was going to bloom at Anfield.

Klopp had been made to sweat on the fitness of Firmino right up to the morning of the game, but he was declared fit to start, which was just as well as Origi was not after picking up a slight knock. The Belgian did make the bench.

Once again Coutinho was deployed in a deeper role, with Lallana, Firmino and Sturridge heading the attack.

One slight surprise from the opposition was that Negredo had been left among the substitutes, with Rudy Gestede starting up front. It was less of a surprise to those who had seen the big aerial specialist give the Reds all sorts of problems for Aston Villa the previous season. It was clear what Boro's tactics would be.

Liverpool arrived to hundreds of fans lining the streets, welcoming their heroes for one last push. It was reminiscent of the games that had led to the league challenge in 2014 and the Europa League run of 2016. For all Klopp's attempts to downplay it, the fans were very much treating this like a cup final.

Noise filled the stadium in the build-up, and as Liverpool emerged on to the field wearing their new home kit, a loud 'You'll Never Walk Alone' led into choruses of 'Liverpool! Liverpool!' as the game kicked off.

As expected, the hosts dominated the ball early on, with 82 per cent of it in the first ten minutes. They had been reduced to half-chances though as Middlesbrough's organisation and the competent partnership of Calum Chambers – on loan from Arsenal – and Ben Gibson kept them at bay.

The noise had been largely maintained, but noticeably dropped when news filtered through from Vicarage Road that Manchester City had raced into an early 2-0 lead. It seemed that third was off the table straight away. Worse news was to follow though as Arsenal scored first at the Emirates. No one had been banking on Everton doing their neighbours any favours, but it made the fact more real that Liverpool were going to have to win this game.

They were toiling though, with Boro coming more into the game and the tension was starting to creep into the crowd.

Coutinho was getting on the ball but struggling to make an impact as the visitors packed their own box. The Brazilian saw a shot from range go wide, before Sturridge worked an opening on his right foot and also missed the target.

Hearts were then in mouths as an error from a Gestede flick-on saw Patrick Bamford in on goal. Lovren chased back and appeared to haul Bamford down in the area. Gasps from the crowd were soon sighs of relief as referee Martin Atkinson waved the appeals away. Replays showed that there had been contact both outside and inside the area, but Atkinson later revealed he felt Bamford had slowed down to invite the contact from the Croatian defender.

Nothing else seemed to be going Liverpool's way though as City were battering Watford, taking a 4-0 lead by half-time, and Arsenal scored a second against Everton despite having had captain Laurent Koscielny sent off. The nail-biting in the stands was getting worse.

One thing that had been noticeable about recent games for Liverpool was how many goals there had been – both for and against – on the stroke of half-time. Whether it was a deliberate tactic to up the tempo in the last couple of minutes before the break was unclear, but there was to be one last example.

Gini Wijnaldum, who had been struggling to even control the ball for most of the first half, played a pass into Firmino. The Brazilian laid it off with perfect weight for Wijnaldum to run on to. All of a sudden he was in the penalty area on his own. Sturridge was making a run to the back post, but the midfielder ignored him and blasted the ball towards the near post. The net rippled furiously and the fans exploded with relief as the Dutchman had given them the lead. Klopp turned and pumped his hands with aggressive glee, trying and largely failing to hide his delight.

It sent his team in ahead at the break, and the mood of the ground was changed entirely. The first goal was always going to be the big hurdle given Boro's propensity for defending and lack of firepower at the other end. Gestede had been limited to one header that he directed wide. Otherwise it had more or less been all Liverpool.

The hope from Reds fans was that their team would come out in the second half as they had done against West Ham, on fire and eager to put the game to bed, and they did just that.

They spent most of the opening ten minutes of the second period in the Middlesbrough half, and during that time Sturridge won a free kick. Coutinho stepped up to take it and guided it into the net to Brad Guzan's right. The American keeper had anticipated the ball going the other way, and couldn't scramble back in time to stop Coutinho's effort making it 2-0.

All of a sudden it was an entirely different game. Liverpool were creating chance after chance, and it wasn't long before it was put to bed. A poor Adam Lallana cross into the box was cleared, but he won a header to divert the ball to Sturridge, and he tried to head it to Nathaniel Clyne, who for some reason was in the centre-forward position. Clyne left it for Lallana, who took it into the area and with his left foot sent the ball into the far corner to make it 3-0.

There was an audible realisation among the 50,000 Liverpool fans that the job was done. Klopp raced down the touchline and decided not to hold back his joy any longer. He punched the air as he faced the jubilant Main Stand. Him roaring at them. Them roaring at him.

Having been fraught with nerves, the latter stages of the game were now like a proper end-of-season affair. Calm, composed and with allowance to be a tad more sentimental than usual. Klopp brought Lucas on for the last 15 minutes, knowing that it could end up being his final appearance in a Liverpool shirt after ten years of service. It was inevitably followed by the home fans urging him to shoot every time he got the ball. As he had managed just one league goal during his time at the club, another didn't seem overly likely.

Liverpool had chances to make the score more emphatic, but that was the end of it. It was of no concern though, and neither was that fact that Arsenal had beaten Everton 3-1 in north London. The final whistle was blown on the campaign and a fourth place finish was confirmed.

It may not have been the title challenge that many dreamt of in the heady heights of late November 2016, but there was no denying that it had been a season of significant progress. In the league Klopp's men had finished with 16 points more than in 2015/16, had scored 15 more goals, conceded eight less, achieved six more wins and four fewer defeats.

The beaming smile of Klopp was clear for all to see after the game, and in his post-match press conference he was keen to praise the achievements of his team and the progress they had made.

He said, 'I'm not sure if that [finishing in the top four] was the target of all the Liverpool supporters, but I think pretty much the second best. For a few weeks we knew that's the maximum we can achieve and we did it. It feels really outstandingly good at the moment.

'I said in the press conference two days ago that everything is good in this club at the moment, it feels good, but of course we have to deliver results. Feeling in a good way is one [thing], showing you're on a good way is another thing and I think again we showed today that we deserve this position; 76 points, that's an outstanding number.

'We all know what happened in January, I'm not sure all of us agree why, but the explanation is injuries and too many games. We cannot change this, it happened, then the problem in February was that we suffered from the games in January, but then in March we were back on track and got to 76 points, so that's it.

'That's the base we created, we learned a lot in this year about ourselves, so we can use it. Yes, if you want, usually at the end of the season you're kind of tired, but I could start – and don't tell the players this – tomorrow because I'm already looking forward to what we can do.

'I'm really proud of the boys, they did well. It was a good start in the game and [then] it became a little bit more stiff. If you don't score in these few moments, you get a bit more stiff, you feel the intensity of all the ways. Middlesbrough defended deep – that's absolutely okay – we had not good timing and then we scored this one goal but the main target was to defend better in the second half, because we thought pretty much each long ball was half a counter-attack – that makes no sense when you have the ball 90 per cent. That was the thing we wanted to change, plus better timing in all our movements because we had the right positions but in the wrong moment.

'After the second goal, I think everybody could see how good we can be and it was never easy, but it looked then very good. That's probably what everybody wished before we started today and now we have it and we should celebrate it.'

On the prestige of getting Liverpool back into the Champions League, where they had featured just once since Rafa Benitez's final season in 2009/10, Klopp said, 'It's the best tournament in Europe, there's nothing better, maybe in the world. For me, it's the best competition, you want to be there and Liverpool needs to be there consistently. I love the perspective, I would not say we're already in because qualification is qualification and we're already looking forward to it.

'We will be really strong and we will really fight for it because we want to be there and it's all good. It's a fantastic competition and I think in the last ten years Liverpool was not part of it too often, three years ago once only maybe. We should try everything to change this, we have to make steps and the step for us to be around the best teams in the world because we are one of the best clubs.'

He was also asked about when he felt his team were capable of finishing in the top four, and replied, 'I didn't think before the start of the season about it, but yes the target from the beginning was to go there so we needed to create a team that could do it. We all know we had no European football, so for us, it was not that [much] an advantage because we had injuries.

'Without injuries like Chelsea – and I don't want to make it too big – we could have had a few points more and it would have looked a little bit different. We had these injuries, but in the first part of the season I knew we were ready. But that doesn't mean anything and you have to do it because there are a lot of games to go after this moment. It was long, it was really long.

'I don't know the specific moment, but I knew after we beat Arsenal there in this manner [on the opening day], it should be possible.

'In a lot of games, we played really outstandingly good football and that showed what we can do. When you don't do it any more, everybody is asking why, why is it not that fluent any more and where is the plan B, C and D? We always knew that the way is okay; we have to accept a few parts of our situation and do work on the other parts of our situation. That's what we did and in the end 76 points is really difficult to get and we have them, so good.'

He ended by talking about what he had learned about his time through the season, and again the subject of belief was at the centre of it.

He said, 'Obviously we are not confident enough in general, that's how it is. Always when something doesn't work it always feels like something slips through your fingers, so it's like, "Oh, again like this, again like this," so I am really happy that we achieved a little bit of something we didn't achieve in the past too often [a top-four finish]. Not because I am vain and want to show we can do it, but because I am interested in the way and for development you need to feel the improvement, you need to feel the next step, that it's right. That's pretty much all and I'm really happy about the situation and to learn. I hope it has given us a little bit more confidence in general and we can work with this. That will be good.'

Immediately after the game saw the traditional end-of-season lap of honour, and thankfully it would be a happy and deserved one as the fans stayed to applaud and show their gratitude to the players, coaches and manager who had delivered a top-four finish. Klopp was stopped for several interviews during it, and one in particular with LFCTV summed up his feelings for the achievement, the fans and the future.

'We will be best prepared and give everything, because these fans deserve European nights and it's really cool to know we will have them,' he revealed.

Neil Atkinson and Gareth Roberts of *The Anfield Wrap* were among those out for celebratory pints after the Middlesbrough game, toasting the ultimately pleasing end to the season. Once they'd had a chance to reflect on things, I asked them for their final thoughts on Klopp's first two campaigns at Anfield.

What have been your highlights of the Klopp era to date?
NA: 'The highlights have been plentiful. The obvious European run and excellent football early this season. Then grinding out the fourth-place finish. But I'd want to give a mention to Old Trafford away this season [the 1-1 draw]. I've seen many Liverpool sides go there and crumble. However, with a debutant at right-back, Henderson on one leg, we went there, were the better side, conceded the equaliser late but grabbed the ball and looked more likely to win the game. The mind set was spectacular in hindsight. Liverpool weren't playing brilliantly in general and didn't play brilliantly in this game, but they knew they could win it. They never took the point.

'The tactical setup that day was brilliant.'

GR: 'The 4-1 win away at Manchester City was fantastic. It was a day when everything seemed to click – Klopp got his tactics spot on, the players carried them out to the letter and we also saw the real Roberto Firmino stand up after many had harboured doubts about his ability and suitability. Dortmund in the Europa League goes without saying, Manchester United in the same competition, too. In general terms, bringing back a feeling that we can beat anyone on our day was absolutely crucial and Klopp has done just that.'

And lowlights?

NA: 'January to mid-February 2017. It was about as dismal a run as could be imagined with shafts of light in massive games such as the above. The pint after Spurs at home was like few I have ever known due to the relief of watching Liverpool win again that everyone felt.'

GR: 'You can never get used to losing in a final. It's such a let-down; a horrible low when you've geared yourself up for a real high. So the two finals are the lowlights alongside the spectacular collapse at Bournemouth, being bullied away at Leicester and losing to Swansea at Anfield.'

Has Klopp achieved what you expected him to in his first two seasons?

NA: 'Broadly yes. He's perked the club up, got us back into the Champions League. I would have expected stronger home form but the away form has more than made up for that.'

GR: 'In a roundabout way, yes. I imagined we would be competing for a place in the Champions League this season, and so it proved. It bizarrely almost feels like an underachievement, such was the quality of football we witnessed prior to the turn of the year. But it's progress nevertheless. I think also he's helped to focus minds at the club – despite a worrying start to the transfer business post-season, it feels like the club is in general terms in good health and much of that is down to Klopp.'

To what extent do you think he has 'turned doubters into believers'?

NA: 'The question remains around the club finding its way post-Hicks and Gillett. Liverpool still haven't clarified that. Do I believe that he is a great manager and has good players who give their all? Absolutely. Within 90 minutes can we ask for any more than that?

Absolutely not. I think Jürgen Klopp can make Liverpool by far the greatest team the world has ever seen, but a lot of stars need to align for that to happen. However, he has brought the clarity of purpose. And that is one of his greatest assets.

'He has to keep enjoying it. And keep being himself. This is the most important thing. And has to be given the room to enjoy it and be himself.'

GR: 'He's done his best on that score but so much of it remains out of his hands. On the pitch, with his best 11 available, I think most fancy Liverpool to give any side a game. Off the pitch, away from Klopp, how the club is run and the people running it still generates some doubt. Liverpool's support is also scarred by the near misses – 27 years of waiting for the title does that to you.

'Klopp remains the best man for the job. In many ways it feels like if he can't do it with Liverpool then who ever will?'

Klopp explained after the game that he and his squad would be travelling to Australia for a post-season friendly with Sydney FC (which they won 3-0), but that once he was back in England he would have a few more things to do before going off on holiday and reflecting on what he and his team had achieved.

What had they achieved though? Even with top four it would be churlish to say that Liverpool fans had been universally won over, that all the doubters were now believers.

Some bemoaned the fact that they had been so good in the first half of the season but so inconsistent in the second; that they had blown their chances of bigger success with a disastrous January and February, and that the season had perhaps been a missed opportunity.

However, with champions Chelsea ending up on 93 points, it turned out that even if Liverpool had matched the record of their first 19 games in their next 19, they still would have finished behind Antonio Conte's Blues.

Their record against the teams around them was imperious, the only team to go unbeaten against everyone else in the top eight of the league. It was the 16 games against lower teams where they had dropped points that had cost them. That would though, in theory, be a far easier issue to remedy than if it were the other way round and they struggled in the bigger games.

At their worst, Klopp's team could look devoid of ideas, sapped of energy and as toothless as a new-born baby, but at their best, their scintillating best, they were rightly talked about in the same breath as Europe's elite in terms of entertainment value and effectiveness.

It was coming together, less than two years into the project. Consistency was the only thing missing.

In the days that followed, the general consensus from the media and wider world alike was that, while not perfect, it had been a very good season from Liverpool. To finish above Arsenal and Manchester United was no mean feat. It was the first time in two decades that Arsène Wenger had failed to make the top four and the first time ever in England that José Mourinho hadn't finished a season in the top three.

When Jürgen Norbert Klopp arrived at Anfield in October 2015, he was taking over a team that had finished seventh the season before, had been beaten 6-1 by Stoke City on the final day of that season, and had started the new campaign in tenth place after winning just three of their first eight games.

The mood was low, optimism was lower and hope was only restored once Klopp was confirmed as the new man to lead the Reds revolution.

He took his new team and fans on a rollercoaster ride that included big wins against big teams, agonising losses against smaller teams, two cup finals, including a European adventure that would end in heartbreak, a spell where his team were seen as title favourites and had the football world purring at their displays, to not knowing where the next win was coming from, and finally to a place in the top four of the Premier League and a chance to once again grace the sunny climes of the UEFA Champions League.

Klopp may have ended up regretting coining the phrase 'turning from doubters to believers' given how often it came back to him in press conferences and interviews, but after nearly two years at the helm he has created far more optimism, hope and indeed 'belief' in the team and the direction of the great club than had existed before his arrival.

There is still work to be done and cups to be won if he is to convert those who still hold doubt in their heart.

But then his work has really only just begun.